M000084297

Albert Cohen

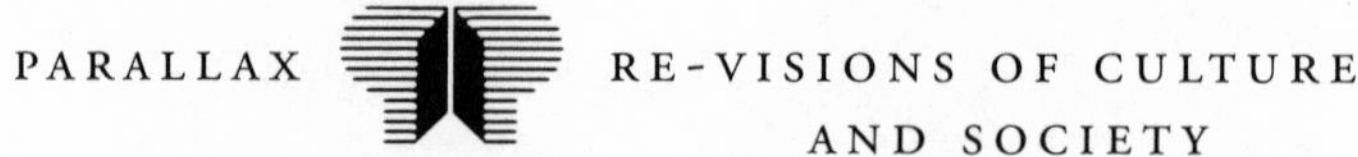

Stephen G. Nichols, Gerald Prince, and Wendy Steiner
SERIES EDITORS

Albert Cohen

Dissonant Voices

Jack I. Abecassis

The Johns Hopkins University Press
Baltimore and London

The production of this book was enhanced with the aid of a Faculty Research Grant from Pomona College.

Printed in the United States of America on acid-free paper
9 8 7 6 5 4 3 2 1

The Johns Hopkins University Press
2715 North Charles Street
Baltimore, Maryland 21218-4363
www.press.jhu.edu

Library of Congress Cataloging-in-Publication Data

Abecassis, Jack I., 1959–
Albert Cohen : dissonant voices / Jack I. Abecassis.
p. cm. — (Parallax)
Includes bibliographical references and index.
ISBN 0-8018-7982-5 (hardcover : alk. paper)
1. Cohen, Albert, 1895–1981—Criticism and interpretation.
I. Title. II. Parallax (Baltimore, Md.)
PQ2605.O24Z52 2004
843′.912—dc22 2004008936

A catalog record for this book is available from the British Library.

For my beloved parents,
Moshe and Lea Abecassis

My suffering is my vengeance against myself.

Albert Cohen, Le Livre de ma mère

Contents

Foreword: Reading Cohen Today

Since we have come to the end of what Eric Hobsbawm called the "short" twentieth century, we should now be able to view it and its artistic productions more objectively.

As a consequence, some widely held opinions may have to be revised, particularly as regards French literature. It is not obvious, however, that the intellectual establishment in France—never amenable to criticism—is ready to reassess the literary heritage of the twentieth century. Asking whether Marcel Proust was really the most prominent French writer of the century, suggesting that André Malraux was better as an essayist than as a novelist, questioning Louis-Ferdinand Céline's importance, or doubting that René Char was indeed the philosophically inspiring poet that so many complacent commentators have described, such questions amount to blasphemy. And yet they still will need to be addressed some day.

In the same vein, sooner or later we need to ask why some outstanding works are still excluded from the canon. Why, for instance, are Marcel Aymé's and Raymond Queneau's fascinating novels, Jacques Audiberti's and Jean Vauthier's baroque plays, and Michel Butor's and Yves Bonnefoy's beautiful essays on painting so little read, and even so little known, in French universities—which, we have to admit, have never been quick to adapt to cultural change?

If and when they do respond, I am confident that Albert Cohen's reputation will be among the first to benefit from such a necessary reevaluation. For no writer, in fact, has been so consistently undervalued over the past fifty years. And even if I believe, with Jack Abecassis and others, that Cohen was one of the most outstanding writers of the twentieth century, this conviction is still far from being widespread.

Cohen never belonged to the French Academy. When he was not involved in his administrative professional life (which was no less productive than his literary output, since he was, for instance, the author of the Inter-Governmental Agreement on Refugee Travel Documents of October 1946), he preferred to live a secluded, rather secretive life. He did not like expressing his opinions in popular newspapers. He never tried to become a "public" intellectual. As a consequence, his death in 1981 did not occasion the kind of public tribute the French usually accord well-known men of letters. A small square in a deserted area of the 15th arrondissement of Paris has been named after him, but not a major street in the French capital. And although his publisher, Gallimard, has brought out his main works in two volumes in the prestigious Pléiade series (1993–94), they have received little critical attention since they appeared.

Cohen is not the kind of historical figure liked by the media. Nor has he formed the basis for a wave of scholarly research. He has few fans. Even though they are available in paperback editions, his major works are too long and too full of blatant eroticism to be read by adolescent readers. Avant-garde critics sometimes look condescendingly at his masterpiece, *Belle du Seigneur:* "this is just another naturalist novel," they say, before returning to their preferred field of investigation, the so-called *nouveau roman.* But although I do not dispute that in many ways the *nouveau roman* had a tremendous impact in its time, I doubt whether it could ever generate the kind of rich, complex, deeply disturbing emotions that any book by Cohen is bound to provoke.

It is not only French intellectuals who are at fault here. American champions of Francophone literature could easily incorporate Cohen into their canon, yet they seem no more interested in him than their French counterparts. Such discrimination is all the more puzzling, since this Swiss citizen who was born in 1895 into a Sephardic Jewish family on the Greek island of Corfu certainly can lay claim to a place among French-speaking writers, just as surely as can Aimé Césaire and Léopold Sédar Senghor, to name but two.

French was not even Cohen's mother tongue: when he arrived in France for the first time, at the age of five, he spoke only a Judeo-Venetian dialect (because his birthplace, Corfu, had been occupied by the Venetians when his Spanish Jewish ancestors, expelled from their country in 1492, arrived there). This meant that, for him—as, more recently, for people like Milan Kundera and Andreï Makhine—it was no easy thing to achieve fluency in the language of Molière and Hugo, where the issue is not simply facility, but mastery of the style that distinguishes a great French writer. It symbolizes a bold conquest, a victory won after a long and passionate struggle. Yet both the struggle and the conquest still await proper recognition.

One problem with Cohen may lie in the fact that he did not come from a "colonial" or "postcolonial" background (although Corfu was a British protectorate from 1815 to 1864). He was primarily a European. And he was, to be more precise, a European Jew. That said, have we found the key to the enigma? Should Cohen's marginal position within the French literary field be attributed simply to anti-Semitism?

As Jack Abecassis shows in the present book, the reality is, of course, much more complex. Proust too was a Jew, as was Nathalie Sarraute. So also were Henri Bergson, and Raymond Aron, and Claude Lévi-Strauss. Yet none of them has for that reason been excluded from the pantheon of great literary or intellectual stars, to which Cohen has so far not been admitted.

Cohen's problem must therefore be of a different order. Without anticipating Abecassis's analysis, which is as brilliant and convincing as it is minutely elaborated, I would like to sum up, in my own words, what I regard as one of his most striking theses.

Let's put it this way: the French establishment's reluctance to regard Cohen's work with the same degree of empathy that it accords Proust arises mainly from the fact that Jewish identity is not a central issue in Proust's work, although it is never absent, whereas most of Cohen's work revolves explicitly around the question of Jewish identity.

Moreover, Cohen never leaves the reader in doubt on this issue. The problem of Jewish identity is always related by him to the fact that the European Jews have to live in a predominantly Christian world, a non-Jewish world that rejects the Jewish law and that may at times show itself to be deeply anti-Jewish—as it happened in Europe from the time of the Dreyfus Affair to the Holocaust, that is to say, during most of Cohen's own lifetime.

Proust, like the vast majority of French "Israelites" (as they used to be called) a century ago, was a so-called assimilated Jew and never questioned the "duty" of assimilation, which the French Revolution had imposed on the Jews. On the contrary, for Cohen—as for the many Sephardic Jews who arrived in France in the 1950 and 1960s fleeing the newly independent North African countries—assimilation was neither obvious nor obviously necessary. For people whose ancestors had not directly shared French history, and who viewed themselves as immigrants in France, assimilation was just an option: an option that some accepted and others rejected, or that the same person might be prone—like Cohen—to accept at times and reject at others, depending on several factors, including the level of French anti-Semitism he encountered at any given moment.

Unfortunately, because of the time in which he lived, Cohen was never able to feel completely at ease in that French Christian world. And, unlike other, more introverted or more cautious Jews, he declined to hide his discomfort.

He wrote rather extensively on what he called ironically "the catastrophe of being Jewish" (let us note that "catastrophe" is the standard translation of the Hebrew word *Shoah,* which is the word the most commonly used in Europe, as well as in Israel, to refer to the Holocaust). He might even be said to have been the first writer to give that catastrophe a metaphysical, epic dimension. And this is probably why the French Christian world, which never fully accepted him as a citizen when he was alive, still has difficulties accepting him as a writer now that he is dead. It is not only that anti-Semites do not like to be called anti-Semites. It is a much deeper issue involving the "clash" of religions which over the past two thousand years has never ceased to be at the core of the tense Jewish-Christian relationship.

I do not think that in saying so I am overestimating the importance of the religious issue in literary matters. Nobody can seriously doubt that religion and theology (including atheism, which in the end is also theological) played a significant role in French literature and philosophy at all times, including the twentieth century. This is self-explanatory in the case of Paul Claudel, Georges Bataille, André Gide, or Samuel Beckett. It is less explicit in the case of Sartre and Queneau, for instance: yet the last book published by Sartre (with the help of Benny Lévy, alias Pierre Victor) was a book on his own spiritual experiences; and it would not be difficult to show through a close reading of Queneau's novels that they illustrate an ongoing discussion of the validity of Gnosticism, the religious doctrine that most attracted him.

This is why, returning to Cohen, we should not be surprised by the fact that many of his works involve a dialectical argument on the comparative merits and drawbacks of Judaism and Christianity—an opposition embodied in his novels by the character of Solal, on the one side, and his blonde, aristocratic, non-Jewish mistresses (Ariane, Aude, et al.), on the other.

Yet once again we should try to delve beneath the surface. Yes, Cohen supported Judaism; but never unconditionally or unreservedly. In fact, few Jewish writers have been on occasion so critical of certain aspects of Judaism. Cohen, as Jack I. Abecassis says, had a double identity: he was both Jewish and secular, occidental and oriental, masculine and feminine. He was able to identify with Solal as well as with Ariane. And this was, in a sense, his existential drama. A drama that echoes, in a way, that of the Christianized Spanish and Portuguese Jews called Marranos.

Besides, Judaism and Christianity were not only, for him, the names of two distinct religious traditions. They also had an anthropological or cultural significance. He used to view them—not without reason—as two altogether different "ways of making the world" and inhabiting it. From that point of view, Cohen's "Jewishness"—and, more precisely, his Sephardic Jewishness, well rooted in the history of his native island—includes cultural features that continue to be at odds, even today, with the Christian worldview.

One of those features is the radiant acceptance of everything that lies under the sun, be it good or evil, as necessary to the whole order of the universe. This kind of Mediterranean outlook, as one might say, allowed Cohen to recognize the central place of sexuality in our lives without feeling ashamed or guilty about it. It also helped him understand, in a psychoanalytical mode, the unconscious mechanisms (narcissism, sadomasochism . . .) at work in what the Surrealists used to call *amour fou*—an understanding that, in turn, explains his critical views on love, faithfulness, and marriage.

Another feature that is equally linked to the male-dominated cultures of Cohen's Mediterranean background is his pessimistic (and sometimes derogatory) conception of his female characters. In fact, it is hard to deny that Cohen's women remain, in too many cases, cultural stereotypes and, at times, very simplistic ones. Cohen was not a big supporter of feminine emancipation. Even his fans must admit it.

Needless to say, these are two more reasons why his fictional work does not much appeal to Christian French readers, and equally disturbs American readers who perceive his indisputable "machismo" as the highest form of political incorrectness.

This will change, and Cohen's "machismo" will have to be put into historical perspective—that is at least what we can hope for. Yet it will take some time. And it will take still more time, I am afraid, for Cohen's preoccupation with the Jewish identity issue to be accepted as a normal reaction to a predominantly hostile environment.

This, in fact, will be especially difficult in France, a country where, sadly enough, anti-Semitism, after being subject to almost unanimous censorship in the aftermath of the Holocaust, started resurfacing in the years following the Six-Day War (1967) under the guise of "anti-Zionism."

Officially, anti-Zionism pretends to have nothing to do with anti-Semitism. We now know—as Martin Luther King Jr. was the first to say—that such a claim is simply untenable. Denying the Jewish people—and them alone—the right to have their own state is a typically anti-Semitic discrimination. Yet although it has been at times sharply criticized, anti-Zionism is not ebbing at all. It is in fact—at least in France—a rising tide, especially since the so-called Second Intifada began in Israel.

As for Cohen, who was the editor-in-chief of the prestigious *La Revue juive* in Paris before World War II, he never hid his sympathy for Zionism. Yet, his own Zionism was more vocal in the 1920s and the 1930s, on the eve of the war, than it was after the birth of the Israeli state. Actually, he never visited that state. And he chose to spend his last days in Geneva rather than in Jerusalem.

I nevertheless doubt whether the complexity, not to say the strong ambivalence, of his relationship to the so-called Jewish question is fully understood in France. And, as I have said, I doubt this situation is bound to change in the very near future.

This is why I can only rejoice that an American scholar like Jack Abecassis teaches us to read Cohen as he has to be read: as a brilliant, provocative—and sometimes disturbing—witness to the catastrophe that the twentieth century was for European Jews.

Christian Delacampagne

Acknowledgments

The idea for writing this book and many of the analyses within originated during conversations with my wife—my intellectual companion and invaluable editor of ideas and language. I thank Professor Stephen G. Nichols for his encouragement of this project from its inception and for the trust he has placed in me since we met long ago. My colleague, Michael McGaha, has been an infallible conversational partner, especially with respect to Judaic, Sephardic, and Crypto-Jewish studies. My research assistants Erik Stettler and Tina Simon deserve enormous credit for text editing, translation suggestions, and myriad other insights. I would like to thank my colleagues Mary Coffey and Susannah Chavez-Silverman for their constant encouragement and valuable suggestions with different drafts of the manuscript. I am grateful to Peter Dreyer, copy editor for the Johns Hopkins University Press, who did a superb job with the manuscript. I would like to thank the Atelier Albert Cohen in Paris and especially Madame Daisy Politis for their warm hospitality and for free access to the Cohen archives. My French colleagues Philippe Zard and Alain Schaffner have provided me with generous and substantive feedback both during Cohen conferences and with respect to the manuscript. All the financial support needed for the completion of this book has been most generously granted by Pomona College since 1997 in the form of various travel and research grants, including the Yale Griffith (1999) and Harriet Barnard (2003) Faculty Travel Grants, and a National Endowment for the Humanities Sabbatical Research Grant (2001–2).

Abbreviations

BdS	*Belle du Seigneur*
LM	*Le Livre de ma mère*
Ô vous	*Ô vous, frères humains*

Albert Cohen

1 Prologue: The Cohen Paradox

Here, in this room, he has the right to do what he wants, to speak Hebrew, to recite Ronsard to himself, to shout that he is a monster with two heads, a monster with two hearts, that he is everything of the Jewish nation, everything of the French nation. Here, all alone, he can wear the sublime silk of the synagogue over his shoulders and even, if he feels like it, apply the red, white, and blue sticker to his forehead. Here, hidden away and lonely, he will not see the distrustful looks of those he loves and who do not love him. *Albert Cohen,* Belle du Seigneur

As one of the most renowned and yet critically unread authors of the French, Jewish, and Sephardic canons, Albert Cohen (1895–1981) presents a rare paradox in academia. The prestigious Bibliothèque de la Pléiade collection, the most visible sign of canonicity in the French print world, has recognized him by publishing an excellent two-volume compendium of his fiction and essays, and quality paperback editions of his works are sold in every well-stocked bookstore in France.[1] Cohen is read by the French-speaking public, and those who read him rarely remain indifferent to his baroque verve, his passion, and his unique style. Yet despite two illuminating biographies in French and a growing body of criticism by a handful of academics associated with the Atelier Albert Cohen and its series *Cahiers Albert Cohen,* wider scholarly interest remains negligible. This is especially the case in the English-speaking world, where only one of Cohen's works, *Book of My Mother,* is currently in print, and there is not a single critical monograph devoted exclusively to Cohen. This is particularly surprising given that Jewish studies and Holocaust studies have become serious components of twentieth-century French curricula in the United States. Why would an author whom Elaine Marks rightly characterizes as "one of the major French writers of the twentieth century who is Jewish by birth and whose narrators are never not conscious of their own Jewishness and the Jewishness, or relation to Jewishness, of most of the important characters in their fictional world" be all but absent from our curricula?[2]

This is the "Cohen paradox," which from the start has motivated me to think about this author. Cohen is known, read, appreciated, but deemed too disturbing for critical inquiry. Why, in fact, is there such a plethora of commentary on Louis-Ferdinand Céline, a great writer to be sure, but such a dearth of commentary about his contemporary Albert Cohen? The two disturb, but Cohen is—consciously or subconsciously—deemed more disturbing. Why? This is the question that I seek to answer in this book through a series of sustained readings of Cohen's fiction and essays. These readings are an attempt at an uncompromising analysis of his dissonant and nightmarish version of the state of being a Jew, which Cohen himself labels a "catastrophe." I take this core sentiment, which is both ironic and literal, as the main theme of Cohen's work.[3]

To enter Cohen's world is to face the multiple facets of recounting this catastrophe, which in Cohen is like a wound that does not heal, notwithstanding the occasional extravagantly colored bandages adorning it. Kafka recounts a variant of this catastrophe, yet his systematic usage of allegories and of parables, his sober style, and his focalization of the narrative from a single point of view allow the reader a hermeneutic space for multiple identifications and transferences.[4] Does one need to think of the specifically Jewish metaphysical and historical predicament to understand *The Trial* or *In the Penal Colony*? Perhaps, but the abstract allegory permits many possible identifications, and oppressed and alienated readers of all creeds and nationalities can thus read themselves into these allegories. The figurative writ large opens that space. Cohen is stylistically precisely the opposite: the hell of being Jewish in early twentieth-century Europe is taken on directly, despite the astounding pains that his readers have taken to avoid seeing the obvious. His comic and baroque novels abound in multiple points of view, complex (and often half-hidden) plots, digressions, streams of consciousness, exuberant styles, constant flaunting of the French prose style, and even transgression of French syntax. Lost in the forest of Cohen's writing, the reader may find it easy enough to forget what is at stake. Although readers may think that they are reading a satire on romantic delusion (as embodied, for example, in *Anna Karenina*), their unconscious knows the truth that they are reading a burlesque epic on the catastrophe of being Jewish in republican France.

Critics thus politely and even deferentially shy away from the task of evaluating Cohen—they may "love" his writing, but they exclude him from their professional conversation, and silence continues to surround his unpalatable description of the Jewish condition in Europe and the searing ambivalence contained in the Jewish response to this condition. For ideological and esthetic reasons, most of his republican/romantic readers persist in seeing primarily a meditation on romantic love and its vicissitudes even where Cohen emphatically states the religious and political reasons for his hero's personal catastrophe (most explicitly in chapters 54, 93, and 94 of his epic and best-known novel, *Belle du Seigneur*).[5] Not a single critic of *Belle du Seigneur* in the three years following its publication even mentions the key episode of the monumental novel, the episode of the dwarf Rachel hiding in her Berlin cellar in 1936. But this determination not to acknowledge the essential was hardly limited to the book's initial reception. A very recent French history of francophone literature summarizes *Belle du Seigneur* as follows:

> The great theme of Cohen's novel is amorous passion, which is at once glorified and demystified, because it too is liable to weaken. With much satirical verve, the novel also portrays the milieux of international diplomacy in Geneva in the anti-Semitic Europe of the 1930s, all while playfully and derisively suggesting the emptiness and illusory nature of sentiments and ideologies. But the novel is dominated by the spectacular figure of Solal, the passionate, although lucid, seducer. The narrative wins us over with its powerful and baroque inspiration, is often lyrical, epic, tragic, but equally comical, even burlesque.[6]

Everything in this synopsis is true, but unfortunately the main plot of *Belle du Seigneur*—that of an ambivalent court Jew, undersecretary-general of the League of Nations, who tries to save his people from Nazi extermination, fails, and therefore commits suicide—has somehow dissolved into the sprawling text, and instead we have the vague allusion to "anti-Semitic Europe of the 1930s," as if it were just an incidental element, a historical footnote. Is Cohen's Solal in the League of Nations of 1936 like Stendhal's Fabrice at Waterloo, or like Flaubert's Frédéric during the revolution of 1848, so absorbed in his own story ("amorous passion") that he does not notice the horror around him? Is history meaningless to him? Is history just sound and fury dissociated from his narcissism? Obviously not! It is precisely against this interpretive tendency, which I see as a symptom of resistance to the meaning of Cohen's work, that I write this book.

At the risk of anticipating many of the arguments of this book, I'll state here, by way of contrast to the republican/romantic reading, the catastrophic Gospel according to Albert Cohen. Cohen's story is that of a boy who loved France but was violently expelled from her bosom; it is the story of how in the specific context of the interwar period, the biblical Josephic and Estheric political plots of salvation through charisma, seduction, and cunning are exhausted, once and for all, and become Purim carnivals of self-mocking, self-hatred, and hopelessness; it is the story of searing ambivalence about the mother and unrelenting hostility toward the father. It is the story of that nightmarish equivocality where Jews are despised in the flesh but embraced in the abstract, where God is recognized and affirmed by a nonbeliever, where the flesh is condemned for its bestiality and forgetfulness of death yet celebrated in the most sensual way, where the state of Israel is fought for, but the French language remains the true ground of being; it is the universe where a rabbinical Don Juan seduces the feminine projection of himself, a Gentile woman, who also represents the absolute hostile other of his Jewish identity. And, finally, this historical, familial, and psychological nightmare ends in a double suicide—suicide being the theme that haunts Cohen's successive narratives from 1930 to 1978. In other words, Cohen tells the story of the Jewish catastrophe in a specifically twentieth-century French context, from libel to appeasement to genocide (Dreyfus, Munich, Vichy), not simply in terms of historical narrative, but in terms of successive masochistic fantasies of a kind that no other novelist, in my opinion, has ever penned. The power of such a vision is obvious, and its capacity to disturb, to unhinge, and therefore to be resisted and repressed, is vastly underestimated.

Paradoxically, it is precisely this scriptural fauna of plots and styles, this exuberant strangeness of Cohen's prose, that allows the reader, even the very sympathetic reader, to become so "lost" as to be unable to see what is clearly on the page: the Jewish catastrophe, the desire to struggle, the longing for death. Cohen is complicit in this obfuscation of the obvious, inasmuch as he himself couples categorical statements with sleight-of-hand concealments, not simply in the texts themselves but especially in his public commentary on them. But the careful reader is in the end pinned down to a reading of a specific catastrophe, and its representation is so disturbing and so dissonant that it constitutes, in my opinion, the root cause of the institutional resistance to the transmission of Cohen's work.

Abraham Albert Cohen was born in 1895 on the Greek island of Corfu (Kérkira), which had been a place of refuge for Spanish and Portuguese Jews since the sixteenth century. Cohen's family was prominent in the community, his grandfather being its religious and civic leader. Cohen's native language was a Judeo-Venetian dialect, a language that he continued speaking with his parents throughout his life and that underlies his strangely oriental French. After centuries of relative calm, as the euphemism goes, the late nineteenth century was not kinder to the Sephardim in Corfu than it was to their Ashkenazi brethren in eastern Europe. Blood libels preceded the threat of violent pogroms, which then precipitated communal disintegration and emigration. (Later, during World War II, the entire remaining Jewish population of Corfu was decimated by the Nazis, one of the few Sephardic communities to perish en masse during the Holocaust.) In 1900, the Co[h]en family immigrated to Marseille,[7] where his parents toiled away in a modest shop selling eggs, while the five-year-old Albert attended a Catholic convent kindergarten, then a state elementary school, and finally the lycée Thierry (with his lifelong friend Marcel Pagnol). The Dreyfus Affair was in its waning phase, but the anti-Semitic virulence in the streets did not spare the young Albert Cohen, who was traumatized for life by the experience of being publicly harassed by a street hawker. During World War I, he studied law and literature in Geneva, rubbing elbows with that city's restless community of foreign students, who ranged from Bolsheviks to Socialists to Zionists. In 1919, he married Elisabeth Brocher, the daughter of a Calvinist pastor, and became a Swiss citizen. He seized on the occasion to alter his last name: Coen became Cohen, making the name even more Hebrew, just as the immigrant became a citizen. In 1921, he published a collection of lyrical poems entitled *Paroles juives* (Jewish Words) to reveal to his wife the verve, vitality, and sensuality of biblical Israel, as opposed to both Calvinism and exilic Judaism, and, more important, perhaps, to affirm his own Jewish identity vis-à-vis (and despite) his Gentile wife. Their only child, Myriam Judith, was born in 1921.

The next year, a relative promised Cohen a paid internship as an apprentice lawyer in Egypt. He traveled there alone, leaving his wife and one-year-old daughter in Switzerland. But Cohen was never actually paid for his internship, and the entire Egyptian episode was a miserable experience for him, except for a chance encounter that dates the beginning of his vocation as a novelist. Walking down the street in Cairo, he saw displayed in a bookstore window Marcel Proust's *À l'ombre des jeunes filles en fleurs,* the 1919 winner of the Prix Goncourt (the French equivalent of the Pulitzer Prize). He entered the store, picked up the book, began reading, and was transfixed for hours (a store clerk offered the penniless intern a chair to sit on). Later, in 1924, Cohen would teach a summer course on Proust at the University of Geneva.

Cohen's career as a professional Jewish and Zionist activist commenced in Paris in 1925, when Chaim Weizmann, head of the World Zionist Congress, conferred on him the responsibility of establishing, directing, and editing a major cultural review to promote Zionist ideas in the francophone world. Thus was born *La Revue juive* (published by the *Nouvelle Revue française*), whose editorial board included many Jewish notables, among them Sigmund Freud and Albert Einstein. The review was successful in its initial year, but soon disintegrated because of Cohen's difficulty in collaborating with other Zionist representatives in Paris and Geneva. This personal discord seems to have been a permanent feature of Cohen's intermittent work for Jewish and Zionist organizations from 1925 until the end of World War II.[8] In 1926, Cohen obtained a post in the diplomatic section of the International Labor Organization, and he thereafter was concurrently a writer, diplomat, and activist. This triple career ended only in 1951, when he retired from his official functions and devoted himself exclusively to writing.

Cohen's first novel, *Solal* (1930), is remarkable for its Dionysian energy, its breathtaking style, and its emblematic plot. It tells the story of a charismatic Joseph-like figure named Solal, who, born on the Greek island of Cephalonia (also one of the Ionian Islands, like Corfu), ascends to political power in France by means of bravery, cunning, and seduction, but whose career (and life, in the first edition) are destroyed when his Sephardic family encroaches on his secular Parisian life, thereby ending his forgetfulness of his origin and destiny.[9] All of Cohen's subsequent works of fiction focus on the adventures of the great European diplomat Solal and his Gentile women, and on Solal's clownish Sephardic kin, whom he calls the Valorous (also the title of a later work, *Les Valeureux*). The function of the Valorous is both to serve as Solal's ethnic and historical id, and, most important in the plots, to remind Solal that he must be true to his full name (Solal des Solal or, alternatively, Solal Solal), that his life and his name form a tautology from which he cannot escape. Whenever the two worlds collide, disaster occurs. *Solal* was a major literary achievement, garnering wide critical acclaim and meriting immediate translation into English and German. The success won Cohen a long-term contract and stipend from Gallimard, the most important French publishing house both then and now.

His next work, the one-act play *Ézéchiel* (Ezekiel), was staged at the Odéon theater in 1931 and won the first prize in the Comoedia competition. Two years later, the Comédie-Française gave ten performances. *Ézéchiel* tells the story of a Greek Sephardic banker (Solal's father), a grotesque combination of Shylock and Molière's Harpagon incarnating each and every anti-Semitic stereotype, while at the same time claiming to represent the eternal spirit of the Jews. The play sparked heated controversy, especially among Jews (even Cohen's closest friends criticized the play for its alleged display of anti-Semitic self-hatred), and when Gallimard published the final version in 1956, the reprobation of the Jewish community continued unabated.

In 1938, Cohen published *Mangeclous* (Naileater), a burlesque novel focusing on the adventures of Solal and the Valorous. Cohen's original authorial intent was different. Since 1935, he had intended to publish a single novel, entitled *Belle du Seigneur,* or alternatively (and very significantly) "La Geste des Juifs" (The epic of the Jews), that would defy all genre conventions by juxtaposing in one narrative most of the established modes of expression, whether of Rabelais, Proust, or Joyce.[10] By 1938, Cohen already had a complete draft of *Belle du Seigneur,* but he was not entirely satisfied with it. Gallimard insisted on publishing something, however, and to satisfy his contractual obligations, *Mangeclous* was thus extracted from the sprawling manuscript. The novel's blatantly disjointed form, along with the unfortunate timing of its publication, on the eve of World War II, explains its lukewarm critical reception.

With the war imminent and a clear sense of urgency, Cohen returned to his diplomatic career as spokesman for a number of Jewish and Zionist organizations. He launched a feverish campaign in 1939–40 for the creation of a substantial Jewish Foreign Legion that would be trained by the French Army and fight at its side. Cohen was rather successful in his negotiations with the higher echelons of the French Army, but the project was vetoed by Quai d'Orsay (the French Foreign Office) and by the British Foreign Office, both representing colonial powers in the Near East and both hostile toward any organized Jewish armed force, which they perceived as the precursor of a future Jewish army in Palestine. (Ironically, this was exactly what happened with the British "Jewish Brigade" that fought in the middle and later stages of World War II). Cohen's prewar effort thus failed. The phony war *(drôle de guerre)* soon commenced, followed by the debacle of the French and British Armies in May–June 1940.

Fleeing the invading German armies and accompanied by his daughter and his second wife, Marianne Goss (his first wife had died of lymphatic cancer in 1924), Cohen escaped from France in June 1940 to London, where he continued his career as writer, diplomat, and activist. In his haste to abandon his Paris apartment on the rue du Cherche Midi, he left behind all his manuscripts, including the first complete version of *Belle du Seigneur;* these were saved, along with the furniture, only by the good graces of the Swiss legation, and stored safely in its diplomatic cellars. In London from 1940 to 1947, Cohen published early versions of his major essays about his mother (who died in 1943 in German-occupied Marseille) and about the traumatic anti-Semitic street incidents he had experienced in Marseille in 1905, as well as various wartime articles, mainly in *La France libre.* He was also very active on the diplomatic front, first serving as diplomatic liaison between the Jewish Agency for Palestine and the Allies, and then, from 1944 to 1947, at the summit of his legal and diplomatic career, working as legal counselor for the London-based Intergovernmental Committee for Refugees. There he wrote *The Refugee Travel Title* (1946), which he considered his most important work, either diplomatic or literary, and which subsequently became the basis for the definitive *International Conventions Relative to the Status of Refugees of the 28th of July 1951.*[11]

Albert Cohen and Marianne Goss officially divorced in 1947, having been separated since 1946, and he pursued his diplomatic career in Geneva until 1951. Cohen returned to literature in 1954 with the autobiographical essay *Le Livre de ma mère (Book of My Mother),* and a revised version of his play *Ézéchiel,* published in 1956. *Le Livre de ma mère* was an instant hit and reestablished Cohen in the French literary world. *Ézéchiel,* however, suffered the same reprobation as in 1933. In the middle 1950s, having married Bella Berkowich, his literary secretary, Cohen commenced an isolated, reclusive existence, punctuated by three surgeries and bouts of depression.[12] During this period of isolation, melancholy, and sickness, he and Bella produced four drafts of his monumental novel *Belle du Seigneur,* and in 1967, he submitted a 1,400-page manuscript of it to his publisher, which was rejected "as is" by the Gallimard editors, who judged it to be stylistically incoherent, technically unmanageable, and literarily unpalatable. Cohen then reconfigured the novel by deleting five hundred pages of seriocomic, Rabelaisian material, and the relatively streamlined *Belle du Seigneur* as we know it today was subsequently published. For this novel he received the Grand Prix du roman de l'Académie française and immediate critical and popular acclaim. After 1968, Cohen become an odd literary celebrity, often sought out for interviews, which he seems to have relished, the most famous of which is the one-hour interview in his apartment for the weekly literary television program *Apostrophes* with Bernard Pivot.[13] These interviews were mostly regrettable: Cohen allowed the interviewer to frame his work in erroneous ways, permitting his "Stendhalization" and "Don Juanization" (Pivot spent an inordinate amount of the *Apostrophes* interview inquiring with great titillation about the ten "moves" of seduction). In other interviews, perhaps under the influence of medication, Cohen proffered perplexing statements, especially about other authors.[14] The deleted fragments of *Belle du Seigneur* were subsequently published in 1969 as *Les Valeureux* (The valorous), a separate, stand-alone novel, which concludes the saga of Solal. In 1971, he published *Ô vous, frères humains* (O you, human brothers), an autobiographical essay about a traumatic anti-Semitic incident he suffered as a child. *Carnets 1978* (Notebooks 1978), a dark and lyrical meditation on mortality and suffering, is a monologue addressed by Cohen to an absent God, whom Cohen sees as the projection of the Jewish prophetic temperament onto the infinite—the delirious cogitations of a man nearing death, but already present in *Solal* forty-eight years earlier. There is an astounding unity to all of Cohen's writings.

Before his death in 1981, Cohen insisted that many thousands of manuscript pages and all his correspondence be destroyed.[15] I suspect that he feared that he might suffer at the hands of others the fate that Proust had suffered at his own. We know that in 1925, Cohen asked Robert Proust (Marcel's older brother) to see the author's archives. And what a disappointment it was! Cohen was sickened by Proust's letters to the princesse de Noailles, and he was henceforth unable to read *À la recherche du temps perdu* without feeling contempt for an author whose personal correspondence was filled with flattery and nonsense.[16] I surmise that he feared the same fate for his own literary posterity—feared that some of his papers that revealed his own foibles might fall into the hands of merciless readers and discredit his work. It would consequently be safer, he felt, to burn the papers and leave the published work to stand exclusively on its own merits, sheltered from traces left behind of the feebleness of an ego enmeshed in what he called the "baboonery" of "the Social," which is always the very petri dish of stupidity. Another reason for burning the manuscripts was that Cohen had created an aristocratic and erotic creation myth according to which his published works were the fruit of spontaneous oral dictation to a loving woman, the Seigneur dictating to his Belle. And while it is true that he dictated much of his work, the myriad manuscripts would surely have revealed a much more belabored writing process. Nothing would have displeased Cohen more than a careful genetic reconstruction of his texts. He was too invested in his own myth.

The foregoing literary chronology underscores an essential thematic and stylistic synchrony in all of Cohen's writings. Albert Cohen recognized this synchrony, and he was fond of saying that he simply masticated *(ressassait)* his own "cud," that is, he endlessly repeated the same (dissonant) montage, only in different keys, scales, and tonalities. The history of the creation of his monumental novel *Belle du Seigneur* bears this out. In fact, the only published novel that adheres to Cohen's original manuscript intent is *Solal,* which best represents his aesthetic choice to juxtapose the dissonant genres of the romantic and the seriocomic in a single text. In other words, *Mangeclous, Belle du Seigneur,* and *Les Valeureux* should be read as one novel, the prototype of which, *in petito,* is *Solal.*

It is impossible today to recover "La Geste des Juifs," the baroque *roman fleuve* that Cohen initially intended, from *Belle du Seigneur.* And, as noted above, Cohen went out of his way to make sure that we would not even be tempted to try. But when reading these texts, one should nevertheless remember the artificiality of their truncated state. This is why I study the dialogical relationship, the astonishing intratextuality, among Cohen's seriocomic novels, (anti)-romantic novels, and autobiographical essays. The same characters—Solal, the Valorous—appear in all four novels, and Cohen seems to assume the reader's familiarity with the unfolding saga at hand. The fifty-year-long dialogue between Solal and Mangeclous, between the competing fantasies of Jew and Gentile, Don Juan and Jeremiah, the Orient and the Occident, insiders and outsiders, is key to any hermeneutics of Cohen's œuvre as a whole. It is all too tempting to read Cohen only through the narrative of *Belle du Seigneur* or only through those of *Mangeclous* and *Les Valeureux,* without seeing their tight dialogical relationship, whatever their aesthetic incongruity.[17] The two most seemingly disparate novels begin in the same manner. Solal contemplates killing himself in *Belle du Seigneur;* likewise *Les Valeureux* opens with Mangeclous deciding that that day is to be his last day, that he is going to finally commit suicide, since he has no prospect of becoming a great man, and that a huge, Rabelaisian meal is therefore called for. Mangeclous does not kill himself but eventually returns to his birthplace, Cephalonia—a return trip that, as the play *Ézéchiel* strongly suggests, is for Solal worse than death.

Even across genre boundaries, Cohen traffics in almost identical fantasies—words, phrases, and images float from one genre to the other; entire fragments transit from his essays, such as *Le Livre de ma mère, Ô vous, frères humains,* and *Carnets 1978,* to his fiction, and vice versa. In *Belle du Seigneur,* Uncle Saltiel, who wants his nephew Solal to marry a Jewess, places a page-long personal ad that reads exactly like the rambling account of the qualities most desirable in a Jewish wife that Cohen attributes to his mother in *Le Livre de ma mère.*[18] Furthermore, many of the metacritical digressions, apostrophes, and mini-essays in Cohen's works of fiction bear a close resemblance to his actual biographical essays. And the essays clearly contain nascent fictional or fictionalized episodes. This is why the whole question of knowing whether the fictional Solal stands for Albert Cohen, which Cohen categorically denied, is beside the point.[19] If anything, Solal, together with the Valorous and the maternal figure, represents *in toto* a collage of Cohen's repeated ghoulish and clownish identity fantasies.

The intention of this book is to study in all its facets the representation that Cohen gives of the "catastrophe of being Jewish," which is the most difficult—and therefore the most repellent—thematic thread in Albert Cohen's literary creation. In a sequence of chapters that range in theme from early trauma to mythic and historical fantasies to mourning and finally to suicide, I cut along the rawest nerves that run through Cohen's work. It may be objected that this suicidal scheme is common enough, especially in introspective novels.[20] True, but my interest lies precisely in what makes Cohen's suicidal schemes emblematic of a collective experience that transcends personal psychology. Too often the critical tendency has been to accept Solal's suicide as the result of disenchantment with romantic love, a view that Cohen did not discourage, because he remains obtuse or even misleading as to the meaning of those suicides to the very end. This view is partially valid, but terribly misleading. Whereas the final double suicide in *Belle du Seigneur* has sometimes been interpreted as a Jewish variation on the theme of *Tristan and Isolde,* I see it as a direct response to the "catastrophe of being Jewish" in the specific circumstances of the 1930s.[21] In my view, Solal commits suicide because he is a failed Joseph and a failed Esther, and not because he is a failed Don Juan or a miserable Julien Sorel. The scheme of the erotic suicide is simply an intertextual Trojan Horse, which transports a specifically Jewish nightmare into the French *cité des belles lettres.* The relevant historical intertext of Cohen's morbidity is more likely to be found in the biographies of Theodor Lessing, Rudolph Loewenstein, and Sander Gilman's self-executing Jews than in *Madame Bovary* and *Anna Karenina.*[22] Solal's suicide is his personal holocaust—and there is no way of understanding *Belle du Seigneur* unless the fate of European Jewry during the Holocaust is both the background and heart of the novel, its partially invisible center of gravity.[23]

Cohen's dissonant baroque aesthetics are also crucial for my argument. His fiction is akin to the carnival of Purim (a general parody of being, or humorous masochistic exercise, that exilic Judaism developed as a survival mechanism) writ large, expressed through the constant play of doubling and concealment. The mythical overlay, the confrontation of a personal journey and concrete historical context (pregnant with the impending catastrophe in those years between the wars), and the baroque performative expressiveness clearly set Cohen's carnivalesque epic novels apart from similar narratives of introspection and make his suicidal schema worthy of close study. In a sense, I am retelling the legend of Albert Cohen in my own manner—trying to account for his spectacular masochistic dissonance.[24]

Sketched thus, Albert Cohen's diplomatic and literary lives, and the motifs of his writings, do not square with the evident reluctance to include him in our cultural heritage, and being included in my view only occurs if an author is not only read (and Cohen is) but also written about, studied in classrooms and graduate seminars, and becomes, in short, part of a living conversation. The musical metaphor of "dissonance" in the title of this book asks the reader to adopt a dynamic mode of thought when approaching this paradox—with respect both to the logic of Cohen's texts and the effect that they have on readers. Dissonance in music refers to the tension in a chord that must, but does not, resolve itself by notes returning to a certain (resting) scale. Inversely, musical consonance refers to rest and resolution, in other words, harmony.[25] Every text contains dynamics of tension and resolution, but what is particular to Cohen are both the specific character of his dissonance and its effect on readers. Every familiar note (say Tristan and Isolde or Don Juan or even Zionist hopes) descends to another key without harmonic resolution, not even in death. That is the repetitive procedure.

Cohen speaks through the juxtaposition of a number of incongruent voices. In Chapter 6, for example, I show how in *Belle du Seigneur,* the protagonist Solal is concurrently a Don Juan who seduces women serially and a Jeremiah who denounces the valorization of all markers of hierarchical physical difference, such as beauty and strength, as a symptom of zoological regression from the human to the animal. Furthermore, in seducing Ariane, his feminized Aryan double, Solal seems to assert that Judaism stands for the massive transvaluation of all pagan values, that is, the victory of the Law over nature, of the human over the animal. And yet Solal does not practice the Law, does not believe in God (the source of the Law), and shuns the company of Jews whenever possible. Historically, this predicament, this systematic masochism, reminds us of the metaphysical and existential double binds of European assimilated Judaism.[26] But Solal's hysterical anti-nature jeremiads also run counter to his own Zionism, which is itself a complete transvaluation of traditional Jewish values in that it advocates a return to nature, beauty, and strength, and a turning away from traditional forms of subservience to the Law.[27]

Furthermore, Solal's metaphysical rants contain strong misogynistic overtones, stemming from both the Don Juan and the Jeremiah dimensions, and I suspect these also play a large part in the institutional reticence about Albert Cohen.[28] In Cohen's fiction, the romantic European woman adores the alpha baboon—and is therefore contemptible, just as contemptible, I may add, as the object of her desire, the baboon. The Jewish woman (read, the mother), on the other hand, stands in opposition to the Aryan lover in that she values the Law over nature. On the face of it, this seems to be the logic of the manifest plot of *Belle du Seigneur.* Yet a close reading of what Ariane actually says in her multiple streams of consciousness renders this argument meaningless. Ariane in fact hates male baboons and yearns for exactly the same feminine paradise as that described in *Le Livre de ma mère,* where Cohen fantasizes about becoming an old woman living with her sister—who is also, incidentally, Cohen's mother. I argue that the character of Solal is a hybrid of Don Juan, Jeremiah, and a feminized son, caught in his own web of historical, metaphysical, and psychoanalytical dissonances, tensions that can only be resolved in suicide—the double suicide of the empirical self (Solal) and its poeticized feminine phantasm (Ariane). In other words, the protean formula of *Belle du Seigneur,* as indeed of all of Cohen's fiction, is *the self-fashioning of death with the other who is at heart the same.*

Finally, writing about a foreign author who is virtually unknown to the English-speaking public presents expository problems that a critic of Flaubert or Proust does not face. Most readers of this book have little or no familiarity with Cohen's texts. Wherever it seemed appropriate, I have therefore included plot summaries and brief biographical details based on the critical apparatus of the Pléiade edition of *Belle du Seigneur* and Jean Blot's and Gérard Valbert's biographies of Cohen.[29] To facilitate further research and study of Cohen, a bibliography of his published writings and comprehensive listings of biographical studies of him and of studies of his works are provided preceding the general bibliography. I have tried to make the book as readable as possible by giving translations of passages cited from Cohen's writings, or sometimes quotations from David Coward's translation of *Belle du Seigneur,* in the body of the text, with the original French given below in the footnotes. I have also avoided using untranslated French terms. By building my study of "Cohen" from the ground up, as it were, I aim to familiarize the reader with Cohen's idiom: his mythopoetic vernacular, linguistic ticks, repetitions, and obsessive echoes of core scenes. I have striven throughout to minimize critical jargon and scholarly clutter and to adopt a vocabulary peculiar to Cohen (e.g., "the Social," "belonging" *[en être],* "baboonery"). All the same, this book is very much indebted to the existing scholarly works on Cohen, to psychoanalytical concepts (especially those of Melanie Klein and Daniel Sibony), to the Bakhtinian poetics of the novel, to narratology (especially Dorit Cohn's work on the stream of consciousness and Peter Brooks's understanding of plots and metaphors), and to the intellectual history of Judaism, especially the concept of the Marrano,[30] the crypto-Jew. In writing this book, I had in mind A. B. Yehoshua's monumental novel *Mr. Mani*, which is a modernist rewriting of the book of *Genesis*, haunted by transgression, insanity, and suicides. Most important, however, I finally got a bearing on the figure of Solal—or was rescued from a "Stendhalian" vision of Solal—through the reading of Thomas Mann's series of four novels on the theme of Joseph and his brothers (1934–44). Mann's expansive treatment of the story of the patriarch Jacob, his wives, sons, and eventually, Joseph in Egypt—all written as an allegory of the predicament of modern Judaism—allowed me to begin to understand the Solal identity montage in all its mythic and historical dimensions and therefore begin to make the necessary connections among the seemingly highly disparate elements of Cohen's works. Mann taught me how to begin to read Cohen.

1 *The Double Bar Mitzvah*

The essential is to be identical to your name, to incarnate it.
Daniel Sibony, Perversions

[The]Father . . . has this obsession of forcing the son to sacrifice.
Daniel Sibony, Psychanalyse et Judaïsme

The Jewish adolescent rite of passage, or bar ("to be worthy of") mitzvah ("commandment"), signifies individuation vis-à-vis parents and integration into a community. Cohen presents two distinct bar mitzvahs—the first, in *Solal,* is a bar mitzvah ceremony during which the father explicitly commands his son, Solal, to estrange himself from all communities except the Jewish community. This demand for communitarian and metaphysical insularity also reminds Solal that, since the destruction of the Temple, Jews have existed outside of history. The second, metaphorical bar mitzvah occurs in *Ô vous, frères humains,* an autobiographical narrative that recounts an adolescent rite of passage in 1905 when the ten-year-old Albert Cohen was subjected to violent anti-Semitic aggression. Here, for the first time, Cohen comes to perceive himself, irremediably, as a perennial universal pariah, not an *Israélite* citizen of the French Republic. (The *Israélite* is an assimilated person of Jewish origin, whereas the *Juif* [Jew] is an unassimilated Jew.)[1] An anti-Semitic street hawker *(camelot)* delivers a message essentially like the one dictated by the father in *Solal:* you are fundamentally different, quintessentially foreign; your place in history is one of permanent exile. Good society in which people are at ease with themselves is forever inaccessible to you. Even when successful in the Social, yours will always be a high-wire act. The street hawker's message is the X-ray negative of the image transmitted by the father: while the father insists on insularity from the inside, the anti-Semite imposes exclusion from the outside—both exclude Solal from Europe, the one community to which he really wants to belong. Cohen thus remains suspended between the Jewish ghetto and the Gentile European city, with no return and no definite departure.

Bar Mitzvah I: Metaphysical Calling-Reminding

In the first part of *Solal,* the thirteen-year-old protagonist, Solal des Solal, celebrates his bar mitzvah. After the Shabbath synagogue service, his father, Rabbi Gamaliel, gives the bar mitzvah charge. Gamaliel plays a pivotal role in the *Solal / Belle du Seigneur* saga, for he is simultaneously the biological father of Solal, the rabbi and patriarch of the Jewish community in Cephalonia, and a renowned expert in Halakah (Jewish Law). He embodies authority and the transmission of the Law. Even so, his bar mitzvah charge simply stuns those present, who had expected a cheerful, hortatory bar mitzvah charge but instead hear a bleak theological diatribe, a lashing of sorts with the spears of the Law. Gamaliel targets his son exclusively, the audience is merely the backdrop: face-to-face, the patriarch summons his son to utter and thereby affirm the Abrahamic and Mosaic *Here I am.*

Solal is no ordinary adolescent. The strength and beauty of his body and the brilliance of his mind mark him as singular—and Gamaliel knows it. At night while looking at the stars, the great rabbi often wonders whether his son is the *L'Attendu* (the Expected), that is, the Messiah, and others, as we shall later see, have the same premonition.[2] So, instead of clichés about the passage from childhood to adulthood, this charge—the affirmation that the father demands from the son—concerns the passage from nature to anti-nature, from history to insularity. Solal is summoned literally to forego what is *at hand* for what is *in memory.* Gamaliel's charge represents what Daniel Sibony calls a calling-reminding *(appel-rappel)* of the father to the son, although here it is a particularly brutal example. The violent charge is a traumatic experience, because it marks the opening of a rift between father and son, pitting the son's concrete exogenous desire against the father's abstract yet brutal demand for fidelity to difference, memory, and location.

The scene is dramatic. Posed majestically under a radiant blue Mediterranean sky, in a courtyard infused with the perfume of citrus trees and jasmine, Gamaliel admonishes Solal to accord his conduct and desire to the strictest version of priestly Judaism by learning to inhabit this abyss between nature and the Law. Gamaliel's charge represents an intransigent priestly vision of Judaism, a strain of Judaism that is insular and impermeable to all foreign intrusion, and, above all, resistant to the romantic ambitions already in an advanced state of gestation in Solal's charismatic and erotic imagination:

> Act justly without hope of reward, so that the people may reap glory. (Pause.) Despise woman and what they call beauty. They are two fangs of the serpent. Anathema on him who stops to look at a beautiful tree. (Pause.) Charity is the pleasure of feminine peoples; the charitable savors the exhalations of his goodness; in his heart of hearts he proclaims himself righteous; charity is vanity and love of your neighbor is of impure origin. The poor man has a legal right of ownership to part of your property. (Pause.) Later, do not be repelled by our deformity. We are the monsters of humanity, for we have declared war on nature.*

This diatribe must be read carefully, for these propositions reverberate throughout the *Solal / Belle du Seigneur* saga, and at the least expected, and most dissonant, moments. I read this discourse as an early metaphysical trauma, the symptoms of which resurface time and again in Cohen's writings.

The punctuation conveys a paratactic rhythm, suspended with clearly marked parenthetical indications "(Pause.)" of silence. Like a stone sinking to the bottom of a deep well, each proposition is given the silent time to reach the bottom and settle. The propositions are delivered in cadence, juxtaposed, with the exception of the last one; they are not reasoned or even coordinated as a series of logical propositions. This is the cadence of the Law, laid down like the Tablets of Moses—oracular words beyond articulated reason. Gamaliel's speech contains five principal propositions:

> 1. "Act justly without hope of reward, so that the people may reap glory. (Pause.)" Justice is decoupled from individual destiny. Justice benefits and thereby glorifies the people, not only the individuals who act justly. Dutiful action does not allow for individual compensation—there is no hope of personal glory, distinction, individuation, or realization of narcissistic desire. The ego is abstracted; only the community stands, the only goal of which is glory gained through obedience to the Law.

*"Sans espoir de récompense agis avec justice afin que le peuple soit glorifié. (Pause.) Méprise la femme et ce qu'ils appellent beauté. Ce sont deux crochets du serpent. Anathème à qui s'arrête pour regarder un bel arbre. (Pause.) La charité est le plaisir des peuples féminins; le charitable savoure les fumées de sa bonté; en son âme secrète, il se proclame supérieur; la charité est une vanité et l'amour du prochain vient des parties impures. Le pauvre a droit légal de propriété sur une partie de ton bien. (Pause.) Plus tard, ne sois pas rebuté par notre difformité. Nous sommes le monstre d'humanité; car nous avons déclaré combat à la nature." (*Solal,* 111)

2. "Despise woman and what they call beauty. They are two fangs of the serpent." Decant the sexual difference of all aesthetic value in favor of the human-divine difference. The religious life probes the presence of the divine in that difference between the world as-it-is and that which gives it meaning; it "manages" this tension by obeying the Law, and, above all, studies its texts. The sensual life, where sexual difference is essential, creates its own value, through adoration of beauty and attention to minutiae. According to Gamaliel, the two differences are mutually exclusive. Woman is the source of perdition. The pronoun "they" *(ils)* is important. It does not refer to those assembled, but to those besieging the ghetto community: the Greeks and, above all, the Europeans, pagan adulators of "beauty." The references to the serpent and its two fangs (woman, beauty) obviously echo Genesis 3, but in a curious way. Gamaliel exhibits an unusually Augustinian reading of the Fall, since Jewish thought does not accord the narrative of Adam and Eve the ontological import attributed to it in Christianity.[3] Curiously, though, Solal repeats the father's anti-feminine diatribe, especially at moments of erotic seduction and/or disintegration, moments when he is seemingly the farthest from the calling-reminding represented by the father. When Solal, for example, harpoons his wife Aude with his spite against the feminine, he transposes the father's bar mitzvah charge without changing the slightest nuance:

> Imbecile, he articulated. You idiot, I paid you the royal tribute of being sincere and disarmed. You have seen me on my knees, me! How right I was always to despise women! Before I was born I detested the servile creatures, who worship the fist, the intonation, and the fame. I loathe my memories of my intra-uterine life. So, what you needed was virile silence, and the virile ice, which you little satin idiots are always dying to break. 'Rat-a-tat, beautiful knight, strong and silent, may I come in?' Imbecile! All this time I have been trying to escape the machinery [of the masculine]. I tried not to treat you as a woman. I honored you.*

3. "Anathema on him who stops to look at a beautiful tree. (Pause.)." This dictum refers to a famous passage from *The Ethics of the Fathers [Pirke*

*Imbécile! articula-t-il. Ô idiote, je t'ai fait ce royal hommage d'être sincère et désarmé. Tu m'as vu à genoux, moi! Le mépris que j'ai toujours éprouvé pour la femme, comme il était juste. Avant ma naissance, je détestais ces créatures de servage qui adorent le poing, l'intonation et le renom. Quel sale souvenir j'ai gardé de ma vie intra-utérine. Donc ce qu'il te fallait, c'était le silence viril et la glace virile que les petites folles de satin meurent d'envie de rompre. "Toc toc toc, beau chevalier énergique et silencieux, puis-je entrer?" Imbécile! Tous ces temps, je n'ai pas voulu faire de la machinerie. Je n'ai pas voulu te traiter en femme. Je t'ai honorée. (*Solal,* 326)

Avot], a compendium of ethical principles authored by some sixty sages between 300 B.C.E. and 200 C.E., which actually reads: "R. Jacob said, He who is walking by the way and studying, and breaks off his study and says, How fine is that tree, how fine is that fallow, him the Scripture regards as if he had forfeited his life."[4] Where Rabbi Gamaliel's proposition seems to apply to all persons in all circumstances, in the original context, this prohibition and anathema are much more circumscribed, applying exclusively to a person who is in the midst of studying the Torah. Perhaps the most surprising of the propositions, this decree almost places Rabbi Gamaliel in Gnostic heresy, where all matter is fallen and only the immaterial spirit is divine. This proposition blatantly contradicts the "And it was good!" declaration at the end of each day of creation in Genesis, which we shall find echoed in *Solal:* "And God rejoices in his creature."* Theology aside, it is imperative here to note the radical estrangement that the Law of the father imposes on the son—not merely estrangement from the feminine, but from everything material and beautiful. Everything is disinvested except for the study of the Torah and the survival of the community. Ironically, these Gnostic-sounding propositions could not be in greater dissonance with the seductive physical backdrop: a sunny Greek island and blue sea; the aroma of trees and flowers permeating everything—including the son's nascent libido.

4. "Charity is the pleasure of feminine peoples; the charitable savors the exhalations of his goodness; in his heart of hearts he proclaims himself righteous; charity is vanity and love of your neighbor is of impure origin. The poor man has a legal right of ownership to part of your property. (Pause.)" Again, the good does not come from individual judgment or choice, but instead from respect for rights and duties placed above any and all intersubjective dynamics. Again, the ego is circumvented, for whatever pleasure it may derive from charitable acts is condemned as feminine narcissism. The masculine is all Law. It does not depend on the vagaries of desire for gratitude, the philanthropist's secret sadism. The masculine gives because of the Law, not because of natural categories such as pity or pride. The poor have a right to a portion of your goods, and when you give them whatever is rightfully theirs, do not bask in the aura of self-congratulating *caritas.* Draw justice from subjective desire and place it in collective obligation, well beyond the vagaries of the will. "Love of your neighbor is of impure origin": The Law does not summon you to love your neighbor, but to

*Et Dieu se réjouissait de sa créature. (*Solal,* 193)

respect him or her. After all, the fifth commandment of Moses reads: "Respect *[Chabed]* your father and mother"—as opposed to "Love your father and mother."[5] Likewise, the essence of Judaism according to Hillel—"Don't do unto others what you do not want done to yourself"—does not necessarily imply any notion of love, but rather a utilitarian concept of cooperative mutuality. Gamaliel again criticizes the utopian ambient Christian theology in which love supposedly eclipses the Law. One of Cohen-the-novelist's voices often echoes Gamaliel's critique, especially in his acerbic satire of high-minded charitable charades: "Versailles, Trianon Palace. Charity ball of the Ladies of the Bloody Cross. On the chests of heavy gunner generals the crosses of Saint John and Saint Peter."*

5. "Later, do not be repelled by our deformity. We are the monsters of humanity, for we have declared war on nature." This is the only proposition that contains within it an argument. Read backward, the logical chain unfolds: Jews have declared war on nature and messianic utopias, and they have thus become monstrous to pagans and Christians. This metaphysical monstrosity has physically deformed the Jews, as Cohen would explain in an extensive and searing stream of consciousness at the end of *Belle du Seigneur.*[6] Although he himself is beautiful, the godlike Solal should learn to interpret correctly, and therefore not be repelled by, his kin's repulsiveness. Cohen's readers will at this point recognize the conceptual origin of his carnivalesque and physically grotesque protagonists: Mangeclous; the band of deformed but ever so entertaining relatives known as the Valorous; Solal's mother; Jérémie; and, above all, the dwarf Rachel. I know of no other Jewish fictional author who exorcises these misshapen demons, whether they are real, self-generated, or an interiorization of the Gentile's hostile gaze, or a combination of all three. Be that as it may, this last proposition in the father's diatribe may germinate and eventually mutate, but its seed will remain a constant programmatic desire in Cohen's writings: to "show the glory of Israel to those who saw only Jews"†—while Cohen remains, at least in the fictional character of Solal, extremely ambivalent about his repulsion from and outright desire for this "monstrosity." Time and again, Solal willingly fabricates situations where he attempts not to be "repelled by our deformity" and repeatedly falls short of embracing this "deformity." Much of the fictional and conceptual drama of Cohen's writ-

*Versailles. Trianon-Palace. Bal de bienfaisance des Dames de la Croix Sanglante. Aux poitrines des généraux d'artillerie lourde les croix de saint Jean et de saint Pierre. (*Solal,* 213)

†dire la beauté d'Israël à qui ne voyait que les Juifs (*Solal,* 291)

ing derives its power from this attraction to and repulsion from Jews. Solal, at least, always falls short of obeying Gamaliel's commands, yet he remains forever mindful of them.

Many of these propositions may seem strange to those familiar with the Hebrew Bible. For example, contrary to Gamaliel's admonitions, the affirmation of the inherent goodness of creation is categorical, although God is caught in the drama of either blessing or scattering, creating or destroying, an in-between dynamic notably absent from Gamaliel's monological dogmatism, which tends to resemble Gnosticism more than Judaism.[7] But the link between greatness and beauty, if not necessarily causal and categorical, as in the Greek sense of *kalon k'agathon* (good and noble conduct), is nevertheless an important and persistent feature of Hebrew and Jewish greatness, as in the cases of Sarah, Joseph, King David (supposedly God's favorite), and Queen Esther.

But I suspect that the real etiology of Gamaliel's rigidity also reflects concrete historical realities. In part, at least, his theology is a symptom of a long history of exile, exclusion, and violence—and therefore intellectual deformation, which explains Cohen's corrective intent in *Paroles juives* (1921) to excavate and recover from the ruins of exilic Judaism a form of positive and sensual Hebraism (but even here he is unable to suppress his aggressiveness):

> Endormie
> Sur ta bouche entrouverte
> Sur tes lèvres fendues de fièvre
> J'écraserai les filles lourdes de la vigne.
>
> Comme l'esclave à genoux je laverai la blessure.
> Et je baiserai ta lassitude royale
> Ô Sulamite.[8]
>
> Asleep
> On your but slightly parted lips
> On your lips cracked with fever
> I shall crush the heavy daughters of the vine.
>
> Like a slave on his knees I shall cleanse your wound.
> And I shall kiss your regal weariness
> O Shulamite.

In these early poems, he expresses a desire to escape from both Gamaliel's rigid rabbinical posture and the equally misanthropic Pauline and Augustinian anthropology. In rejecting both, he desires to "show the glory of Israel to those who saw only Jews," exhibiting the Zionist will to excavate the Hebrew beneath the Jew. This Jewish-Hebrew fault line, along with his budding European identity, gives rise to Solal's own particular dissonant identity montage. But, as Alain Schaffner correctly asserts, these straightforward "Solalic" poems represent the "Cohen before Cohen," that is, the Albert Cohen before he adopted a much more Pauline anthropology, which always undermines the excavation of the Hebrew beneath the Jew and therefore circles back to a moribund conception of Judaism.[9]

In saying "No!" to his father's charge, Solal resists (self-)sacrifice to the father's Law and the imperative slavery to memory. The father wants to sacrifice his son to the Law and to the exilic community. But Solal is no Isaac; he is more of a Joseph; he does desire at times to serve his kin, but always reticently, at arm's length. To reach this position in the outside world (the courts of Pharaoh or Ahasuerus, or the League of Nations in Geneva), the father must be eclipsed. Joseph's luck was to have lost his father, at least for a long while. That is not to say that Solal rejects the father's Law or the memory of kin outright, merely that he entertains a very ambiguous relationship to them, oscillating between fidelity and rejection, attraction and repulsion. This dissonance will mark Solal's fictional career; he will violate all the "Thou shall not(s)" of the father, all the while holding on to the father's Law in some perverse, fanatical fashion.

Why dissonance? Because each and every point of the father's Law estranges Solal from the secular European world he so desires; and, later on, each advance into this coveted European Social remains always precarious in nature. The Law estranges him from the world; the world estranges him from the Law; when he is with the one, he opposes to it the other, and vice versa—but no resolution to this conflict is ever offered, except for the perpetual repetition in all minor and major keys of the dissonant chord, culiminating in suicide.

Alongside rabbinical training, Gamaliel allows his son a secular French education. The French high school is a gateway to the outside, a bridge to the mainland. Among other things, French literature teaches Solal about romance, about an erotic ideal notably absent from the Cephalonian ghetto, where all the Jewish women are distinctly unerotic. By the time of his bar mitzvah, Solal is erotically obsessed with the island's French consul's twenty-four-year-old wife, Adrienne de Valdonne. Romance is a form of religion, a binding to a feminine seductive ideal.[10] In fact, every aspect of Gamaliel's charge opposes Western romance. Whereas the severe rabbi is hostile to feminine beauty, spontaneous emotional impulses, and highly mannered rituals of desire and coitus, romance prizes these indulgences above all else. An extreme, but reasoned, formula: romance represents the reintroduction of the pagan, while the rabbi represents priestly monotheism bordering on Gnosticism and xenophobia. Solal, Adrienne, Gamaliel (and all their various permutations in Cohen's fiction) henceforth form an agonistic triangle. The Mediterranean sun-boy desires the Aryan; a desire rebuffed by the lawful patriarch, Gamaliel: "Adrienne de Valdonne. Why did she want to see the rabbi? What did this goddess and that ill-natured man they called the 'Rabbi of the Mediterranean' and the 'Light of Exile' have in common?"* Add to this mix the specific historical backdrop of the Dreyfus Affair and the drama is complete. The aristocratic Adrienne is by definition anti-Semitic and anti-Dreyfusard. When she invites the rabbi to a charity reception, he politely but firmly refuses on account of Dreyfus. But for the thirteen-year-old Solal, Dreyfus is of no consequence: "Solal decided that he would go to the reception. This Blum should not have been an officer in the first place!"†[11] Rather than vibrate with the verb of the father, Solal resonates with desire for the blonde anti-Semite.

The estrangement accomplished, Solal's most familiar surroundings suddenly seem repulsive and absurd: "Solal . . . rose and went out. He could no longer bear his uncle's bare feet and the snoring of Salomon stretched on his guitar. And it was for this race that he had had many a fight with Christian schoolfellows at the French high school who made his life a misery and laughed at his beauty, which they envied. Why was he a Jew? Why was he so unfortunate?"‡ At thirteen, Solal already wonders about the catastrophe of being Jewish; his fantasy then and there, which reoccurs throughout his fictional life, is to shed his origin as a snake sheds its skin.

And nothing enables you to shed your identity better than adopting a new origin altogether, acquiring an Aryan substitute mother, whom you (actually) seduce and make love to. Solal viscerally abhors his biological mother, Rachel, and adores his erotic mother, Adrienne de Valdonne. "Solal then analyzed his mother trait by trait. Rachel's eyes, in her broad sandy face, had the gleam of cleaved coal. Why did he feel repelled by this woman, who watched him with

*Adrienne de Valdonne. Pourquoi voulait-elle voir le rabbin? Qu'y avait-il de commun entre cette déesse et ce méchant homme qu'ils appelaient le "Rabbin de la Méditerranée" ou la "Lumière de l'Exil"? (*Solal,* 109)

†Solal décida qu'il irait à la réception. Ce Blum n'avait qu'à ne pas être officier! (*Solal,* 115)

‡Solal . . . se leva et sortit. Il ne pouvait plus supporter le pied déchaussé de son oncle et les ronflements de Salomon gisant sur sa guitare. Et c'était pour cette race qu'il s'était battu plusieurs fois au lycée français contre ses condisciples chrétiens qui lui faisaient la vie dure et se moquaient de sa beauté qu'ils convoitaient. Pourquoi était-il juif? Pourquoi ce malheur? (*Solal,* 123)

such odious clairvoyance?"* What could possibly cause Solal to abhor his own mother? She bears the marks of a tortured and tormenting history on her body—the horror is inscribed on her, in her, it hovers around her terrified gaze.

> At the age of ten, he was still innocent, eager, kind; but bitterness and relentlessness had come the day of the Jewish massacre. The disarrayed skirts of murdered women; children's brains in the streams; gaping bellies. He smiles wearily, knowledge in his eyes. And his mother who had been afraid ever since; her odious prudence, that ignoble acceptance of misfortune. Would he too become one of the persecuted? His mother would certainly die mad.†[12]

The mother's body bears the trace of this violent massacre, and Solal dreads her precisely for that reason. Every time he looks at her, he sees her hysteria and wonders whether this curse also represents his own destiny: "Would he too become one of the persecuted?" Solal does not want his mother's past to be his future—he does not want to carry forward her terror and hysteria. In resisting the mother's gaze, he seeks to break this chain of symptoms, this transmission of horror from generation to generation: again—"Would he too become one of the persecuted?" The answer is a resounding No! The mother's body points toward insularity and terror, while the lover's body points toward conquest and joyfulness. Solal has the illusion of making choices, but his "choice" between Rachel and the Aryan is always undone by the father's word, stubbornly pursuing him.[13]

Prior to this massacre, Solal bathed in innocence; he was not estranged and hostile to his kin. But at age ten, Solal witnessed horror: death, pillage, and perhaps the rape of his own mother ("the disarrayed skirts"). Thus the "catastrophe of being a Jew" becomes primary in his consciousness and provides the impetus for the rejection of the father's bar mitzvah charge, which is simply the theological correlative to the mother's "ignoble acceptance of misfortune"—a negative metaphysics for a terrifying existence. Solal resists the necessity of assuming the transmission of this physical violence and metaphysical estrangement. If there is an urgent necessity in Cohen's writing, it can be

*Ensuite, Solal détailla sa mère. Dans la large face de sable, les yeux de Rachel lançaient l'éclat du charbon taillé. Pourquoi avait-il de la répulsion pour cette femme qui le considérait avec une odieuse clairvoyance? (*Solal,* 109)

†À dix ans, il était encore si pur, si émerveillé, si bon; mais l'amertume et l'inquiétude étaient venues le jour du massacre de Juifs. Jupes soulevées des femmes assassinées; cerveaux d'enfants dans les ruisseaux; ventres troués. Il sourit avec fatigue et une science dans le regard. Et sa mère qui avait toujours peur depuis ce temps-là; sa prudence odieuse; cette habitude ignoble du malheur. Plus tard, serait-il un traqué lui aussi? Sa mère mourrait folle certainement. (*Solal,* 123)

located in this oscillating acceptance and rejection of Diaspora, Jewish calling-reminding. Sibony's definition of a symptom captures the dynamics of the palpable and repetitive urgency in Cohen: "A symptom is a repetitive montage, it signals what does not pass, what is repeated, it replaces this repetition. Analysis liberates us from *belonging* to the symptom."[14] The fracture between Jew and Gentile, mother and lover, Asia and Europe forms the contours of Cohen's novelistic terrain, the resistance to the parent's desire to continue the intergenerational transmission of symptoms. Cohen obsessively revisits this scene in his autobiographical essays and in his novels, unable to resolve it once and for all. In a sense, he belongs to this symptom, or at least to his ambivalence about it.

Bar Mitzvah II: Violent Calling-Reminding

The "symptom" of hysterical deformation, the radioactive traces of which fall into all of Cohen's fiction, has a real biographical origin. Cohen alludes to it in an essay in 1945, "Le Jour de mes dix ans" (My tenth birthday), and again, most notably, in 1971, in his book-length autobiographical essay *Ô vous, frères humains,* where he returns to his own origin-as-violence—origin of estrangement, scene of his own personal pogrom, and his own figurative rape—and expands it greatly.

The event itself was a rather commonplace one. Toward the end of the Dreyfus Affair in 1905, the ten-year-old Albert Cohen was verbally harassed in the streets of Marseille. Such scenes occurred across the whole of France during that period, as they still occur in France at the moment of writing these lines, a century after Cohen's baptism into Judaism.[15] This aggression marked Cohen for life, for it stripped him of the illusion he had entertained about his relationship to France. In one swift stroke, the aspirant French boy became a guilty Jew, bar mitzvah-ed onto hate, worthy of the commandment of . . . assuming his priestly name, COHEN, and all the misery that such a name promised an immigrant Jew in 1905 France. But to assume the name in the most symbolic sense of Cohen (priest) meant permanent estrangement from the Gallic fantasy of becoming like the others—a French citizen, an *Israélite,* and perhaps even, as in the young boy's daydreams, a colonel in the French army. In early twentieth-century France, a Cohen could hardly be an unsuspected citizen, let alone a trusted officer. The child was not yet aware of the horror of exclusion and suspicion—or, more accurately, he did all he could not to be aware of it, because all around him the walls were scribbled with slogans such as "Mort aux Juifs" (Death to the Jews). It was the street hawker who forced the boy literally to see the writing on the wall.

Before describing the event, a word about this ten-year-old Albert Cohen, this "French boy" who will soon be expelled from the bosom of his beloved Gallic homeland. Albert was, in fact, never a happily integrated French boy. This expulsion at the hands of the street hawker was not so much a fall from paradise as a fall from hope, the sudden deflation of a phantasm. A poor immigrant child whose French squeezed through his thick accent, Albert was always alone and aloof, with only his mother for best friend, his favorite hideout being the small apartment above the egg and oil shop where his parents scraped together a meager existence working fourteen hours a day.

When he arrived in France at the age of five in 1900, he only spoke Judeo-Venetian. Albert learned his French in a Catholic convent. He and the good sisters shared a strong mutual affection, and they taught him not only French but also good manners: how to walk with dignity, hold oneself erect, and be self-possessed. The nuns were his second feminine conquest, his mother being the first, "I was paradoxically the favorite of the gentle Catholic sisters."* But alas, even with them, reticence hangs in the air, for the nuns recognize Albert's beauty, ability, and natural finesse, but regret nevertheless his exclusion from possible salvation: "Yes, the Mother Superior . . . would sigh looking at my black locks and murmur from time to time 'what a pity,' thus alluding to my Jewish origin."† This sense of difference and exclusion continued in public school due to his accent, religion, and strange mannerisms. Yet the ten-year-old Albert still found himself enraptured with France—its traditions, its inclusive republican ideology, and, above all, its language. While imaginary, this inclusion always flowed richly with possibilities. Albert imagined himself primarily as French: his chief ambition was to become a colonel—Colonel Abraham Albert Cohen!

Albert's imaginary attachment to France grew so strong that he secretly assembled an altar to the Republic. Carefully enclosed in his closet, he hid

> an altar of repose, a patriotic crib, a sort of reliquary of all the glories of France surrounded by small candles, fragments of mirrors, chips of marble, shards of colored glass and nice shapes that I had made with tinfoil. The relics were portraits of La Fontaine, of Corneille, of Racine, of Napoleon, of Victor Hugo, of Lamartine, of Pasteur . . . I loved France, I despised the

*J'étais paradoxalement le préféré des douces sœurs catholiques. (*LM,* 714)

†Oui, la mère supérieure . . . soupirait en regardant mes boucles noires et murmurait parfois 'Comme c'est dommage', faisant ainsi allusion à mon origine juive. (*LM,* 714)

> Prussians, I was revanchist and jingoist, and I loved Joan of Arc. France was in me, it was my passion.*

> in the evening, before lying down in my small bed, I double-locked the door to my room, I took the key of the sacred cupboard . . . and opened the holy of holies. I lit the small candles on the shelf that I called the pantheon of France, and, down on my knees . . . I lifted my soul toward the lofty France that I so loved.†

The little boy literally constructed a totemic representation to serve his imaginary inclusion in the Republic: the altar with its many candles no doubt mirrored Catholic altars seen at the convent; the French pictures and figurines certainly derived from the iconography of the republican school; the reference to the "holy of holies" recalls the Jewish synagogue. But at the heart of this sacred altar lay the French language: images of Corneille, Molière, Hugo—icons of French literature, his first (and only) home in France. The mature writer Albert Cohen later affirms that the French language constitutes his only true homeland: "[France] you gave me your language, the highest flower in the human crown, your language, which is mine and the country of my soul, your language that is also for me a homeland."‡[16] The French language lies pregnant with possibilities, especially this "crazy desire to belong,"§ that is, to belong to the language, not just in performance but in a heroic sense to the quasi-missionary republican ideology of universal and secular culture *(civilisation).* The figurative bar mitzvah that follows thus takes on multiple meanings: it is not just expulsion from *a* community, as it could have been for a Polish Jew at around that time (as Romain Gary explains so convincingly),[17] but expulsion from *the* secular and inclusive linguistic, cultural, and political ideal that was embraced so universally by the Jewish community in France—and indeed across the world.[18]

*un reposoir, une crèche patriotique, une sorte de reliquaire des gloires de la France qu'entouraient de petites bougies, des fragments de miroir, des billes d'agate, des bouts de verre coloré et de mignonnes coupes que j'avais fabriquées avec du papier d'étain. Les reliques étaient des portraits de La Fontaine, de Corneille, de Racine, de Molière, de Napoléon, de Victor Hugo, de Lamartine, de Pasteur. . . . J'aimais la France, je détestais les Prussiens, j'étais revanchard et cocardier, et j'adorais Jeanne d'Arc. La France était à moi, était mon affaire. (*Ô vous,* 1062)

†le soir, avant d'aller me coucher dans mon petit lit, je fermais à double tour la porte de ma chambre, je prenais la clef de l'armoire sacrée . . . et j'ouvrais le saint des saints. J'allumais les petites bougies du rayon que j'appelais le panthéon de la France et, à genoux . . . je faisais monter mon âme vers la haute France que j'aimais. (*Ô vous,* 1063)

‡tu m'as donné ta langue, haut fleuron de l'humaine couronne, ta langue qui est mienne et pays de mon âme, ta langue qui m'est aussi une patrie. (*Ô vous,* 1065)

§fou désir d'en être (*Ô vous,* 1063)

This civic-literary ideal, the republican Marianne, has its erotic corollary in the daydream fantasy of Albert's first fictional heroine, "Viviane, my true love, which began at the start of my ninth year and lasted until the day of the street hawker. Afterward, I no longer had the heart to see my Viviane again, because I knew that she could not henceforth love me, that I was spiteful and vile, bad like the scabies."* Loving Viviane proves no less a delusion than believing himself to be French, for—just like his Frenchness—she is pure fiction. Both imaginary objects of desire operate almost at the same infantile level as a result of either overinvestment in transitional objects or invention of imaginary companions: "When the clock sounded ten, Viviane wished me goodnight, allowed me to kiss her hand, and we swore to love each other for the rest of our lives."† If we are to take Cohen at his word and believe that he had really imagined Vivianne at age ten as he portrayed her in 1971, then he had already at the age of ten invented the matrix plot for his romantic novels: an outsider momentarily forgets or surmounts his exogenous position, seduces a feminine insider (Vivianne, Adrienne, Aude, Arianne), and constructs, either with or around her, a utopian erotic zone impervious to the hostile world; this utopia collapses, and both must disappear. Thus, in one permutation of the stories he invents, after a devastating earthquake, Albert hides out in an Ali Baba–like cave with the fictional Viviane, where the two then lead a life of utter bliss, protected from all outside incursions.

And so, on the day of his tenth birthday, August 16, 1905, at 3:05 in the afternoon precisely, Albert is returning home from summer school. On his way, he is drawn toward a street hawker *(camelot),* who, with great verbal agility, sings the praises of a universal stain remover *(détacheur universel)* displayed for sale in his stall. But Albert's facial features betray his ethnic origin, and the street hawker turns on him and aggressively apostrophizes him. Albert internalizes each term, repeating it often, conjugating it in the rest of the book in all its possible permutations.

> "You there, you are a Yid, aren't you?" said the blond street hawker with the thin mustache whom I had gone to listen to with faith and tenderness on leaving school, "you are a dirty Yid, aren't you? I can see it from your snout, you don't eat pork, do you? no, I suppose pigs don't eat each other, you are

*Viviane, mon grand amour qui commença au début de ma neuvième année et qui dura jusqu'au jour du camelot. Après, je n'eus plus le cœur de revoir ma Viviane car je sus désormais qu'elle ne pouvait pas m'aimer, que j'étais un méchant et un vilain, mauvais comme la gale. (*Ô vous,* 1065)

†Lorsque la pendule sonnait dix heures, Viviane me souhaitait une bonne nuit, me tendait sa main à baiser, et nous nous jurions de nous aimer toute la vie. (*Ô vous,* 1067)

miserly, aren't you? I can see it from your snout, you guzzle gold, don't you? love it more than candy, don't you? you're not quite French, are you? I can see it from your face, you are a dirty Jew, aren't you? a dirty Jew, right? your father is into international finance, no doubt? [Did you] come to eat the bread that belongs to the French, I suppose? ladies and gentlemen, may I introduce you to a crony of Dreyfus, a little thoroughbred kike, a guaranteed member of the brotherhood of clippers, cut it down where it matters, I recognize them from the first move, I have an American eye, and we hate Jews here, they're a filthy race, a bunch of spies working for Germany, look at Dreyfus, they are all traitors, they are all rotten bastards, putrid like a scab, bloodsuckers of the poor world, rolling in gold and smoking large cigars while the rest of us tighten our belts, isn't it so, ladies and gentlemen? you can slip by, we've seen enough of you, you don't belong here, this is not your country, you have no business being here, off you go, clear out and keep your eye to the ground a little while, get the hell out of here go to Jerusalem and see if I'm there."

. . . A few minutes earlier I had walked up to the street hawker's table with a childish smile, now I left with that of a hunchback.*

There is no need to explain at length the content of this classic compendium of anti-Semitic libels. Our interest rather resides in Albert's perspective. The hawker speaks exquisite French with succulent, flowing, and natural verve, which is the very ideal that the child adopted, and thus the hate exuding forth from this speaker violently excludes Albert from the community of French speakers, their Republic, and their erotic ideals. Mastery of the French language is the sine qua non for seducing both Marianne and Viviane. For him, henceforth, the French language still remains *the* poetic medium, but it disaggregates as an integrative instrument and is no longer associated with the "Israélite" political and cultural

*"Toi, tu es un Youpin, hein?" me dit le blond camelot aux fines moustaches que j'étais allé écouter avec foi et tendresse à la sortie du lycée, "tu es un sale Youpin, hein? je vois ça à ta gueule, tu manges pas du cochon, hein? vu que les cochons se mangent pas entre eux, tu es avare, hein? je vois ça à ta gueule, tu bouffes les louis d'or, hein? tu aimes mieux ça que les bonbons, hein? tu es encore un Français à la manque, hein? je vois ça à ta gueule, tu es un sale Juif, hein? un sale Juif, hein? ton père est de la finance internationale, hein? tu viens manger le pain des Français, hein? messieurs dames, je vous présente un copain à Dreyfus, un petit Youtre pur sang, garanti de la confrérie du sécateur, raccourci où il le faut, je les reconnais du premier coup, j'ai l'œil américain, moi, eh ben nous on aime pas les Juifs par ici, c'est une sale race, c'est tous des espions vendus à l'Allemagne, voyez Dreyfus, c'est tous des traîtres, c'est tous des salauds, sont mauvais comme la gale, des sangsues du pauvre monde, ça roule sur l'or et ça fume des gros cigares pendant que nous on se met la ceinture, pas vrai, messieurs dames? tu peux filer, on t'a assez vu, tu es pas chez toi ici, c'est pas ton pays ici, tu as rien à faire chez nous, allez, file, débarrasse voir un peu le plancher, va un peu voir à Jérusalem si j'y suis." (*Ô vous,* 1052)

Quelques minutes auparavant, je m'étais avancé vers la table du camelot avec un sourire d'enfant et je partais maintenant avec un sourire de bossu. (ibid., 1053)

ideals of assimilation into the Republic. This event transforms Albert, worshiper of all things French. While he was once a child who harbored certain fantasies, he now becomes forever disillusioned, forever excluded, "expelled and condemned to remain foreign."* The event—bar mitzvah by the anti-Semite—precipitates his coming into awareness of his irremediable foreignness, and when the ten-year-old child finally retreats from the assault, he immediately becomes another person, in fact, *the* ultimate other—the hunchback with the frightened and solicitous smile who will haunt him for the rest of his life in the shape of the nightmarish fictional characters Jérémie and the dwarf Rachel:

> And I left, an eternal minority, my back suddenly bent and the usual apologetic smile, I left, forever banished from the human family, bloodsucker of the poor world and putrid like a scab, I left, the laughter of the satisfied majority upon me, good men who loved [one another] by hating together, inanely communing in a common enemy, the stranger, I left, keeping my smile, my dreadful trembling smile, my smile of shame.†

The text abounds with metaphors. The street hawker sells a universal destainer, capable of removing all stains from fabrics, and yet he stains the child. A universal destainer may wash away all sins, except for those of the murderers of the Savior and traitors to the Fatherland. But the child desires to bask in the semi-religious aura of the street hawker's open air performance, for he resembles a magical priest officiating over his altarlike display; the destainer itself stands for a magical totem; the jovial spectators recall the ecstasy of collective communion—and, above all, there is the use of the "sacred" French language. Albert wants to commune with the crowd and the priest, and so he tries to purchase the destainer, but they do not accept his symbolic transaction, do not admit him into the destained society, justified by faith and patriotism. Albert Cohen rightly affirms in *Ô vous, frères humains* that without the street hawkers, that is, the Camelots du Roi and the *Action française,* there would have been no Auschwitz, to which I would add that, without the mocking crowd communing with the street hawker, there would have been no Vichy France.

The next link in the metaphorical chain occurs when, frightened and disoriented by the incident, Albert runs to the train station, and locks himself up

*expulsé et condamné à rester étranger (*Ô vous,* 1063)

†Et je suis parti, éternelle minorité, le dos soudain courbé et avec une habitude de sourire sur la lèvre, je suis parti, à jamais banni de la famille humaine, sangsue du pauvre monde et mauvais comme la gale, je suis parti sous les rires de la majorité satisfaite, braves gens qui s'aimaient de détester ensemble, niaisement communiant en un ennemi commun, l'étranger, je suis parti, gardant mon sourire, affreux sourire tremblé, sourire de la honte. (*Ô vous,* 1053)

in the bathroom, soiled as he must be by his religion, for by definition he cannot be destained. He tries to flush his stained self down the toilet but cannot; he thinks of leaving but cannot. There in the bathroom of the Marseille train station, the child first thinks of this "sinfulness of being born," or, more precisely, the sin of being born Jewish, and thus, this potential candidate for citizenship in the Republic becomes instead a Jewish drifter who contemplates death, who would like to flush himself down the toilet. Soiled, humiliated, and impotent, he goes home to cry with his parents, themselves bewildered, absolutely frightened by what has happened and capable of no succor. Albert becomes suicidal, viewing his only prospects as those of a drifter who runs from train station to train station. He thus wishes his father would kill him—"Yes, father was good, he would kill me"*—so that he would not suffer the fate of being that eternally stained being, destined to a life of fear, humiliation, and wandering. In chronological terms, this is the first instance of his desire to die, to flush himself down the toilet, a leitmotif in the whole œuvre.[19]

The street hawker transforms the child's self-perception. The signifier "Jew" *(Juif)* forever haunts the little Albert and later on the mature Albert Cohen

> Ever since the day of the street hawker, I have not been able to read a newspaper without immediately locating the word that says what I am, immediately, at first sight. And I even locate the words that resemble this terrible word *[Juif]* that is at once agonizing and beautiful, I immediately locate June *[juin]* and soot *[suif]*; in English, I immediately locate *few, dew, jewel.* Enough.†

Cohen is marked for life by this violent redescription of himself as the stained, the ontologically unassimilated, undestainable other—the "kike," "pariah," "financier who rolls in gold," and so forth. All language is henceforth filtered through this paranoia, the feeling of always being on trial, and from that day on language will always be *suspect,* a potential source of aggression. Moreover, on his tenth birthday, Albert Cohen becomes a masochist who takes secret delight in searching for arbitrary combinations of phonemes so that he may once again relive the street hawker trauma.[20]

In *Ô vous, frères humains,* Cohen seeks to catalogue every bit of anti-Semitic

*Oui, Papa était bon, il me tuerait. (*Ô vous,* 1099)

†Depuis ce jour du camelot, je n'ai pas pu prendre un journal sans immédiatement repérer le mot qui dit ce que je suis, immédiatement, du premier coup d'œil. Et je repère même les mots qui ressemblent au terrible mot douloureux et beau, je repère immédiatement juin et suif et, en anglais, je repère immédiatement *few, dew, jewel.* Assez. (*Ô vous,* 1064)

invective and ruminate upon the absurdity of each, but this hardly liberates him from their grip, from being the prisoner of the symptoms that this trauma elicits in him. Here, knowing leads not to overcoming but only to ruminating, to further exploration of a festering wound, whose blood and pus nourish the successive texts, all responses to the event, but responses-*cum*-symptoms of re-living (and relieving) the trauma without ever "resolving" it. Hence, like the father's bar mitzvah charge on the metaphysical level (but they are of one cloth, really), the street hawker's discourse leaves its traces in all of Cohen's work whenever the questions of belonging and exclusion surface; it stains all his characters poetic, fictional, and autobiographical, from *Paroles juives* to *Ô vous, frères humains*; from the grotesque of the play *Ézéchiel* and the novel *Mangeclous* to the sublime lyricism of the Solal motif from 1930 in *Solal* to the mature Solal protagonist of the 1960s. And nowhere can this autobiographical "pariahization" be seen articulated more clearly than toward the end of *Belle du Seigneur,* when Solal's illusions of assimilation and success come to yet another catastrophic conclusion. He reads a negative comment in a magazine and notes with obvious satisfaction and relief that the object of derision "is not Jew, it's only June."* Wherever he goes in Paris that fateful day, Monday, September 10, 1936, he perceives the hatred of the Jew. Just as on the day of his tenth birthday in Marseille, in 1905, he reads "Death to Jews" scribbled on public walls, and he notes with some relief that another bit of graffiti shows some mercy, because it only reads "Down with the Jews." Down *(à bas)* is better than dead. Tired, incapable of withstanding more assaults, he returns to his room at the hotel George V, his "chic ghetto," where he locks himself in his lonely sanctuary, only to continue yet again harping on his horror and curious delight at the words of the street hawker, whatever his latest metamorphosis.

In this sense, striving to make up for the dumbfounded silence of the ten-year-old, Cohen's writings constitute a permanent response to the street hawker. Cohen's "golden quill" compensates for the words he lacked on that fateful day. More precisely, Cohen's texts compensate in the pure act of responding, but this responding does not overcome the trauma—it only turns the textual magma of the street hawker's harangue into a lifelong response. At least the silence of the ten-year-old Albert is overcome, if not his wounds. Eva Miernowska is right to affirm that Cohen's writing exists in tight dialogical re-

*n'est pas juif, c'est seulement juin. (*BdS,* 852)

lationship with anti-Semitic invectives.[21] No doubt that this is Cohen's signature dialogical experience, and the aspect of Cohen's work that seems the most obvious, but that is the most consistently overlooked by readers and critics alike.

And thus the street hawker sends Albert back home, back to his private world, encased in a cocoon of words that are forever organically decoupled from their genuine Gallic culture. While this was in large part the case even before the street hawker episode, once the incident has occurred, Albert cannot even return to his hopes of possible integration, back to his symbolic sanctuaries: the private worship at the republican altar, the veneration of military officers admired in the streets, the erotic fantasies about Viviane. Isolated he will be; in language he will live—but the narratives underpinning this language must change. Cohen must locate new narratives to replace those of Corneille, Stendhal, and Hugo that he had hoped to appropriate. He will henceforth be *hors chapelle,* outside the chapel of the Republic, although physically present within it. (To this day Albert Cohen remains in the same limbo.) The post-Israélite Cohen would find his narratives elsewhere: in certain biblical "moves" (the subject of the next chapter) and in a baroque aesthetics of the novel that is as far removed as one could be from tight, elegant, classical French aesthetics. But no one escapes initial desire, and, however different these new narratives are in content and mode, they remain dialogically tethered to the original longing to become a Frenchman and the bitterness of being expelled from the Social, the one word Cohen uses throughout his work to signify Gentile European culture. If Cohen is forced to write a "Sephardic" French, then he can at least mercilessly parody French style and aesthetics, which is a way of remaining within it by taking the *via negativa.* But this was not his first choice, and to the end, he partly regrets his "outsider's" position: "There was my love for France and my crazy desire to belong. There was an absurd and sacred enthusiasm that I am not ashamed of and will never abandon. For, beneath what I look like, I am still that child."* No doubt this self-conscious estrangement from France is one of the main reasons why Albert Cohen is still an outsider to the French canon—and to this extent, the street hawker's success was considerable, for he made Albert's assimilation impossible. Referring to the street hawker trauma, Cohen told Gérard Valbert,

*Il y avait mon amour pour la France et mon fou désir d'en être. Il y avait un enthousiasme absurde et sacré dont je n'ai pas honte et qui ne m'abandonnera jamais. Car, sous mes airs, je suis resté cet enfant (*Ô vous,* 1063)

"It's a story that happened to me and that says everything."[22] This is doubtless one of Cohen's most incisive insights into his own psyche and writing.

Cohen's narratives, all his successive baroque montages—Solal, Mangeclous, Ézéchiel, Jérémie, the lucid narrator who intervenes—would, ultimately, be determined neither by the father's metaphysics nor by the anti-Semite's invective, but rather by the necessity of operating between them, and, when necessary, beyond them. Cohen would operate in between the father, the street hawker, and Viviane, and also in between fantasies of secular preeminence and tribal marginality. He "fabricates" bridge narratives in order to create a narrative space of his own, yet always orbiting around a dialogue with the father's Law and the omnipresent anti-Semite; always in a dialogical relationship with the two catastrophic bar mitzvahs.

2 Identity Montage, or Solal as an Estheric Joseph

For I am and am not just because I am I.
Thomas Mann, Joseph the Provider

Joseph . . . is the experience and the problematic of Israel to assemble itself, form a people, construct its multiplicity and give it sense.
Shmuel Trigano, La Philosophie de la Loi

We have seen two bar mitzvah stigmata branded onto Solal. His symbolic difference, by way of the father, includes him in the Jewish covenant, while his violent difference, by way of the street hawker, excludes him from what Cohen calls "the Social."[1] In between these two primary traumas lay his initiations to desire, first with the autobiographical (but imaginary) Viviane and then with the fictional Adrienne de Valdonne, wife of the French consul in Cephalonia, with whom the sixteen-year-old Solal escapes to Europe. To become the persona he wishes to be, Solal must escape and then refashion himself as a charismatic figure: "The smooth sea separated Solal from the beautiful foreign lives. The island now discovered was stupid with beauty."* Each dislocation—within traditional Judaism and eventually within European modernity—is linked to a highly symbolic geographical space: Judaism festers in the Ionian island ghetto, while modernity, including virulent anti-Semitism, flourishes in Paris and Geneva. On the surface, Solal's trajectory resembles the typical itinerary of any ambitious romantic hero. But Solal is no ordinary Balzacian country chap intent on conquering the city by means of erotic exploits and manipulations. Solal's narrative differs essentially from that of a Rastignac or a Julien Sorel. Beneath the romantic veneer, Cohen conceals a mythic dimension, underwritten by Scripture, rendered intelligible when read against a well-defined historical tradition whose roots are much deeper than classicism and romanticism or, for that matter, Greco-Roman typology. Solal's "lost illusions"

*La mer lisse séparait Solal des belles vies étrangères. L'île, découverte maintenant, était stupide de beauté. (*Solal,* 91)

are completely different in nature; they connect the deeply ingrained historical self-consciousness of a community whose history goes back three thousand years.

This displacement in geography and in identity is defined in opposition to the father, the anti-Semite, and the seductive European woman. Their interaction results in multiple dissonant juxtapositions, in existential parataxis that is in dire need of mythic coordination. This mythic "coordination" does not eliminate conflict, but does provide an epic trajectory from traumas to domination . . . to dissolution.

Too often, in the desire to demonstrate Cohen's "Frenchness" and "Frenchworthiness," discussions of intertextuality, influence, and inspiration have centered on analogies with classical myths and romantic and modern novelists.[2] Interestingly, Cohen's own complicity in this romantic reading of his work. In many ways, as the following chapters will show, the misreading is programmed into the rhetorical strategies that the author deploys. Furthermore, once he attained fame and notoriety after the publication of *Belle du Seigneur,* Cohen allowed the romantic reading to go unchallenged, or, rather, unqualified. Perhaps he was basking at last in the comfort of *en être,* having made it, in the French literary world and mass media and did not wish to compromise it with a much-needed . . . yes, but there is more here than a passionate love story![3] But, in my view, Stendhal or Proust remains secondary in Cohen's work to the biblical romances of Joseph and Esther. All the analogies with Stendhal and Proust collapse as soon as one tries to tie together Solal's individual romantic dimension with his political, historical, and indeed messianic dimensions. After all, Cohen's first publication, *Paroles juives,* is explicitly biblical in inspiration; and his last book, *Notebooks 1978,* deals with his desperate struggle with and against Yahweh, the quintessential Jewish experience (Isra-el means "struggle with God"). In between these two dates, the question of being Jewish in modern, secular European settings, while being fully conscious of the horrors that are either about to take place or have taken place, remains urgently omnipresent. Although barely mentioned, the Shoah is the black hole that sucks in all of Cohen's narratives.[4]

This argument implies the existence of a mythical narrative that authorizes an authentic Jewish existence for an epic modern hero. Gérard Valbert, Jean Blot, and others correctly view Cohen as the first fully "Jewish" French novelist.[5] My intention is to show exactly how Albert Cohen is that Jewish author in terms of his own self-conscious placement within biblical narratives and the political logic of exilic Judaism operating in the historical context of early twentieth-century France. I contend that the Solal saga—which, as we have seen, Cohen originally intended to title "La Geste des Juifs" (The epic of the Jews)—is quintessentially a Hebrew-Jewish or even Sephardic hybrid, masterfully adapted to the genre of the modern novel. Throughout the saga, Solal retraces the paths of archetypal biblical personages (including its main protagonist, Yahweh); he is contradictory, incongruent, ontologically alienated from himself, from kin, and from strangers. More specifically, he represents the phantasms of the seductive Jew, a fine *trafiqueur* of identities sojourning among disparate communities, being both an insider and an outsider in a perilous world. In short, Solal practices the art of seduction in the service of providence. Solal is essentially the heir of Joseph, although with the temperament of Esther, and maybe even of the matriarch Sarai.

To cover the entire spectrum of biblical matrix narratives in Cohen's poetry, fiction, and essays (e.g., the metaphysics of death) would derail our discussion of the charismatic, sexually seductive identity-phantasm of Solal. Our topic is solely the narratives that authorize Solal's initial posttraumatic displacement from Cephalonia to Geneva and his relative concealment of his Jewish kin once in political power, which results in a series of theatrical existential and identity crises, the subject of the following three chapters.

I shall start with the prototypical story of Sarai in Egypt, because it is both the first in the genre and the blueprint. I shall then point out the parallels between the story of Joseph in Egypt and the story of Solal in Geneva. Next, the Book of Esther combines motifs of concealment and sexuality from the Sarai and Joseph narratives and serves as the basis of the carnival of Purim, a prominent chronotope in Cohen's baroque fiction.

In a recent study of Marrano (crypto-Jewish) culture, Shmuel Trigano shows that Joseph and Esther became "the symbols and the archetypes of their faith [because of] the fundamental gesture of their faith: the fracture of the existential unity of the inside and outside."[6] Furthermore, the narratives of Sarai, Joseph, and Esther show that Marranism, as an existential condition, may not necessarily be of medieval or early modern vintage, but rather integral to the logic of exilic Judaism. If the Solal character represents the collage of a quintessentially Jewish identity-phantasm, it is here in the biblical roots of this identity, and in the almost theatrical *habitus* that history has inscribed upon the Jews, that the core elements of Cohen's particular montage should be located. In the guise of a synthetic (and highly comic) conclusion to this chapter, I shall analyze a scene from the novel *Mangeclous* where Cohen masterfully combines the structure of the most dramatic scene in the story of Joseph with the carnivalesque phenomenology of Purim, thus creating an idiosyncratic hybrid of biblical allusion, contemporary satire, and personal nightmare, the signature of his style.

Sarai's Concealment and Conceit

The story of Sarai in Egypt provides the earliest example of beauty and sexuality as a means of survival, told with frankness and economy, and devoid of any theological varnish.

> And it happened as he drew near to the border of Egypt that he said to Sarai his wife, "Look, I know you are a beautiful woman, and so when the Egyptians see you and say, 'She's his wife,' they will kill me while you they will let live. Say, please, that you are my sister, so that it will go well with me on your count and I shall stay alive because of you." And it happened when Abram came into Egypt that the Egyptians saw the woman was very beautiful. And Pharaoh's courtiers saw her and praised her to Pharaoh, and the woman was taken into Pharaoh's house. And it went well with Abram on her count, and he had sheep and cattle and donkeys and male and female slaves and she-asses and camels. (Gen. 12: 11–16)[7]

This is the "J" layer of Genesis: direct and pragmatic.[8] Pure unsentimental realism. The founder of Judaism asks his wife to become a courtesan so that he can survive and prosper. From its inception, then, the house of Abraham owes its very survival to deliberate concealment, adultery, and prostitution. A hard initial lesson is thus learned: outside the Promised Land, the survival of the Hebrews will depend at times on the seductive powers of a borderline Hebrew, or "a court Jew or Jewess," often operating through concealment. We can say of Sarai's comic heroism what Trigano says about Esther's choice: "It is because she becomes an abstraction to herself, 'does not sacrifice herself,' that Israel is saved. . . . Her abnegation is the principle of the plenitude of Israel."[9]

Abram profits immensely from his access to Pharaoh's court, and at the end of his stay in Egypt, he returns to the Promised Land a very rich man. Hence Sarai's beauty stands between not only survival and perdition but also penury and abundance. Gamaliel himself, when faced with Solal's de facto assimilation into the fabric of French society, chooses to sanction it, provided the wayward son creates a place—concealed and even subterranean, if need be—for his kin. Like Abram, when faced with a concrete set of choices, Gamaliel is pragmatic, interested more in ends than in means. He knows that survival is paramount, death final and pointless. "I shall stay alive because of you" and

"And it went well with Abram on her count"—that is, "I survive because of your transgression; and in your transgression, I am with you, knowing that because of it, I shall live to see tomorrow."

One can only imagine the comedy of Abram periodically visiting his stunning "sister" in Pharaoh's harem, which closely parallels Mordecai loitering around Ahasuerus's palace in hope of catching a glimpse of Esther, his cousin/daughter, now wife of a Gentile king. But this grotesque farce—a husband visiting his wife in a courtly harem—allows Isaac to be born, and thus the individual Abram becomes Abraham the father of nations, and, likewise, Sarai becomes Sarah. In the flow of this Hebrew invention called providential history, all is permitted in the name of survival.[10] At one point, when Solal suffers a particular calamitous reversal of fortune, he self-consciously assumes Abram's perspective: "Unhappy, he was unhappy but he lived, he lived, and it was today that he lived and he went toward a miracle and he was a miracle."* Reversal, cunning, and providence comprise the cadence of this seminal sexual and political intrigue, and are repeated with much amplification with Joseph and Esther and to a lesser degree with Tamar and Ruth. These narratives are highly comic, relying on dissimulation, deception, and play as their main theme and device. Providence, at least in Genesis, is a comedy.[11]

Joseph the Savior

> *Ah, it's the wife of the one who is my grandchild in the country of the Franks and like Joseph in power and brilliance?*
>
> *Albert Cohen,* Solal†

The Joseph novella in Genesis (37–50) is one of the great narrative masterpieces in world literature and is the clear intertext of Cohen's Solal saga. Joseph is the first son of Jacob and his beloved wife Rachel. His beauty, charisma, and intellect make him his father's favorite, and he dreams of becoming superior to his kin—that they all, including his father and mother, will prostrate themselves at his feet. Jealous of their father's esteem for Joseph and fearful that the latter's dreams of dominance, which he describes quite vividly to them, may come to pass, Joseph's brothers, as dimwitted as they are wicked, contemplate

*Malheureux, il était malheureux mais il vivait, il vivait, et c'était aujourd'hui qu'il vivait et il allait vers un miracle et il était un miracle. (*Solal,* 241)

†"Ah, c'est la femme de celui qui est mon petit-fils en pays des Francs et pareil à Joseph quant à la puissance et l'éclat?" (*Solal,* 298)

killing him, but compromise by selling him as a slave and telling Jacob that he was killed by a wild beast. Joseph is purchased by passing traders and then becomes the head steward of Potiphar, captain of Pharaoh's guard. Potiphar's wife covets Joseph and, when rebuffed, she falsely accuses him of seduction. Joseph finds himself in jail, where he correctly interprets the dreams of both Pharaoh's own butler and his baker.

Two years later, Pharaoh is haunted by two persistent dreams, neither of which his courtiers manage to interpret to his satisfaction. Joseph is summoned from jail. His interpretation immediately rings true, and he quickly becomes Pharaoh's vizier. Joseph anticipates future risk of drought and famine, and through wise planning and financial acumen, he enables Egypt to survive and Pharaoh to prosper greatly. Twenty-one years pass; Joseph does not send word to his kin; yet Jacob mourns his absence daily.

In the second year of the famine, Jacob, who still resides in Canaan, sends all his sons except for Benjamin to buy food in Egypt, where Joseph immediately recognizes them. They, however, do not recognize the seventeen-year-old shepherd they sold as a slave in the garb and persona of the second most important man of Egypt. Thus the third major deception of the story occurs when, without revealing his identity, Joseph accuses his brothers of being spies and orders them to bring Benjamin (his younger full brother) down to Egypt. Benjamin accompanies his brothers on their next trip, but as Benjamin prepares to leave Egypt, Joseph has one of his servants place a silver cup in Benjamin's pouch; Joseph's servant pursues the twelve brothers and accuses Benjamin of stealing the cup, because Joseph wishes to keep Benjamin at his side. Judah finally makes an eloquent speech on behalf of Benjamin and the brothers. Joseph is so moved that he lifts his Egyptian mask and finally reveals his identity. At last, Jacob with his clan of seventy goes down to Egypt, safe from starvation and possible extinction. Unfortunately, tragedy strikes when Pharaoh dies, and the new sun king does not know Joseph. Thus the Hebrews fall into slavery for the first time.

Albert Cohen does not simply graft this gripping narrative to a modern setting in the abstract way in which James Joyce transposes *The Odyssey* into *Ulysses* or through the expansive psychology and anthropology with which Thomas Mann mines the Joseph novella. Reading the Solal saga, the reader does not immediately recognize the parallels with Joseph for three possible reasons: In the first place, the Joseph narrative is so ubiquitous that it is uncritically and perhaps even subconsciously taken for granted. Secondly, Cohen bypasses the explicit dream motifs and transposes the sibling rivalry motifs into the lifelong play between an elected only child (Solal) and a band of hapless relatives (the Valorous) in lieu of brothers. Finally, Cohen inverts many Josephic traits. Solal's sexual recklessness inverts Joseph's prudence as the means of attaining political power. Nevertheless, from the first line of *Solal* (1930) to the last line of *Les Valeureux* (1969), Solal's trajectory constitutes a performance of the Josephic principle writ large, down to its exhaustion and violent decanting—of which the Shoah is the most resounding proof. Under Cohen's pen, Joseph's dreams become nightmares.

Both Joseph and Solal are their fathers' favorites. Both are beautiful men. Both hold themselves superior to their kin. Joseph's first two dreams reveal his megalomania: "And, look, we were binding sheaves in the field, and, look, my sheaf arose and actually stood up, and, look, your sheaves drew round and bowed to my sheaf" (Gen. 37: 7). His second dream goes further: "[L]ook, the sun and the moon and eleven stars were bowing to me" (Gen. 37: 9). All are to bow down to Joseph, including his brothers and father. The adolescent Solal also daydreams: "Solal had taken his place [in the synagogue] in the chair reserved for descendants of Aaron. He contemplated his future. When he was grown up, he would throw money at the heads of the wretches and he would give a car made of gold to his Adrienne."* And later, "He rose, his eyes brilliant, suddenly certain that he would always be victorious."† At twenty, Solal promises himself, "He would see [his father] again only if famous."‡ In short, unconditional superiority will be the precondition to Solal's reconciliation with his father.

This sense of superiority, or outright Josephic megalomania, translates into a quasi-messianic predestination that people perceive in Solal even in his younger years. An aged Christian clairvoyant asserts: "[T]he child bears the sign."§ A rigorous legal mind, hardly prone to mysticism, Rabbi Gamaliel wonders nevertheless while gazing at the stars whether "his son was the Expected one."|| And when, penniless and aimless, Solal errs with the old Roboam on the roads of Europe, the mystically inspired Roboam "quivered with admiration as he listened to his young relative dream in Hebrew. Could He be the one?"#[12]

*Solal avait pris place dans le fauteuil réservé aux descendants d'Aaron. Il songeait à sa vie de plus tard. Quand il serait grand, il lancerait l'argent à la tête des ignobles et il offrirait une voiture en or à son Adrienne. (*Solal,* 116)

†Il se leva, les yeux brillants, sûr tout à coup qu'il serait toujours vainqueur. (*Solal,* 120)

‡Il ne le [son père] reverrait qu'illustre. (*Solal,* 145)

§[L]'enfant porte le signe (*Solal,* 114)

||son fils était l'Attendu (*Solal,* 135)

#frissonnait d'admiration en écoutant son jeune parent rêver en hébreu. Serait-ce Lui? (*Solal,* 147)

Clearly, both Joseph and Solal are variants of the divine-child archetype. For Joseph, matters are clear: his mother Rachel is Jacob's beautiful and favorite wife. Jacob knows that aristocracy of true election flows in Joseph's veins, while the other half-brothers—sons of Leah and her servant Bilhah—are born of contingency and expediency. Their inferiority is borne out at every step (with the possible exception of Judah) in their intermittent wickedness and permanent mediocrity. Joseph, on the other hand, recognizes his innate superiority, because he was born of Jacob's beloved Rachel. Solal presents another inversion of this canonical narrative. He sees himself as a divine child, but he views his mother, whose name is also Rachel, as repulsive and anxiety-ridden—the very opposite of Jacob's majestic Rachel. Thus, throughout his life, the megalomaniac divine child searches for a substitute mother to redeem the sinfulness (sexual desire) of all women and to crown him king. (Precisely as the dwarf Rachel does in the very last paragraph of *Belle du Seigneur.*) In a very intimate psychological sense, the Josephic narrative here provides the most apt juxtaposition to Solal's messianic and erotic drives.

His messianic vocation allows Solal to overcome the trauma of the double bar mitzvahs, of symbolic and violent stigmata. It also affords him great license, a teleological alibi for all manner of egomaniacal mischief; the messianic is a perfect vector for a transfer ("carrying across") of identities. From the messianic imaginary, Solal needs a transcendence of locality and tribe, a geographic and ethnic passport out of the island ghetto, a perfect excuse for apostasy, adultery, robbery, kidnapping, and theft. It is all done for the sake of this "Me later on" *(Moi de plus tard).*[13]

Joseph and Solal become grand bureaucrats, although by different means. Joseph rises principally by resisting adultery, interpreting dreams, and governing effectively. Put in modern terms, Joseph leverages his ability to anticipate rare events (a seven-year bounty followed by a seven-year drought) to great political and financial advantage. Solal's meteoric rise results from his unbound, almost Davidic energy and resourcefulness, bordering on recklessness: he breaks up marriages, joyfully humiliates his cuckolds, and, except for Aude, drives all his lovers (Adrienne, Isolde, Ariane) to suicide. Solal employs recklessness where Joseph relies on prudence. Where Joseph resists temptation largely on prudential and pragmatic grounds, Solal seduces Aude, his benefactor's daughter, who is already engaged to her childhood sweetheart, for the sake of sheer provocation.[14] Solal nevertheless possesses Joseph's skill of making himself indispensable to his benefactor, Aude de Maussane's uncle, a powerful French senator. The parallels are self-evident:

> And the Lord was with Joseph and he was a successful man, and he was in the house of his Egyptian master. And his master saw that the Lord was with him, and all that he did the Lord made succeed in his hand, and Joseph found favor in his eyes and he ministered to him, and he put him in charge of his house, and all that he had he placed in his hands. And it happened from the time he put him in charge of his house that the Lord blessed the Egyptian's house for Joseph's sake and the Lord's blessing was on all that he had in house and field. (Gen. 39: 2–5)

> Yes, [Solal] knew how to work, and within six months Maussane had grown in influence and wealth. Vanity of vanities. . . . Life was not unpleasant. The journalists, the banks, and all the useless trembling of people who would die tomorrow. . . . His father. And yes, his father was an old man with a beard, he was not the Eternal. . . . In truth, Maussane could no longer do without this young boy, whom he loved.*[15]

Yet the real drama of this narrative occurs not when Joseph or Solal rises to power but rather in their attempts, once in power, to reconcile the conflicting demands of a foreign court and ancestral kin. Solal does not have brothers but instead a band of relatives from the Greek Jewish ghetto of Cephalonia—the Valorous—who shadow him throughout his saga. Joseph's brothers are portrayed as mean-spirited simpletons, while the Valorous are fools, but of a more kindhearted variety. They represent in Cohen's fiction what Judith Kauffmann terms the "marginal grotesque."[16] Solal invites them to most settings of his successes, so that their embarrassing presence can undo his carefully constructed, but tenuous, position. Socially and politically, they represent a death drive with which Solal simply toys as he totters between his life-affirming messianic phantasms and his self-destructive drives of regressing to the womb, where ends equal beginnings: "How I crave sometimes to return to this ghetto, to live among rabbis who are like women with beards, to live there this loving life, impassioned, full of vain reasoning [*ergoteuse*], a bit destitute [*nègre*] and insane."† Like a masochist who delights in almost losing it all, Solal repeatedly inflicts the Valorous on himself, only to send them away with remorse and resignation. This is his obsessive *Fort! Da!* game of "having my worldly

*Oui, [Solal] avait su travailler, et en six mois Maussane avait grandi en influence et en argent. Vanité des vanités. . . . La vie n'était pas désagréable. Les journalistes, les banques et tout le tremblement inutile des gens qui mourront demain. . . . Son père. Eh bien oui, son père c'était un vieux avec une barbe, ce n'était pas l'Éternel. . . . En réalité, Maussane ne pouvait plus se passer de ce garçon qu'il aimait. (*Solal,* 172–73)

†Parfois, comme je voudrais retourner dans ce ghetto, y vivre entouré de rabbins qui sont comme des femmes à barbe, y vivre cette vie aimante, passionnée, ergoteuse, un peu nègre et folle. (*LM,* 738–39)

position and . . . almost losing it."[17] They also function as a repository of grotesque humor that deconstructs the pristine surface of European bourgeois mores just as Jacob's sons' faith in their ancestral God, despite their obvious personal limitations, foiled Egypt's Religion of the Dead. To the heroic and romantic narrative of seduction and power, they juxtapose their carnivalesque presence, forever decrowning Solal of his self-dramatizing delusions. They are, therefore, absolutely integral to Cohen's baroque poetic vision of Solal's self-dramatization.

The Valorous, however, are merely surrogates, substitutes—foils against which the true conflict unfolds. True psychological drama takes place between fathers and sons. The burlesque fools are just witnesses, vectors for action, thematic and stylistic arabesque. I would say of the Solal saga what Harold Bloom says of the Joseph story:

> [J's] central interest in this story is the relation between Joseph and Jacob rather than that between Joseph and his brothers. The brothers, after all, are not an elite, except for the hapless Judah; they are instead the ancestors of the unruly horde in the Wilderness. Joseph and Jacob are the elite, the natural aristocrats with whom the Davidic-Solomonic J sympathizes most readily.[18]

This holds true too of the tortuous relationship between Solal and Gamaliel, as witnessed at the bar mitzvah. And when, disobeying his father, Solal runs away with Adrienne de Valdonne, wanders across the continent, and eventually becomes a political maverick—his father remains forever in his mind, always representing to Solal the symbolic, a calling-reminding of origin (Israel) and destiny (Savior of Israel). Yet Gamaliel's predicament is much bleaker than Jacob's. Whereas Joseph presents Jacob to Pharaoh at the palace, Solal cannot invite his father, the oriental rabbi, to the Quai d'Orsay or the Palace of the League of Nations in Geneva. When Gamaliel encounters de Maussane in Paris, he is violently humiliated, both by de Maussane himself (Solal's adopted father) and by Solal (see next chapter). Even when reconciled with his father, Solal can only keep the old rabbi hidden in a Paris basement or, as in *Mangeclous,* in a suburban house, tucked away from the Judeophobic world.[19]

But beyond the psychological subtleties of the comic megalomania, jealousy, betrayal, concealment, and reconciliation, the "Josephic principle" is more political than psychological. The father-son drama points clearly in that direction, as Bloom has correctly suggested: "Joseph's only agon is the aesthetic enterprise of precisely how and when he will gather his father and brothers in to him so as to become their worldly savior."[20] For Shmuel Trigano, the Joseph story is emblematic of a persistent political principle in the history of Israel: "Joseph—as his name testifies ('that which adds')—is the experience and the problematic of Israel to assemble itself, to form a people, to construct its multiplicity and give it a sense."[21]

The paradox of Joseph resides in his name: he adds, but remains absent; he acts, but remains invisible. Trigano terms this political motif the *augment,* the "leavening." Absent and in retreat vis-à-vis his kin, Joseph is the invisible leavening that guarantees that the bread will rise. "In the absence," Trigano writes, "there remains a surplus that escaped the counting, and [this absence] will become the pivot of salvation at the heart of a generalized loss."[22] Thomas Mann, in his multivolume *Joseph and His Brothers* (which is perhaps the best commentary ever written on Joseph) has Jacob say to Joseph: "You are the set-apart, severed from your stem, you are and shall be no stem."[23] For Joseph is the severed branch that allows the very survival of the tribal "tree." He is the sacrifice that saves; the *pars pro toto* upon which everything hinges. Later, Mann adds to this penetrating observation: "Joseph was the one set apart, at once lifted up and withdrawn. He was severed from the tribe and was not to be a tribe."[24] Joseph will not be a head of one of the twelve tribes (but his first two sons will), yet the very existence of Jacob's descendants was made possible by his active absence. A clear progression exists in the logic of the *augment:* Sarai saves Abram; Joseph saves a clan of seventy; Esther saves a whole people in exile. In the context of Cohen's narrative, we must ask, will Solal, the undersecretary-general of the League of Nations, save millions in Europe?

A Joseph-like figure is, of necessity, concealed but active, pagan in appearance, Hebrew in destiny. He must cultivate a careful duality, forever surveying the ratio between the visible and the invisible, perfecting the duality of being and appearance.[25] It is easy to see that the whole psychology of the "Marrano," the crypto-Jew, is present at the very inception of Hebrew Scripture, a permanent background trace emanating from the earliest Hebrew experience, and is therefore not limited to a secondary trait or symptom of exilic Judaism. Regardless of how well Joseph seems to be integrated into the Egyptian elite, he remains the son of Jacob, and his fidelity to his father's God makes Joseph ontologically hostile to paganism. Joseph, then, is not simply another Syrian Semite who succeeds in Pharaoh's palace. Outwardly a good pagan, Joseph knows that sooner or later he will reunite with Jacob and accomplish his role in the history of Jacob, which becomes the history of Israel. Thus family romance merges into an allegory of exemplary historical existence for the Hebrews—these *passeurs,* forever estranged from their hosts and enemies.

It is therefore not surprising that peninsular Sephardic Jews should essentially transform the figure and story of Joseph (and Esther) into a central and sustaining narrative, symbolically sanctioning an outward Christian appearance and an inward faith in Yahweh. Joseph's role as a major motif for Jewish existence in the Diaspora has an extensive history that predates the year 1391, when the Jews of Spain first became undesirable. In a book describing the different Josephs of the Jews, Muslims, and Christians of medieval Spain, Michael McGaha affirms: "The author(s) of the account in Genesis seem to have viewed it primarily as the wonderful story of a heroic ancestor who embodied the virtues most highly esteemed by the Jews. For later generations of Diaspora Jews the story would take on even greater importance, since it described how a Jew triumphed over adversity and became spectacularly successful in a non-Jewish society, yet always retained his loyalty to his people and used his position of power to help them."[26] Peninsular Jews adopted the Joseph story to fit their needs, as against the more restrictive readings of rabbinical Judaism, but the Sephardic license with the scriptural Joseph coincided rather better with the original Hebrew reality than the more defensive rabbinical commentaries would let on. The rabbinical interpretations would have had to be defensive and ambivalent, since Joseph and Esther as exemplary figures sanction many transgressions of the Law. These marginal but pivotal figures become in fact a necessary counterweight to the Law, to the authority of the rabbis, and to the figure of the father.

There will thus be a visible Israel, Rabbi Gamaliel, and an invisible Israel, Solal. The proper name "Solal" is an ironic inversion: it clearly refers to the sun, to light, to power, and yet the bearer of the solar name labors in the hallways of diplomacy, the invisible "cut-off stem" that shines upon the visible stem, the father. Although superficially at odds, father and son mutually ensure the survival of Israel. Visible Israel obeys the Law, interprets the Torah, and remains within the confines of its voluntary or involuntary ghetto. Invisible Israel transgresses the Law, appears worldly, but remains obliquely true to the one God and loyal to His people. The two Israels are complementary, mutually dependent. Once Gamaliel understands Solal's position, he does not demand that his son return to the ghetto, but rather encourages him to continue leading a double life, just as Jacob recognized that Joseph, besides being his son, was also an Egyptian and thus essentially different. We can see at once why such a narrative should thus profoundly appeal to successive generations of crypto-Jews, down to the discreet and assimilated French *Israélite.*

The political, historical, and tribal dimensions of the Joseph story point toward Cohen's main narrative plot, that of the estranged son who, because he is so ambivalent about his kin, struggles with the idea of gathering them to him and thereby saving them. Cohen's plot succeeds in representing power and politics just prior to the Shoah from a Jewish point of view, using the most archaic Hebrew texts as leitmotifs in a complex modernist montage.

We wish to read the Joseph story as a triumphant U-shaped comedy (stasis, crisis, stasis), because it satisfies our desire to recognize this narrative masterpiece, emblem of the history of the Hebrews, as life-affirming.[27] But the Joseph story as told in Genesis and the beginning of Exodus also alludes to the exilic Jewish nightmare of being constantly suspected or accused of occult knowledge, conspiratorial intent, and disloyal conduct.

From these charges, the whole delusional montage culminating in the *Protocols of the Elders of Zion,* for example, is easily derived. Joseph rises to power through his ability to see what is evident to no one else in the whole of Egypt. "[Pharaoh] sent and called in all the soothsayers of Egypt and all its wise men, and Pharaoh recounted to them his dreams, but none could solve them for Pharaoh" (Gen. 41: 8). Joseph's epistemic singularity propels him toward power and wealth, yet the origin and nature of this empowering knowledge remain shrouded in "alchemical, occult, cabalistic" mystery, to use the classic language of Judeophobes.

In the strict sense of the word, Joseph could be seen as "disloyal," since Pharaoh's good is not an end in itself, but a contingent means to guarantee the survival of Israel. Joseph's ambiguity about Egypt per se is overdetermined by his historical memory, the memory of the monotheistic difference that his father represents and that he must somehow preserve, even though outwardly he leads the life of a pagan. His destiny is therefore neither individual nor national but tribal, bound to the promise Yahweh made to Jacob. He will never cease to be the son, the son of Jacob, and therefore the servant of Jacob's God:

> And Joseph said to his brothers, "Come close to me, pray," and they came close, and he said, "I am Joseph your brother whom you sold into Egypt. And now, do not be pained and do not be incensed with yourselves that you sold me down here, because for sustenance God has sent me before you. Two years now there has been famine in the heart of the land, and there are yet five years without plowing and harvest. And God has sent me before you to make you a remnant on earth and to preserve life, for you to be a great surviving group. And so it is not you who sent me here but God, and he has

> made me father to Pharaoh and lord to all his house and ruler over all the land of Egypt. (Gen. 45: 4–8)

Joseph is categorical: I am who I am for your sake—not for my sake or for Pharaoh's; my lordly situation and Pharaoh's added wealth are just coincidental to the main plot, which is centered on Jacob. Can Joseph concurrently be Jacob's faithful son and Pharaoh's trusted vizier? Might he be suspected of double allegiance? Can Israel's salvation always be consistent with Egyptian interests? Can we say with Hitler and Stalin that the Jew is by definition a "cosmopolitan"? Or in today's thinly veiled anti-Semitic language—very current in Europe and in particular in France—the Jew is a conspiratorial "globalist" and/or a bellicose "settler" or a "neoconservative"? This question still hovers over each and every successful man or woman of Jewish origin. It is a particularly pertinent question here, since the street hawker claims that, by definition, a Jew cannot be a Frenchman. His allegiance will never coincide perfectly with French interests, whatever they may be. The whole logic of the Dreyfus Affair implicitly hinges on this proposition. In 1905, when Cohen's dream of being a Frenchman comes to a traumatic end, the question hovering in the air of Marseille is not "Who is a Jew?" but rather "Who is a Frenchman?" In *Belle du Seigneur,* set in 1936, the bourgeois ladies knitting and chatting politely in the hotel lobby sing the same tune: The Jews sow trouble, are disloyal, and are responsible for the coming war. And they conclude, "Really, better Hitler than [Léon] Blum."*

Scripture is surprisingly explicit about Joseph's economic exploits. During the initial seven years of abundance, Joseph advises Pharaoh to buy and safely store substantial amounts of grain so that when the prophesied drought and famine arrive, Pharaoh will save his people from starvation by selling grain to them. First, the people purchase grain with gold and silver. As time wears on and the drought continues unabated, Joseph exchanges grain for ownership of land:

> And Joseph took possession of all the farmland of Egypt for Pharaoh, for each Egyptian sold his field, as the famine was harsh upon them, and the land became Pharaoh's. And the people he moved town by town, from one end of the border of Egypt to the other. . . . And Joseph said to the people, "Look, I have taken possession of you this day, with your farmland, for Pharaoh. Here is seed for you, and sow the land. And when the harvests come, you shall give a fifth to Pharaoh." . . . And they said, "You have kept us alive! May we find favor in the eyes of our lord, in being Pharaoh's

*Vraiment, plutôt Hitler que Blum. (*BdS,* 739)

> slaves." And Joseph made it a fixed law, to this very day, over the farmland of Egypt, that Pharaoh should have a fifth. (Gen. 47: 20–26)

Through occult wizardry—predicting rare events and leveraging this knowledge into economic power—Joseph helps Pharaoh to enslave the Egyptians and enrich his kin. (Strictly speaking, the Egyptians do not become slaves but rather tenants of Pharaoh's lands.) In response, Egypt enslaves Joseph's kin: "Now a new king arose over Egypt, who did not know Joseph. He said to his people, 'Look, the Israelite people are more numerous and more powerful than we. Come, let us deal shrewdly with them, or they will increase and, in the event of war, join our enemies and fight against us and escape from the land.'" This is not *Mein Kampf*'s paranoid delirium but Exodus 1: 8–10! This same motif (among so many others) is reworked into the mouth of the wicked viceroy Haman in the Book of Esther, who tells the king of Persia: "There is a certain people scattered and separated among the peoples in all the provinces of your kingdom; their laws are different from those of every other people, and they do not keep the king's laws, so that it is not appropriate for the king to tolerate them" (Est. 3: 8).

This theme of the occult, auriferous Jew in Cohen's fiction has aroused the ire of many critics. Repeatedly, Cohen places his protagonists in repulsive Shylockian positions, perhaps nowhere more so than in his play *Ézéchiel,* where a rich Jewish banker loses his beloved son (Solal) but is soon enough consoled and returns to concupiscent speculation and procreation.[28] Solal's own financial acumen is clearly a clownish parody of Joseph's stately and providential gravitas. Time and again, Solal speculates in the stock market, accumulates thousand dollar bills, and then burns them contemptuously in the fireplace. And while most people in the 1930s wallow in financial ruin, "starved" (like the Egyptians) by the decade-long depression, Solal earns 40 million francs in a single episode in *Solal,* which he then theatrically gives away to the staff of the Ritz Hotel, to the Valorous, to eastern European Jewish hobos. Each of these Josephic triumphs turns to ashes in Cohen's novels.

The Joseph story is clearly the dominant, overarching motif embedded in Solal's epic, for both characters are in a permanent state of estrangement, torn and double, at home in neither Canaan nor Egypt. Living in two worlds simultaneously, the discourse of Joseph and Solal is always a symptom of their "in-betweenness"; they must be in a constant state of displacement for—as borderline figures passing repeatedly from Canaan to Egypt, Cephalonia to Geneva—their identity can never be stable. Thomas Mann, a Christian, understood that Joseph represents the richest allegory for the modern Jew. And perhaps I would have never sufficiently appreciated Solal's Joseph-like existence but for my study of Mann. It is not by accident that Mann explores the subject in four rich volumes, the period of composition of which roughly coincides with the rise and fall of the Third Reich. In one enigmatic formulation, he captures the existential drama of Joseph and of his heir Solal: "For I am and am not just because I am I."[29]

Our Patron, Saint Esther

The Joseph story thematically and textually parallels the Book of Esther so closely that it often serves as the basis for many of the plays composed for Esther's feast of Purim.[30] Esther fuses Sarai's sexual transgression with Joseph's political charisma, and her story is recounted with even more frankness, because the text implies the transgression of many more taboos. Esther is, after all, already a Jewess living under the Law, whereas Sarai and Joseph were Hebrews with a far more flexible identity. Esther's self-conscious playfulness represents a canonically enshrined principle of political and existential action, the traces of which—the masquerades, gambling, hierarchical inversions, and grotesque play—define the rite of Purim and, furthermore, allude to aesthetic principles that Cohen adopts, either explicitly, as in *Belle du Seigneur*, or implicitly, in his consistent usage of masquerades and buffoonery. Similarly, Esther's regal beauty and femininity are relevant for an understanding of Solal's complex gender identity, examined in chapter 6. If the Joseph story anchors the political narrative of exilic Judaism, the Book of Esther grounds the particular modalities of the practice of survival in the foreigner's land. As the following sexual and political *Thousand and One Nights* Arabian fairy tale demonstrates, Esther is indeed the matrix narrative at the heart of Solal's tragicomic performance of his dissonant identity-phantasm.

The story takes place subsequent to the Hebrews' first exile (570 B.C.E.). The Persian King Ahasuerus kills his wife Vashti because she refuses to appear (naked?) before the drunken king and his court. In search of a replacement, the most beautiful virgins in the empire, including a young maiden named Hadassah, are gathered in the palace harem. On the advice of her older cousin Mordecai, she hides her Jewish origins and calls herself Esther, a Persian name from the root *str,* "to conceal," but also possibly from *sthara,* Persian name for the sun, the star par excellence.[31] After undergoing a year-long preparation, each concubine is afforded one night with Ahasuerus: "When Esther was taken to King Ahasuerus in his royal palace. . . . the king loved Esther more than all the other women; of all the virgins she won his favor and devotion, so that he set the royal crown on her head and made her queen" (Est. 2: 16–17). Haman, a wicked and influential courtier, detests Esther's cousin Mordecai because the latter will bow only before Yahweh and never before a courtier. His pride deeply wounded, Haman persuades the hapless Ahasuerus to decree the annihilation of all Jewish men, women, and children in all the provinces of the Persian empire. Astrologers draw lots and the propitious date of the 14th of Adar (in the Jewish calendar) is chosen for the royally decreed genocide. Secretly, Mordecai informs Esther, entreating her to intervene on behalf of her people. At first the queen hesitates. Then, after a three-day fast, she cleverly tricks Haman into disgrace and finally reveals her religious origin. Haman is executed and the king, unable to break a standing royal decree, allows the Jews the right of self-defense, which they employ vigorously, killing many of their enemies, including all of Haman's children. Mordecai replaces Haman as vizier, and seeks "the good of his people and intercede[s] for the welfare of all his descendants" (Est. 10: 3). Thus, in commemoration of Esther's propitious action, the carnival of Purim (Lots, *La fête des Sorts* in Cohen's texts) is celebrated annually on the 14th and 15th of Adar.[32]

This carnival is explicitly theatrical. Every year survival is reenacted, not through the celebration of divine intervention, as is decidedly the case with the Passover Haggadah, but through the usage of the mask and of gambling (fate), both explicitly forbidden by canonical Jewish Law. Here is a description of traditional eighteenth-century Sephardic Purim activities: "At nightfall began the masquerade shows. . . . A week earlier, several groups got together to pick and arrange the program, which included plays, songs, speeches. Then after the holiday meal these groups, wearing masks, visited several houses where they performed certain excerpts of their repertoire, one dressed as Ahasueros, another as Haman, another as Mordechai, another as Esther."[33]

Whereas the performance ritual of the Passover Seder retells the wonders of God's direct intervention in history, the Purim performance ritual refers to the intervention of humans in history without any miracles or divine assistance, and is celebrated by reading the Book of Esther and, more important, by the performance of a carnival. Purim is, at its origin, a performance by masked actors, all too human, who transgress taboos to save the nation. In the playfulness of these *jugadores de Purim,* the masquerade thus becomes a performative principle enshrined in historical memory, an important secular correlative to the pious principle of the Passover Haggadah.

With Esther, the principle of leavening [*augment*] becomes much more explicit and purposefully self-conscious. Salvation does not come from an active God who intervenes in history as in the manner of the Exodus from Egypt, but rather from the resourcefulness of a Jewish woman married to a Gentile king. The crypto-Jewish body of Esther, like the crypto-Abramic body of Sarai, constitutes the battlefield of collective survival or destruction. Esther plays the part of the ultimate insider and outsider, figure of estrangement and salvation, encrusted in palace deceit, sex, and politics. The beautiful queen is the "leavening"—invisible Israel—that renders the survival of visible Israel possible. Yahweh is all but absent from the episodes of Sarai in Pharaoh's harem, Joseph in Egypt, and most conspicuously from the Book of Esther—the only book in the Hebrew Bible where Yahweh (or alternatively Elohim) is not mentioned even once. Absent from the Book of Esther are also explicit references to prayers, worship, sacrifice, the Law, and the covenant.

In a contemporary analysis of Purim, the writer Adam Gopnik recounts how, ignorant apparently of all things Jewish (apart from jokes and bagels), he was asked to be Purimspieler at a Jewish museum ball. And so he finally reads the Book of Esther and becomes perplexed as to the meaning of the story. Wishing to relieve his anxiety, he visits Rabbi Schorsch, chancellor of the Jewish Theological Seminary in New York. The rabbi's explanation deserves full quotation:

> [The Book of Esther] is a spoof, a burlesque, really . . . Mordecai is a classic Jew of the Diaspora, not just exiled but entirely assimilated—a court Jew, really. It's a book for court Jews. Why doesn't he bow to Haman? Well, it might be because of his Judaism. But I think we have to assume that he's jealous—he expects to be made first minister and then isn't. Have you noticed the most interesting thing about the book? . . . It's the only book in the Bible where God is never mentioned. . . . This is the book for the Jews of the city, the world. After all, we wonder—what does Esther eat? It sure isn't kosher. But she does good anyway. The worldliness and the absurdity are tied together—the writer obviously knows that the King is a bit of an idiot—but the point is that good can rise from it in any case. Esther acts righteously and saves her people, and we need not worry, too much, about what kind of Jew she was before, or even after. She stays married to the Gentile King, remember. This is the godless, comic book of Jews in the city, and how they struggle to do the righteous thing.[34]

Gopnik's reaction to the rabbi's interpretation is conclusive: "I was stunned. This was, as they say, the story of my life. A funny book about court Jews . . .

I had been assigned to burlesque it, when the text was pre-burlesqued, as jeans might be pre-shrunk." This burlesque Book might in fact be the only biblical text that makes sense to a contemporary non-orthodox Jew; it is a biblical text he can assimilate into his own real life instead of the opposite, the usual calling to adapt one's fallen life to the ideal of a text. In short, the Esther story represents the world of urban Western Solals—a world of the dim remembrance of the Law without God and the ambivalent allegiance to a tribe without land.

Nowhere else does Scripture so programmatically split the exterior and interior as in the Esther story. Blending together the guile of a romantic heroine, the politics of Jewish survival, and the historical basis for a ritual carnival rich in baroque devices, the Book of Esther constitutes *the* text of predilection for Cohen: survival hinges on doubling and concealment, masquerade and buffooneries—all underwritten by historical necessity. Inherent in the Book of Esther are the tense dissonances of Cohen's fiction, characterized by acute historical consciousness, family romance, protean charisma, and hypersensuality as the vector to power. For formal and historical reasons, Purim underwrites the *performative* principle of Cohen's picaresque Sephardic novel, which at times may seem unhinged, but, like Purim, always remains in memoriam—that is, lodged deep in a historical and existential Jewish consciousness that has become a Marrano-like habitus inscribed in bodily gestures, the farcical and tragic fabric of daily life.[35]

Nevertheless, the Book of Esther is particularly disturbing in that what was exceptional in earlier narratives here becomes the norm, if not altogether a canonized principle. That Abram and Sarai, facing imminent danger, should conceal their married status may seem prudent. That, due to violent sibling jealousy, Joseph should become an Egyptian seems at least fortuitous. But that Hadassah, under no impending danger, presents herself (or is presented by Mordecai) under an assumed name in the harem of a Gentile king marks a new threshold in the Jewish romance of survival. Concealment advances (or regresses) from an opportune and temporary device, to an enduring phenomenology of being. Armand Abécassis writes:

> [T]his manner of representing oneself behind a mask is characteristic of the Jew, that is, of the Hebrew in exile. It is impossible in the Holy Land, where everybody knows the origin of its inhabitants. The time of the Torah is one of revelation, the time of Purim, time of Judaism, is one of occultation. All the religious feasts of Israel celebrate the dazzling manifestation of the divine, except for Purim, feast of exile par excellence, of a new historical time marked by the absence [of the divine].[36]

That Purim should play such a crucial role in Cohen's work is hardly coincidental. The name has its root in *pur,* "lot," or, in this context, the casting of lots. Fate can be lethal, but it also can be outflanked by cunning dissimulation at times.[37] Esther therefore becomes the divine "saint" and Purim the most meaningful holiday for Marranos from 1391 until the end of the eighteenth century. Like Esther, the Marranos had to dissimulate themselves, to publicly break Jewish religious taboos, all the while remembering their ancestral religion, rituals, and mental habits. Their lot *(pur)* was that of wearing masks everywhere and at all times, preferring the wearing of masks to exile or death. They could not, of course, celebrate Purim openly, with its all-too-detectable carnivalesque masking, playacting, and revelry, but would instead observe the queen's fast, commemorating her three-day fast prior to her pleading with Ahasuerus. For those who had to appear Christian while remaining internally Jewish, Esther is ideally suited for identification and transference of affect. Her prayer in the Septuagint mirrors their very condition: "You know my necessity—that I abhor the sign of my proud position, which is upon my head on days when I appear in public. I abhor it like a filthy rag, and I do not wear it on days when I am at leisure" (Esther, Apocypha, 14: 16). Cecil Roth is categorical on this point: "The fast [of Esther] . . . attracted the Marranos in an especial degree; and in the Inquisitional records it has an importance second to no other day in the Marrano calendar."[38]

But, as has already been suggested in regard to Joseph, it would be a mistake to think of the Marranos in a restrictive historical chronology, roughly from 1391 to Napoleon. A public Jewish author and Zionist activist, Cohen himself remains, throughout his life, unambiguous as to his public identity. Nor is the fictional Solal ever strictly speaking "crypto," in the sense of one who hides his Jewish origins, although he literally hides his family. Yet his whole dissonant psychology is nevertheless Marrano. When Solal hits bottom, destitute and almost homeless, he goes job hunting with this searing interior monologue: "It's my fault if I don't find any work. When I ask for work, this stupid pride. I parade a slew of Hebrew first names that I invent, if I'm speaking to Christians. Or I say with pride that I'm married to a Christian, if I'm speaking with Jews."*

In a sweeping delimitation of the psychological patterns inherent in Marranism, Yirmiyahu Yovel lists the following characteristics: "a this-worldly dis-

*C'est ma faute si je ne trouve pas de travail. Quand je vais demander du travail, cette fierté stupide. Je leur défile des prénoms hébraïques que j'invente, si je parle à des chrétiens. Ou je dis avec orgueil que j'ai épousé une chrétienne, si je parle à des Juifs. (*Solal,* 318)

position; a split religious identity; a metaphysical skepticism; a quest for alternative salvation through methods that oppose the official doctrine; an opposition between the inner and outer life, and a tendency toward dual language and equivocation."[39] Solal displays all these attributes: living opulently, he is clearly this-worldly; he hesitates between Judaism and Christianity (overtly in *Solal*); in contrast to his father Gamaliel, the orthodox rabbi, he is an atheist; he is always self-consciously split between Cephalonia and Europe; and he continually displays the rhetorical art of inhabiting multiple languages and practices (universal and ethnic, diplomatic and coarse, seductive and abrasive, and so forth).

To be a modern, secular, politically "assimilated" Jew (an *Israélite*), is to be in a de facto Marrano-like condition.[40] The modern Jew-*cum*-Marrano is almost by definition nothing but the limit case of a this-worldly, skeptical, antinomian modern person. Is it a coincidence that this "modern person" was in part invented by Michel de Montaigne, that descendent of Iberian Marranos, who published the first volume of his *Essais* on the *exact* date of Purim, March 1, 1580, or the 14th of Adar 5340 in the Jewish calendar?[41] No wonder that the "libidinal, cosmopolitan, atheist" modern, so hated by the anti-moderns of all shades and strides, is perennially assimilated to the figure of the secularized Jew. (The opposite is also true. Voltaire, the greatest cosmopolitan man of the Enlightenment, was casually anti-Semitic and rabidly anti-Judaic in the most profound sense. For the Jews, traditional or secular, visible or concealed, the room for maneuver in any case remains tight.)[42]

There is one additional correlation among Scripture, Cohen's fiction, and his biography that warrants special commentary, since it so perfectly matches the Joseph-Esther identity-phantasm. Even after her victory over Haman, we recall that Esther cannot reverse the royal decree allowing the massacre of the Jews throughout the Persian empire. She does, however, win for the Jews the right of vigorous self-defense. The invisible spine of the novel *Belle du Seigneur,* obliquely explained by the narrator long after the fact, concerns Solal's fall from grace in 1936 as the undersecretary-general of the League of Nations. Subsequent to a nightmarish hiding in the Berlin underground with terrified Jews, the well-trusted diplomat—trusted not to "embarrass" his superiors, trusted to be a "good court Jew," not too pushy with his narrow ethnic concerns—publicly demands urgent action to save German Jewry. His superiors are dismayed by his "inappropriate" audacity and immediately dismiss him "without notice for conduct prejudicial to the interests of the League of

Nations."* All else in the novel, and chiefly the suicide by Eros, or suicide by Ariane, is a consequence of Solal's failure at Joseph(ing) and Esther(ing) his way into history. As for the biographical level, just prior to the outbreak of World War II, as a Zionist diplomat negotiating on behalf of Chaim Weizmann and the World Jewish Congress, Albert Cohen deployed all his ingenuity to organize a substantial International Jewish Legion within the French Army.[43] In essence, Cohen as a Zionist diplomat simply wanted to give the Jews of Europe what Esther and Mordecai gave those of the Persian empire—the means of self-defense. But he failed.[44]

Although always stigmatized by this historical failure, the novels remain true to the performative principles of the Josephic-Estheric montage. This Marrano aesthetic points toward another dissonance in Cohen. As a novelist, his world is defined by the phenomenology of the mask. As a Zionist activist and diplomat, he strives for a time where, for the Jews, masks will have their *necessary* place only on the 14th day of Adar. The Solal saga operates (at least in the initial deployment of each narrative) as a series of fairy tales, performed with all the rhetorical and dramatic devices that have defined an important strand in modern sensibility since *La Celestina, Les Essais,* and *Don Quixote.* By way of illustration of the Josephic-Estheric montage hypothesis, I shall turn next to the central scene in the novel *Mangeclous* and show how it masterfully combines the most dramatic scene from the Joseph story with the most effective performance principle from the Book of Esther to create its own pre-Shoah masquerade.

A Joseph Purim Play in Geneva

> *And Joseph came into the house, and they brought him the tribute that was in their hand, into the house, and they bowed down to him to the ground. And he asked how they were, and he said, "Is all well with your aged father of whom you spoke? Is he still alive?" And they said, "All is well with your servant, our father. He is still alive." And they did obeisance and bowed down. And he raised his eyes and saw Benjamin his brother, his mother's son, and he said, "Is this your youngest brother of whom you spoke to me?" And he said, "God be gracious to you, my son." And Joseph hurried out, for his feelings for his brother overwhelmed him and he wanted to weep, and he went into the chamber and wept there. And he bathed his face and came out and held himself in check and said, "Serve bread." (Gen. 43: 26–31)*

*sans préavis pour conduite préjudiciable aux intérêts de la Société des Nations (*BdS,* 873)

[Jacob's blessing] Blessings, blessings on Joseph's head, and in your name shall they sun themselves who come from you. Songs shall stream far and wide singing the story of your life, ever anew, for after all it was a sacred play and you suffered and could forgive. So I too forgive you that you made me suffer. And God forgive us all!

Thomas Mann, Joseph the Provider[45]

In 1938 Cohen hastily published *Mangeclous* by cutting and pasting fragments from the first rough draft of the 3,500-page *Belle du Seigneur* manuscript. The novel begins when Solal anonymously sends his Uncle Saltiel a bank check for 300,000 drachmas, accompanied by a strangely coded thirty-line cryptogram, which ends in:

404 + 4 − 4 − 4 + 4
303 000 000 francs
204 + 200 = 100 + 50!
151 500 000 francs
444
(*Mangeclous,* 385)

After much collective effort, the Valorous finally decipher the code correctly as an invitation to a mysterious midnight meeting with Solal in a Geneva cemetary. At the end of *Solal,* subsequent to a calamitous visit from his clan (the subject of Chapter 3), Solal has lost his social and political position, as well as his wife and child, and has become an itinerant messianic figure. In *Mangeclous,* he has arisen from his ashes to become the undersecretary-general of the League of Nations in Geneva. And, like Joseph, he makes no effort to inform his family and clan of his meteoric ascent. For six years, no one in Cephalonia has heard from Solal. It is now time, Solal thinks, for a reunion with the Valorous.

Before proceeding we must, finally, introduce the cast of our Purim play, the celebrated French Valorous: Mangeclous, Saltiel, Mattathias, Michaël, and Salomon. They are part of the junior branch of the Solal clan (the senior branch is apparently operating in central Europe and England). After five centuries of wandering in France, they settled in Cephalonia at the end of the eighteenth century, keeping their French "current" by reading aloud among themselves the books of Villon, Rabelais, Montaigne, and Corneille, "so as not to lose the habit of the 'elegant turns of phrase.'"* Needless to say, their French is archaic and colorful—a logorrhea of bombastic and pathetic nonsense, in-

*pour ne pas perdre l'habitude des "tournures élégantes." (*Mangeclous,* 390)

terspersed with surprising insights.[46] They remain patriotic French citizens; Mangeclous and Michaël serve in the French Army.

Mangeclous, the false advocate. Given Mangeclous's importance in Cohen's fiction, I shall introduce him by quoting in full his business card, found at the beginning of *Solal:*

> Carte de visite de Maître Pinhas Solal
> Des Solal originaires de France Bénie
> Mais en Exil depuis des Siècles Hélas
> A Céphalonie Ile grecque en Mer Ionienne
> Citoyen Français Papiers en Règle
> Surnommé Parole d'Honneur
> Dit Mangeclous Professeur Très
> Emérite de Droit Avocat Habile
> Docteur en droit et médecine non diplômé
> Rédige des Contrats Excellents
> Et des Conventions Empoisonnées
> Que Tu ne peux plus T'en Sortir!
> Appelé aussi le Compliqueur de
> Procès Qui un jour fit mettre en
> Prison une Porte de Bois On Le Trouve
> Assis sur les Marches des Divers
> Tribunaux entre Six et Onze heures du
> Matin le plus grand Jurisconsulte de
> Céphalonie homme Honnête Les versements
> En espèces sont Préférés Pour les
> Ignorants on Donne l'explication de
> L'expression élégante Espèces veut Dire
> Argent Mais on accepte Aussi la Nourriture
> On le trouve chez Lui la nuit Et il Se
> Charge d'autres Affaires Il aurait Pu
> Etre Diplômé s'Il avait Daigné Mais il
> N'a pas daigné Ne pas détruire La Carte
> Qui a coûté Extrêmement d'Or et d'Argent[47]
>
> Calling Card of Master Pinhas Solal
> Of the Solals originally from France the Blessed
> But in Exile for centuries now, Alas
> In Cephalonia Greek Island in the Ionian Sea
> French Citizen Proper Documents

Named Word of Honor
Said Mangeclous Professor Very
Emeritus of Law Able Advocate
Doctor in law and medicine without diplomas
Drafts Excellent contracts
And Poisoned Conventions
That You could never Get Out of!
Also called the Complicator of
Trials Who one day had a Wooden Door
put in prison He can be Found
Seated on the Steps of Diverse
Tribunals between Six and Eleven o'clock
in the morning the greatest jurist of
Cephalonia an Honest man Payments
in cash are Preferred for the
Ignorant one Gives the explanation of
the elegant expression Cash means
Money But one accepts Also Food
He can be found in His house at night And He
Takes on other Affairs He Could have been
holder of diplomas if He had Deigned But he
did not deign Do not destroy The Card
Which cost a Great Deal in Gold and Silver.

Michael Weingrad succinctly sums up Mangeclous as "an outrageously self-involved, ever-scheming, ever-inventing, money-and-fame-obsessed ne'er-do-well with a long list of dubious titles and doubtful professions with which to impress the naïve populace of Cephalonia and get rich. He is a combination of Shylock and Falstaff, with a good deal of the Marx Brothers thrown in, and though he manifests most every human failing, it is possible to have, through sheer force of personality, a vitality we might call Shakespearean, or Rabelaisian, or even biblical, this irrepressible character delights [the reader]."[48]

Saltiel, the inventor. Second in command, he plays an especially important role as the surrogate for Rabbi Gamaliel, Solal's father. Saltiel is a little old man who is "boastful and useless" (*Solal,* 392). An admirer of Napoleon, he always wears a frock coat, with a flower in the buttonhole. Saltiel's brain is forever simmering with useless inventions, such as "a fan-powered sailboat" (*Solal,* 293). And, like all of the Valorous, he is perpetually penniless. Ridiculous and touching with his naïve probity, Saltiel is the most endearing of the Valorous, a character whose function is to substitute for the severe father and to speak the words of Cohen's autobiographical mother, albeit in a slightly transposed manner.

Mattathias, the miser. The former head of a "maritime enterprise" consisting of about a hundred kids fishing with single lines, whom he paid with the currency of marbles, matches, and pencils, this man is so stingy that "when he borrowed ground coffee, he dried it in the sun after having used it and returned it the next day to the obliging neighbors, making them believe that it was new coffee."*

Michaël, the giant. A large physical specimen and guardian of the synagogue, he is the courageous strongman of the bunch; he engages in multiple seductions of Jewesses, Greeks, and tourists and helps the adolescent Solal in all of his nocturnal gallant activities, including his final escape with the wife of the French consul.

Salomon, the peddler of apricot water. In contrast to Michaël, this member of the Valorous is plump and short and makes a living peddling syrupy drinks from an ambulatory stand that he pushes and pulls all day long in the sinuous alleys of the island ghetto. He is dimwitted but goodhearted, and when he is not daydreaming about winning the national lottery, he is always eager to engage in the next Valorous adventure.

And so on the appointed night, the Valorous are waiting for Solal at the cemetery, but Solal, unable to overcome his revulsion from these "grotesque men," whom he has himself invited, remains hidden in the back seat of a taxi.[49] The Valorous continue to search for Solal in Geneva. And Mangeclous, overcome by his perennial diplomatic ambitions, decides to play a trick on the Valorous by faking a telegram from Chaim Weizmann, head of the World Zionist Congress in Jerusalem, which supposedly empowers Saltiel and his Valorous to negotiate the size of the future Jewish state with the undersecretary-general of the League of Nations, without knowing that that this "viceroy of the world" is their very own nephew—just as Joseph's brothers did not recognize their kin hidden beneath the cloak of an Egyptian viceroy.

Thus, by the time the Valorous enter the Palace of the League of Nations in Geneva, they are already willy-nilly actors in a farce within a farce: in Solal's farce, which has brought them to Geneva in the first place and then in Mange-

*lorsqu'il empruntait du café moulu, il le séchait au soleil après s'en être servi et qu'il le rendait le lendemain aux obligeants voisins en leur faisant croire que c'était du café neuf. (*Mangeclous,* 393)

clous's farce once they are in Geneva. Saltiel believes that the destiny of Israel hangs in the balance, and that they must dress appropriately for the solemn, if not fateful, occasion. Each of the clowns therefore assembles a diplomatic garb of sorts and they enter the Palace: "Salomon as a tennis champion, Mattathias as a cod fisherman, Mangeclous as a civilized African king, Michaël as a comic opera policeman, and Saltiel, inexpressible in his courteous gravity."* They come dressed for a costume ball or a Purim festival and will not be disappointed.

Solal peeks at his kin through a hole in the door. He knew that sooner or later, they would reappear in his life. They are, after all the willed and willing toys in his own deadly *Fort! Da!* game: "now I am undersecretary-general, now I am not." Seeing them in their Purim costumes (which they take for real diplomatic attire), he decides to lock them up in the waiting room, so that for a while longer at least, these clowns will be "for the moment unable to do any harm."† He then orders his chauffeur to take him to a carnival shop, where he quickly selects a costume of his own, that of a gravely wounded monster. Meanwhile, the Valorous realize that they have been locked in and become increasingly anxious. But suddenly, the door opens and a hideous monster appears:

> On the threshold of the door stood an undersecretary-general in a black dressing gown and black gloves, lacking a human face. On his shoulders rested a white ball of dressing bandages, which hid his face and hair. He wore a pair of dark sunglasses, and a russet-red beard sprouted from between the bands of gauze. He was really a very ugly and dreadful undersecretary-general.‡

Just as the Valorous's ridiculous diplomatic costumes reveal their utter remoteness from the European social scene, Solal's costume illustrates his own ambivalence: a wounded monster is the perfect metaphor for him. He is clad in black, his face partly hidden by bandages and a rusty beard, his voice husky and strained, his speech slurred, and his eyes hidden behind dark sunglasses. Sadistically toying with the Valorous, he becomes a monster, but a wounded monster cutting into his own flesh, his own kin, visibly tortured and delighted by sadistic and masochistic ambivalence.

So heavily disguised is Solal that the Valorous have no hope of recognizing

*Salomon en champion de tennis, Mattathias en pêcheur de morues, Mangeclous en roi nègre civilisé, Michaël en gendarme d'opérette et Saltiel, inexprimable de courtoise gravité. (*Mangeclous*, 553)

†l'impossibilité momentanée de nuire (*Mangeclous*, 553)

‡Sur le seuil de la porte, un sous-secrétaire général en robe de chambre noire et gants noirs, privé de face humaine. Sur ses épaules reposait une boule blanche faite de bandes à pansements qui cachaient son visage et ses cheveux. Il portait des lunettes noires et une barbe rousse coulait hors des bandes de gaze. C'était un sous-secrétaire général vraiment très laid et très terrible. (*Mangeclous*, 557)

their lost kinsman in this Joseph disguised as the evil Haman. The Jewish boy from Cephalonia, disguised as the undersecretary-general (he calls himself "le sous-bouffon général"), disguised in turn as a monster-*cum*-diplomat, can now terrify these odious beloveds, this detritus from an earlier life, with impunity. Everything is thus in place for a sham misrecognition and cruel humor, followed by reconciliation, which is itself then short-circuited. The Mediterranean simpletons are so gullible that they actually imagine that a diplomat might appear as grotesque as this slurring monster. Is it not a Haman who is standing at the door? Have they not been trained to outmaneuver such a monster on each and every Purim? Is not each of them a potential Mordecai? But in fact they are closer to being Joseph's hapless and dimwitted brothers than the cunning courtier Mordecai. The scene is set; actors in costume are in place—and the plot of this farce within a farce within a farce unfolds.

The sight of this disfigured monster stupefies the Valorous, who bow before this "divinity with a head of gauze" *(divinité à tête de gaze)* and prove too frightened to respond to his question regarding the purpose of their visit. At last, Saltiel presents the *machine humaine* (this is how the Valorous perceive the monster) with the phony letter of introduction. The monster asks Saltiel to introduce his colleagues, as if he did not already know them intimately. Then, imitating Judah's eloquent speech in front of the "masked" Joseph (Gen. 44: 18–33), Saltiel makes an impassioned plea for Israel, which is worth citing:

> "Back when Geneva was no more than a putrid marsh . . . with a few huts rising at its borders around which men ran naked, alas, catching game with their teeth, a superb city rose from the Orient, majestic and crowned, and peopled by myriad children of God, who waved palm fronds in the air and read the Commandments that God has sent down to man so that he may truly become human." . . . "This city was named Jerusalem, capital of the kingdom of Israel!" . . . "In short, your excellency, this nation is about to be reconstituted. She has honored me by naming me her tourist guide, and this honor I bear entirely myself."*

Upon hearing this plea for the archaic aristocracy of Israel, which is another variation of the theme of his father's bar mitzvah charge, the "sous-chef du monde"

*"À l'époque où Genève n'était qu'un marais putride . . . au bord duquel s'élevaient quelques huttes autour desquelles des hommes hélas nus attrapaient du gibier avec leurs dents, une ville superbe s'étendait en Orient, majestueuse et couronnée, et peuplée d'une multitude d'enfants de Dieu qui agitaient des palmes et lisaient les Commandements que Dieu a envoyés à l'homme pour qu'il devienne homme." . . . "Cette ville . . . avait nom Jérusalem, capitale du royaume d'Israël!" . . . "Bref, Excellence, cette nation est à la veille d'être reconstituée. Elle m'a fait l'honneur de me nommer son cicérone et cet honneur je reporte tout entier sur moi-même!" (*Mangeclous,* 558–59)

(all these bombastic epitaphs occur in the text) momentarily breaks down and makes the unexpected gesture of taking Saltiel's hand and kissing it (still without revealing himself), just as "Judah's speech has its effect on Joseph who can no longer control himself and at long last reveals his identity to his brothers."[50]

What a hopeful sign! Saltiel, the hapless dreamer, overcomes Haman's resistance! But at the sight of this apparent victory, Mangeclous, consumed with envy of Saltiel's apparent success, interrupts this touching scene, proves impatient and therefore allows the *machine humaine* to recover from his momentary compassionate lapse and resume his role. Mangeclous explains to the terrible "divinity with a head of gauze" that the area of land in Palestine offered to the Jews by the British is insufficient and, although unable to quote the precise percentage of the English offer, he nonetheless declares that the League of Nations should double it. To egg Mangeclous on (he has quickly recovered from compassion and has become sadistic again), Solal feigns reluctance and states that one must also think of the Arab natives. To this Mattathias, always at hand where bargaining is concerned, responds:

> —"Make an offer," Mattathias said.
> —"Ten perfent [Solal slurs] more than England."
> Mangeclous raised his arms heavenward.
> —Highness, you must be kidding!" he cried.*

Their haggling parodies the comic scene in Genesis where Abraham bargains with God over the number of people to be saved from Sodom and Gomorrah (Gen. 22: 27–33). To everyone's amazement the "civilized African king" (Mangeclous) offers to bribe the "Sous-chef de l'univers" with a suitcase full of cash. Quite aside from wanting to save the Jews, Mangeclous is sincerely convinced that if the plea succeeds, he will be appointed prime minister of the new state, and, like Sancho Panza, will at last rise to the regal status of a corrupt judge, living off bribes and stuffing himself with delicacies from dawn to dusk.

Bemused, the monster allows Mangeclous to discuss the matter with him for a while. He then takes the Weizmann telegram, counts the words, turns toward the grotesque "Complicator of trials" and abruptly calls him a crook ("vous êtes une crapule"). Solal orders the other four Valorous to exit the room and confronts Mangeclous, who quickly admits to the forgery of the telegram.

*—"Faites une offre" dit Mattathias.
—Dif pour fent *[sic]* de plus que l'Angleterre."
Mangeclous leva les bras au ciel.
—"Altesse, vous voulez rire !" s'écria-t-il. (*Mangeclous*, 560)

Mangeclous only regrets the pomp, bribery, and the food he will be missing now that he will no longer be elevated from *shtettle shnorrer* (ghetto bum) to prime minister:

> And what a prime minister I would have been, Highness! What inventions! What prosperity for my people and for myself! What a navy and what bribes! And, finally rich with billions, what food, and how my bottomless soul would have satisfied itself passionately with glorious little sesame fritters, dispatched each day for me from Cephalonia by Jacob Without Handkerchief, who is the only pastry chef in the world good enough to make them! O sublime fritters that instill such enthusiasm in my heart, O deliciously disgusting little fritters, filled to the very core as they are with syrup.*

This plethoric logorrhea of delusional regrets continues over six pages. Yet the "viceroy of the world" persists throughout in his cruel indifference. This grotesque Mangeclous incarnates and gives (ample) voice to Solal's origins, his cultural id, as it were. No wonder, then, that the novel *Mangeclous* is dedicated TO MY FATHER. Solal's ambivalence holds him in place; even disguised as a freakish monster, he remains as frozen as he was in the back of the taxi when he intently gazed at the Valorous, unable to force himself to step out and greet his guests.

At this point, Mangeclous expresses regret over the pain that this latest debacle will inflict on Saltiel, who, he notes sadly, is already suffering terribly from the loss of his nephew, a man named Solal, whom the Valorous are desperately trying to locate. Up to now, the similarities with the Joseph story have been obvious, yet somewhat oblique, but here they become textual and warrant a fuller examination. Jacob's reaction to the loss of Joseph mirrors Saltiel's reaction to that of Solal: "And Jacob rent his clothes and put sackcloth round his waist and mourned for his son many days. And all his sons and all his daughters rose to console him and he refused to be consoled and he said, 'Rather I will go down to my son in Sheol mourning,' and his father bewailed him" (Gen. 37: 34–35). Here is Mangeclous explaining Saltiel's grief at the loss of Solal:

> The poor man, he doesn't speak to me about anything other than his nephew whom he lost and wants to find. . . .

*Et quel Premier ministre j'aurais été, Altesse! Quelles inventions! Quelle prospérité pour mon peuple et pour moi-même! Quelle flotte et quels pots-de-vin! Et, étant riche enfin à milliards, quelles nourritures et comme mon âme sans fond se serait rassasiée amoureusement de glorieux petits beignets au sésame, expédiés chaque jour pour moi de Céphalonie par Jacob Sans Mouchoir qui est le seul pâtissier du monde à bien les réussir! Ô sublimes beignets dont mon cœur est fervent, ô petits beignets délicieusement dégoûtants tant ils sont bourrés de sirop jusqu'à l'âme interne! (*Mangeclous,* 564)

. . . Oh, poor Saltiel, if only you could see him at our feasts eating all alone with a plate for his nephew Solal before him, a plate on which he places the choicest morsels! And against the pitcher there is a photograph of his nephew! Ah, highness, if you had known the former Saltiel, sharp and such a liar that it was a pleasure, with an invention always resting on his lips like a flower. While now, highness, ever since he lost his nephew, he's such a pale figure of a man! This broken man no longer utters anything but the truth, and as a result his days are numbered!*

It is clear that we are again at an inflection point. Solal is called upon to affirm once again the perennial "Here I am" and will no longer be able to hide behind his masks. He will have to reunite, however fleetingly and incompletely, with the despised beloved. The still silent Solal "made a sign to the grotesque that he should rejoin his kin [*ses pareils*]."† Alone and despondent, in the lucidity of an interior monologue Solal finds the perfect metaphor for his relationship to his kin: "The Jews were his mistresses and his adulteries."‡

The reader is now ready for a genuine reconciliation scene, prominent in Genesis, but absent in *Mangeclous.* The triumphant scene of reconciliation is seen from Saltiel's point of view, and is therefore discredited, somewhere, both for the narrator and the reader, between the amusing and the abject. The narrator's ambivalence cannot quite find the correct third-person perspective for this narrative climax. The banquet scene, in which all participants reunite, does take place, but again with one important reversal. Unlike Joseph, Solal will not break bread with his brethren: "'Lord Solal, will you not honor us by sharing our modest meal?' asked Salomon. . . . Solal replied that he was not hungry, but that he would keep them company. He seemed numb, only half alive."§

Even in this scene of reticent recognition and reconciliation, there is contiguity between Solal and the Valorous but no transfer of affect. Instead of eating *with* the Valorous, he looks *at* them eating, as in the midnight scene where

*Le pauvre, il ne me parle que de son neveu qu'il a perdu et qu'il veut retrouver. . . .

. . . Oh pauvre Saltiel si vous pouviez le voir aux fêtes manger tout seul avec, devant lui, une assiette pour son neveu Solal, assiette sur laquelle il met les meilleurs morceaux! Et contre la carafe il y a la photographie de son neveu! Ah, Altesse, si vous aviez connu le Saltiel d'autrefois, vif et si menteur que c'était plaisir, toujours une invention à la bouche comme une fleur. Tandis que maintenant, Altesse, depuis qu'il a perdu son neveu c'est un individu pâle! Cet homme désemparé ne profère plus que des paroles véridiques et par conséquent ses jours sont comptés! (*Mangeclous,* 568)

†fit signe au grotesque d'aller rejoindre ses pareils (*Mangeclous,* 569)

‡Les Juifs étaient ses maîtresses et ses adultères. (*Mangeclous,* 569)

§"Seigneur Solal, ne nous ferez-vous pas le plaisir de partager notre modeste repas?" demanda Salomon. . . . . . Solal dit qu'il n'avait pas faim mais qu'il leur tiendrait compagnie. Il paraissait engourdi, vivant à demi seulement. (*Mangeclous,* 596)

he just gazed at them frozen by his shame and shame of shame. Now, once the masks have been removed, in the immediate presence of the Valorous, Solal not only stands apart but seems "numb, only half alive." This is not exactly the classical comic closure that we would expect to a very tense farce! After this scene, Solal bestows much money on the Valorous in the half-articulated hope that they will never return, unless, of course, he chooses to play his deadly *Fort! Da!* game, in which case they just become actors in his sadomasochistic theater.

In contrast to the narratives of Joseph and Esther, the present flux of synecdoches and metonymies (encoded letters, faked letters, fried sesame honey doughnuts, masks, and costumes) never coagulates into that perfectly articulated metaphor of the banquet: the breaking and ingesting of bread face-to-face. In the absence of such a banquet, the ritual of reconciliation in bread and wine (the mass of reconciliation), the sequence of events remains suspended in midair. The narrative is thus short-circuited, truncated. At most, Solal can be obliquely contiguous vis-à-vis his brethren, but a real metaphorical transaction, in Peter Brooks's model of narrative, never occurs.[51]

Consequently, "Purim in Geneva," the central scene in *Mangeclous,* is a scene "whose tenuous readability depends directly on its intertextual support."[52] It must be read thematically (through the theme of the "leavening") and phenomenologically (through the chronotrope of the mask) against the Joseph and Esther narratives. Without reference to this intertextuality, it reads as a bizarre, pathological joke, and ignores the essential intertextual force at work beneath the surface: the problem of gathering a people, constituting one nation from a multitude, all the while being doubled, concealed, and masked—and, in a thoroughly modern fashion, wishing to remain individuated. In Genesis and the Book of Esther, these are successful transactions, and we can therefore see them as the reaffirmation of the basic logic of Genesis, "[the] reaffirmation of the divine purpose to bring about good in the face of evil, life in the midst of death. So good continues to be wrought."[53] Yet, in Cohen, this providential perspective is self-consciously decanted of meaning. The comedy of dissimulation and (temporary) salvation of the biblical intertext becomes monstrous dissonance in *Mangeclous.* Cohen does not repeat and amplify the matrix narrative. Rather, he empties it of all its historico-political potency (the logic of the *augment*) and shows the phenomenology of the mask to be the most alienating of existences when imposed as a permanent state—so alienating that only the poetically grotesque can represent it. On the eve of the Holocaust, Cohen is a genius when it comes to adopting the Mannian dictum for the modern Jew: *For I am and am not just because I am I.*

3 The Jewish Saint-Germain

Joseph's dilemma is always between presence and absence, always confronted with this choice.
Shmuel Trigano, La Philosophie de la Loi

As *Solal,* Cohen's first novel (1930), unfolds, its protagonist, Solal, engineers a meteoric rise in French political life, which culminates in his new status as the theoretician of the Socialist Party, deputy in the French National Assembly, and minister of labor, as well as an influential newspaper editor. Solal, in short, is at last the consummate insider. He is now married to Adrienne de Valdonne's niece, Aude, whose father, a French senator and government minister, greatly assists Solal's ascent to power. Distraught over Solal's abandonment of her and over his refined cruelty, Adrienne de Valdone—the woman who originally facilitated Solal's passage from Cephalonia to Europe and then his introduction into the inner circles of power in Switzerland and France—commits suicide by throwing herself in front of a train. Seemingly indifferent to the suicide of his mother/lover and liberator, the charismatic and very opportunistic Greek Jew leads a blissful life. The illusion of a stable and durable identity as a high-class European socialist seduces him no end.

But one does not become oneself ex nihilo. Past and present inevitably intersect, and Solal's European identity, so eagerly willed and constructed, quickly unravels. He will not be a Mediterranean Disraeli, as he painfully reminds himself in *Belle du Seigneur:* "She then suggested she read a biography of Disraeli to him. Oh no, not that sly [*rusé*] fellow, . . . who knew, he, how not to waste his life."* This failure to become a Disraeli and Solal's acute awareness of it allow Cohen the novelist to masterfully weave competing nar-

*Alors, elle proposa de lui lire une biographie de Disraeli. Ah non, pas ce rusé bonhomme, . . . et qui avait su ne pas gâcher sa vie, lui. (*BdS,* 776)

ratives of idiosyncratic narcissisms and phantasms into historical and theological paradoxes. In *Solal,* this tragic awareness still has a comic and hopeful tinge to it, which will completely disappear in *Mangeclous* and *Belle du Seigneur. Solal* still harbors the hope that a charismatic Jew may be able to negotiate multiple identities, exist in between inclusions and exclusions, and ascend and descend the ladder of identities, following his self-creative comic will, all while secretly and obliquely saving his people from perdition. Solal wants to be the invisible one who will make the presence of Israel possible. But the sudden bursting of Israel into his life makes this all but impossible.

Like Joseph, Solal keeps his worldly success secret from his kin. When his father and his uncle Saltiel finally visit him in Paris, he humiliates them by keeping them waiting in a shabby hotel. The old father and rabbi, Gamaliel, loses patience and decides to force the issue. Uninvited and dressed in traditional rabbinical garb, Gamaliel (accompanied by Saltiel) attends an elegant diplomatic reception at the Quai d'Orsay (the French foreign ministry), thereby calling into question his son's fictional new self. This irruption of the past into the present, of the Jew into the quintessential Gentiles' space (Quai d'Orsay, Palace of the League of Nations, elegant receptions and late-night parties), is a frequent nightmare scenario in Cohen's fiction and essays. Solal's reaction to Gamaliel's intrusion is violent (as it will be with his mother in *Le Livre de ma mère)*: "[T]his man [Gamaliel] who, after making him look ridiculous and *shattering a painfully constructed life,* had the stupid audacity to smile. Mad with shame, he moved to strike. A sudden inspiration stopped him. His eyes blazed malignantly, and, gloating over the act, he slowly made the sign of the cross."*

I cannot overstate the symbolic power of this act of apostasy. For a Jew, making the sign of the cross in front of one's father in public is an act even more spiteful than physically striking one's father in public. Gamaliel becomes so distraught that, once back at his hotel, he slashes his own eyes with a knife. In so doing, Gamaliel enacts upon his own flesh the symbolic erasure of the father that the son has carried out in gesture. Without his eyes, Gamaliel can no longer witness Solal's transgression, a sign of the father's symbolic impotence. The purpose of Gamaliel's life lies in the assurance of a Jewish transmission, assured (in this case) through the symbolic link between the father and son. Solal brutally severs this link to the past and transmission to the future, thus

*[C]et homme qui, après être venu le ridiculiser, *briser une vie péniblement construite,* avait la stupide audace de sourire. Fou de honte, il s'approcha pour frapper. Mais une inspiration subite le fit s'arrêter. Les yeux ardents de malignité, il fit, lentement et avec délices, le signe de la croix. (*Solal,* 280; emphasis added)

castrating the father with a single sign of the cross. Gamaliel responds to this public castration by symbolically castrating himself by mutilating his eyes.[1]

But Solal quickly regains his lucidity. Perched at a window watching his humiliated father and uncle saunter away, the apostate realizes what he has done. "Yes, he understood everything now. When he leant out of the window last night, he had seen the two rejected old men walking in the snow, stumbling, supporting each other and walking away, the two despairing old men."* The high-perched window as a site of truth is a stock trope in philosophical discourse. It was from such a window that Descartes wondered whether the things with hats coming toward him were human or robots; and Pascal's most radical articulation of "What is the Self?" occurred when, perceiving people from a high window, he was struck by the contingency (and ultimate narcissism) of all perception.[2] The high and wide angle permits the viewer to confront the strange familiarity of the other. The familiar becomes absurd, and existentially urgent in its phenomenal and ontological absurdity.

Once drawn out of the diplomatic circle where oriental, religious Jews are considered as the ultimate others, Solal realizes how true to themselves these "despairing old men," those sad silhouettes now drifting away from him, but from whom he sprang, are. Solal does not, however, need a God to guarantee that these are not mere phantoms (Descartes); nor does he need to be reminded of the fragility of their contingency and of his own narcissism (Pascal)—origin and destiny are far more powerful impulses than feeble philosophical moves. The face-to-face encounter, paradoxically enough, does not yield imperative identification. Rather, distance and perspective allow father and uncle to exit Solal's field of self-absorption (the diplomatic reception) and regain their status as kin: as origin and destiny. Standing at the high window, Solal cannot help but exit his narcissism and sadism and become perfectly lucid, as revealed in this interior monologue: "O my Sol, ours is a very ancient people; quite distinct from the Crusaders who are of the day before yesterday; a very pure, very holy, and very faithful people. Poor Solal, you had sold your soul. Kneel at Gamaliel's feet and beg for his forgiveness!"† Again, the proximity-distance paradox stands out as a leitmotif in Cohen's writings and transforms

*Mais oui, il comprenait tout maintenant. Lorsqu'il s'était penché à la fenêtre hier soir, il avait vu les deux vieux renvoyés qui allaient sur la neige, trébuchaient, s'appuyaient l'un sur l'autre et allaient, les deux vieux désespérés (*Solal,* 282)

†Ô mon Sol, ce peuple est un peuple très ancien, autre chose que les Croisés qui sont d'avant-hier, un peuple très pur, très noble et très fidèle. Pauvre Solal, tu avais vendu ton âme. Aux pieds de Gamaliel et demande-lui pardon!" (*Solal,* 283)

the father-uncle figure into a necessary abstraction, thus producing this renewed allegiance. By abstraction, I simply mean that the paternal figures (father and uncle), or the Valorous in general, are not desired as real, concrete individuals in all their concrete "thereness," but only as members of a community obsessed with the transmission of its culture, of its Book. Solal identifies with the Jews as a collective ("a very pure, very holy, and very faithful people"), that is, as historical and theological abstractions—as conveyors of a religion and culture that define him, bind him, and sacrifice his worldly and sexual desire—but never as individuals desired in a differentiated face-to-face encounter. Henceforth Solal's ego bifurcates radically, as all his collective identification focuses on the Jews and his individual desire directs itself toward the Gentiles. Pulled between Rabbi Gamaliel and Aude de Maussane, Solal will vacillate between the two—a comic situation where clans with different codes of conduct clash in a confined space—the Château Saint-Germain.

Once Solal resurfaces from the depths of his self-absorption, his wife, apartment, routines, and political power—all the attributes of his "painfully constructed life"—seem absurd to him. Solal's predicament throughout his novelistic life (1930–69) is represented well in this triple movement: the familiar becomes absurd; the desired is always in conflict with the symbolic (the father and all his surrogates); and therefore everything seems to be vanity—unworthy of life, but deserving a highly stylized death.

The arrival of the oriental Jewish father momentarily disrupts the equilibrium of his new life, and Solal perceives everything around him as a Kafkaesque nightmare: "How strange. An apartment. And this apartment belonged to him. Comic . . . armchairs. A little brush for the fireplace. He had things. . . . Funny. Want to laugh. . . . Solal, the 'theoretician of the party.'"* Solal's laughter is tragic. It is the bleak negation of all desired venues. It is the expression of his contempt for all possible scenarios: the transmission of Judaism, so desired by the father, seems to him just as contemptuous and absurd as his fashionable apartment and pretentious political title, "theoretician of the party."

But returning to his origins proves an impossible fantasy. Although born oriental and Jewish, Solal has also become a European: he is both a secular politician and the son of Rabbi Gamaliel, bearer of the father's blessings and all the duties thereof. Solal's "vanity of vanities" harangue against Aude and Europe thereby acquires a complex character. He does not reject Europa

*Curieux. Un appartement. Et cet appartement lui appartenait. Comique. . . . Fauteuils. Petit balai pour la cheminée. Il avait des objets . . . Comique. Envie de rire. . . . Solal le "théoricien du parti." (*Solal,* 281, 232)

(Aude) on its empirical merit, on the level of a face-to-face existence, for he indeed ardently desires Europa. He instead rejects the anti-Semitic foundation of this Europe—the belief that for Europe to exist, the Jews must be kept alive but remain contemptible, be present but hidden.[3] Upon seeing the Valorous who visit Solal at the Quai d'Orsay, Aude's father, a liberal socialist, directly suggests this desired disappearance of the Jews to Solal: "Scram, you and your tribe [*smalah*]."* Aude has a more nuanced understanding of Solal's inner ambiguity: "All was vanity, except the Law of which he spoke, the hypocrite, eyes distraught and mouth open too wide."† The Law (of his father) renders odious the desired European. Each proposition in the father's bar mitzvah charge now haunts the son's interior monologue: "Marriage. Very well, marriage. And now he was locked in a cube with her. . . . There were bones and they both chewed. Tra-la-la, let us chew and brush our teeth conjugally. And he was, naturally, expected to feed her, to bring meats and grass and serve her. Later, perhaps, he might have to build a nest with his mouth, sit on it to warm up the little snakes, warble to amuse the female, and feed the little sharks with his beak."‡

Solal then slips out of this interior monologue (a nihilistic Manichean dualism between fallen matter and godly spirit, not a dominant feature of Jewish thinking) and ridicules Aude, going so far as to tell her that "music was intercourse and an abomination," which closely echoes Gamaliel's bar mitzvah curse: "Anathema on him who stops to look at a beautiful tree." It would be out of place here to discuss the problematic nature of these beliefs from the point of view of Torah-based Jewish thought.[4] But we can say in brief that the tension between the world as it is and its ontological foundation, managed by the norms of the Law, modulates relationships, whether human to divine, human to human, or human to things, but does not ontologically degrade matter and desire per se, and is therefore rarely nihilistic.[5]

Thus, instead of differentiating Jewish and Christian points of view (which Solal inverts), these outbursts suggest Solal's searing self-dissonance, if not outright hysteria, which Cohen underlines by focalizing Solal's actions through

*"Vous allez déguerpir avec votre smalah." (*Solal,* 239)

†Tout était vanité, sauf la Loi dont il parlait, l'hypocrite, avec des yeux égarés et en ouvrant trop la bouche. (*Solal,* 286)

‡Mariage, bien mariage. Et maintenant il était enfermé dans un cube avec elle. . . . il y avait des os et ils mastiquaient tous les deux. Gai gai mastiquons et brossons-nous les dents conjugalement. Et naturellement, il était tenu de la nourrir, d'apporter des viandes et des herbages et de la saillir. Peut-être même que plus tard il devrait construire un nid avec sa bouche, s'asseoir dessus pour chauffer les petits serpents, gazouiller pour faire passer le temps à la femelle et nourrir les petits requins à la becquée. (*Solal,* 282)

Aude's interior monologue: "the hypocrite, eyes distraught and mouth open too wide." Solal cannot modulate intelligently; he can only swing violently from extreme to extreme: "[H]e could only express himself brilliantly under the impulse of passion."* Here Solal is perverse on all accounts. Perverse when he humiliates his father. Perverse when he humiliates his wife. Narcissism exacts its toll. "[Solal] reveled in the unconscious treasons of which he accused her."† Within two pages, the young minister has deeply wounded his father and his wife, and events become even more comic when we learn that they are destined to share the same dwelling.

Cohen the novelist has found in the Château Saint-Germain the perfect chronotope (ratio of time-space projection) to convey Solal's *in-between* existence.[6] To satisfy the two dominant paternal figures, Gamaliel and de Maussane, the two mutually exclusive spheres must coexist in the symbolic space of the late medieval Château Saint-Germain. The day after he makes the sign of the cross in public, Solal drops to his knees and begs his father for forgiveness. Gamaliel accepts but commands Solal to "build a secret abode in [his] European one."‡ Solal obeys. Gamaliel understands that there is no returning to the ghetto of Cephalonia for Solal. This is why he demands of Solal the active exercise of conflicting identities. By day a visible political maverick, by night a ghost—Solal becomes the obedient son, reenacting the Sephardic nightmare of crypto-Jewish existence.

A château is a worldview reduced to its architectural expression. It represents a collective spirit, a collective discourse. Its ideological arrangement of space signifies a vision of the whole: the meaning of the past, the practices of the present, and the possibilities of the future. Châteaux, in particular, have a number of significant attributes. They dominate ("La Commanderie" is the name of our château), and their size—the invisible underground cellars and multiple compartments—makes them forbidding, hence their gothic potential, so richly exploited here. As symbolic representations, they are meaningful spaces where the visible gives way to the invisible, where hidden passages lead to secret worlds, where appearances often deceive.

In his initial description of the château, Solal twice underlines its religious significance, and hence the relationship between chronology and spatial arrangement in his "European abode." The Château Saint-Germain dates back to "the fifteenth century after Jesus Christ," he notes with precision, and then

*[I]l ne savait s'exprimer que génialement, sous la poussée de la passion. (*Solal,* 288)

†[Solal] se repaissait des trahisons inconscientes dont il l'accusait. (*Solal,* 286)

‡faire une demeure secrète dans [s]a demeure d'Europe. (*Solal, 291)*

sarcastically asks the reader, "Why do you dispose of so few centuries?"* In this context, the sixteenth century can only be of the Christian calendar; no need, therefore, to underline it, unless this reference is the key to understanding the symbolic layout of the Château Saint-Germain. In other words, the chronological order of Judaism and Christianity is replicated in the vertical structure of the château: in the cellar below live the human relics of the period before Christ; above them lives Aude de Maussane, incarnation of the New Israel; and, between the old and new, between the "Before" and the "After," Solal shuttles up and down.

Thus when he describes the château to Aude, Solal emphasizes that "even the ground that is below will belong to us,"† adding sarcastically: "The people of the Middle Ages have arranged everything very well."‡ Unlike moderns, medieval Christians made no pretense of even the theoretical acceptability of non-Christians in the visible realm; thus, they separated Jews from Christians as a matter of law and fact, just as the Germans were about to undertake to do three years after the publication of this novel. As early as 1930, Cohen understood how the medieval and the modern would soon merge in the National Socialist state. Most anti-Jewish Nazi laws were merely a more systematic and efficient rendition of medieval Christian practices.[7] In this Jewish ghetto that Solal constructs for his kin within his "European abode," Cohen locates and mines the most apt chronotope both for his existential identity struggle and, more important, for the fate of his people.

The motif of the underground cave or cellar recurs often in Cohen, and for profound reasons. First there is the obvious ontotheological dimension: the Jews have been superseded and remain blind to the (new) truth; their place remains in the ground, slithering along with the other blind insects. Medieval imagery makes frequent references to the blindness of the Jews.[8] In architectural and iconographical terms, the synagogue lies literally beneath the cathedral, as it is most famously represented in Chartres cathedral. And likewise, the living arrangement in Saint-Germain, where Christians live above and Jews below, stands for the ontological priority of Christians over Jews. The embarrassing relics are best kept below and out of sight.[9]

This ontotheological construct of the château also recalls the superego, ego, and id topology. "A biblical city swarms under His Excellency's house,"§ just

*"Pourquoi disposez-vous de si peu de siècles?" (*Solal,* 283)

†"même la terre qui est dessous nous appartiendra." (*Solal,* 283)

‡"Les gens du Moyen Âge ont tout très bien arrangé." (*Solal,* 291)

§Une ville biblique grouille sous la demeure de Son Excellence (*Solal,* 291)

as Judaism festers under the house of Christianity, like a disturbing unconscious, provoking fits of aggression, fascination, deep ambivalence. The Jews are an origin that resists supersession; an origin that is a crucial element of Christian identity, allowed to remain present but held in contempt.[10] "For the Jews of the cellar are not only the cultural unconscious of the West, they are also the most archaic layer of the personality of [Solal], who attempts without success to do away with it."[11] But let us return to the Jewish Saint-Germain, a name revealing all: château, Saint-Germain, but also in the final analysis Jewish. All the codes collide here.[12]

In order to prepare his "European abode" for its dual existence Solal sends his wife away from Paris and has the château refurbished, particularly its underground. Once this is completed and Solal's kin are settled in the underground *(souterrain)*, Aude returns from Geneva to inhabit the upper part of the château with her husband, while Solal's family and extended kin are hidden below in a cellar. But Solal is edgy, secretive, and paranoiac, and the already precarious existence of this Jewish-Gentile couple becomes strained. To conceal the living relics teeming below, Solal fires the staff, except for one maid. Every night he sounds a gong, after which no one is to move in the castle. Aude is confined to her room, and Solal takes a secret passageway leading underground, where his ancestry awaits him, as nightmares await a madman falling asleep. Every night Solal ascends and descends the ladder of prehistory and history (B.C./A.D.), struggling in the most self-dramatizing fashion to reconcile the impossible.

Yet Aude knows that something is afoot. She hears very strange sounds: "Cries or singing seemed to surge from the depths of the earth. Stumbling phrases, then rapid notes would rise sharply. Was she prey to hallucinations?"* After a thorough search of the castle, she comes into Solal's study and finds him asleep with a golden key in his hands. She understands at once that the golden key unlocks the passage to the forbidden part of the house. Unable to resist her curiosity, Aude descends for a quick first look and discovers the occupants of the underground. She returns upstairs and confronts Solal.

A comic exchange of fantasies follows. Solal and Aude share a vision of "biblical man" quite at variance with the reality of European Jews circa 1930. When she becomes conscious of the chants rising from the basement, Aude is eager to encounter these extraordinary relics of the "Old Testament": "[T]he

*Des cris ou des chants semblaient surgir des profondeurs de la terre. Des phrases butées puis des notes rapides qui s'élevaient avec acuité. Était-elle en proie à une hallucination? (*Solal,* 287)

wonderful world her beloved [Solal] had described. She advanced reverently toward the pure and warrior kingdom of the Old Testament. She advanced toward the prophets."* Solal never hides his Jewish origin and is thus never truly a "crypto-Jew." But he constructs his own "biblical" legend concerning his sunny Cephalonian origins, never mind the one hundred generations of displacements and persecutions separating modern Jews from the last Hebrew "pure warriors and prophets."

As a highly educated Genevan Protestant, Aude knows her "Old" and "New" Testaments and is a competent accomplice in Solal's romantic self-invention. Although converging from opposite directions, they both traffic in similar fantasies. Aude sees her "Hebrew" kin as proto-Christians, while Solal interprets his mythic biblical heritage as a predisposition for a messianic vocation in Europe for which Aude is an important sexual and political vector: "We have given you the greatest wise man. And so many others. And me, among others. *And me later.*"† Aude thus imagines that she will encounter her own proto-Christian origins, just as one might rush to meet Achilles and Patroclus on the shores of Troy. Perhaps these "biblical" figures will resemble the rustic menagerie of Bethlehem in Christmas nativity scenes, exotic and festive Swiss chocolate figurines?

The climax of this black comedy occurs when Aude casually opens the Bible and reads from the Book of Ruth: "[Y]our people shall be my people, and your God my God" (Ruth 1: 16). Aude is eager to rediscover mythic origins that will be a bridge between her world and that of her husband; she identifies with Ruth the Moabite, and she is in that sense eager to convert to Judaism. But in interpreting Ruth's eagerness as doctrinal in nature, Aude comically misreads the text. Indeed, nowhere does the Book of Ruth involve theological argument or assent, so foreign to pre-Hellenic Hebraic texts. Ruth, a poor widow, simply recognizes as superior—or simply as more expedient—the ways of her late husband and of her mother-in-law, whom she follows back to Judea from the desert kingdom of Edom. Aude's theological reading of Ruth amounts to a droll inversion of the biblical text (a common feature of Cohen's rhetoric); she understands the literal meaning of Scripture as theological allegory. On the very next page, Cohen highlights this reversal when Gamaliel asks Aude whether she is ready to convert to Judaism. She replies

*[L]e monde merveilleux que son aimé lui avait décrit. Elle allait avec respect vers le royaume pur et guerrier de l'Ancien Testament. Elle allait vers les prophètes. (*Solal,* 291–92)

†Nous vous avons donné le plus grand sage. Et tant d'autres. Et moi, entre autres. *Moi de plus tard.* (*Solal,* 306; emphasis added)

that before deciding, she "wishes to be initiated into the Israelite doctrine"; to which he sarcastically replies: "Good. Go and share our people's meal. Look at them. Afterward, you will let me know your decision."* In ordering Aude to share a meal and simply observe the others in all their (subterranean) materiality here and now, Gamaliel gives Aude a first lesson in Jewish "doctrine," as well as a correct reading of the Book of Ruth.[13]

But let us return to Aude's imminent descent underground, through which Cohen weaves together two classical chronotopes: that of the château-underground and that of the Dantesque descent to hell. Far from being completely deluded, Solal knows the painful yet comic incongruity that lies between Aude's Calvinistic fantasies about "Old Testament" Hebrews, on the one hand, and modern Jews, on the other. Indeed, while she first views her new kin as sunny, Mediterranean "biblical men," her image of them changes in the end to one of "insufferable losers" *(bonshommes impossibles)* and even "these worms" *(ces larves).*

Solal's own initial description of the underground is chilling. "Where are you going?" Aude asks him. "Into the den," he replies. "To the kingdom of the dead. To the land of the dreadful smile."† Down below, Aude finds searing deformation instead of conformity with "biblical" fantasy. Every detail in her perception of the cellar and its inhabitants conforms to the blood-soaked monstrosity attributed to Jews in anti-Semitic hallucinations, be they crude libels or fine theological arguments.

The first level of the cellar leads Aude to the eczematic, lymphatic, fat, bewigged "women of Judea": "To the right, set apart from the men by a railing, women sitting in profile. A Byzantine empress scratched away at her eczema. A lymphatic was showing her jewelry to a restless corpulence. An old woman wearing a wig gone brown was reading approvingly and shaking her chin."‡

The next step in the descent leads to the menagerie composed of Judean women: "Misshapen *[avachies]* women breast-feeding their babies drew their teat[s] away. The frustrated infants whined."§ The indefinite plural noun

*"Bien. Allez partager le repas des nôtres. Regardez-les. Ensuite, vous me ferez connaître votre décision." (*Solal,* 292)

†"—Et où allez-vous?" "—Dans l'antre. Au royaume des morts. Dans la contrée du sourire effrayant." (*Solal,* 289)

‡À droite, séparées des hommes par une balustrade, des femmes assises de profil. Une impératrice byzantine grattait son eczéma. Une lymphatique montrait des bijoux à une corpulence agitée. Une vieille à perruque roussie lisait en approuvant et remuait le menton. (*Solal,* 290)

§Des femmes avachies qui allaitaient leurs enfants écartèrent leur mamelle. Les nourrissons frustrés se plaignirent (*Solal,* 298)

"women" *(des femmes)* underscores their misshapen lack of differentiation; they breast-feed and then briskly pull *(écartèrent)* their nipples away from the suckling babes.

Third step in the descent into hell—blood: "A mother lulled a newly circumcised infant and took pride in the blood that ran along the thighs of the sturdy little chap. Girls of the tribe were congratulating the mother."* Here is a full account of the bloody ritual of the "old covenant"; the brutality of circumcision accentuated by the adjective "freshly" *(fraîchement).* The warm blood drips down the infant's thighs, while the "girls" of the "tribe" congratulate the mother for the ritualistic mutilation. Each detail evokes age-old blood libels and deeply ingrained phobias. Jews remain underground because they still include sacrificial blood in their covenant,[14] whereas the Gentiles are exempted from the blood ritual by Pauline theology—and therefore remain ontologically above ground. Blood flows in ritual, as in history, because the blood of Jesus drips forever on the Jews, as per medieval Christian theology.[15] Thus we metaphorically descend from disease to animality and finally to blood rituals. In the end, these women are simply part of a misshapen "tribal" whole, writhing like worms in a tin can sloshing about with warm milk and blood, buried alive by a world that, subconsciously at least, wants them dead.

If the females are akin to animals, the males oscillate among the arrogant (Gamaliel), the burlesque (the Valorous), and the insane (the three "superior" brothers), and it is the Valorous who take the comic center stage. As described in Chapter 2, each of the Valorous embodies a distinct aspect of the ridiculous "shlumiels" (false advocate, inventor, miser, giant, peddler of apricot water). It is in the Saint-Germain underground where Cohen best deploys their double function as the conveyors of Solal's repressed horrific contempt of them, as well as the projections of his own genuine joy in their subversive foolery, the perfect foil for his colossal narcissism, which, in their absence, he recreates for himself in his masochistic Purim rituals.

Confronted with Aude, the Valorous run the gamut of their repertoire. Saltiel, who is the most mindful about saving appearances, leads Aude away from Rabbi Gamaliel, and presents her with an elaborate bouquet of flowers as "a tribute from a charmed uncle," the kind gesture being accompanied by "([t]hree pointed smiles, one behind the other. Three bows").† Aude accepts

*Une mère berçait un nourrisson fraîchement circoncis et s'enorgueillissait du sang qui coulait sur les cuisses du petit vaillant. Des filles de la tribu congratulaient la mère. (*Solal,* 300)

†(Trois sourires en pointe, les uns derrière les autres. Trois courbettes.) (*Solal,* 293; parentheses in original)

graciously, but Saltiel promptly demands that she return the flowers "lest the bouquet should be damaged . . . 'I'll keep them for you in my lap, and after dinner you can have them back, don't you worry.' "* Then, seated next to her at dinner, he catalogues all his fantastic inventions, capped by his latest—"fan-powered sailing!" After dinner, Aude descends to yet a deeper underground chamber where the false advocate Mangeclous, the peddler of apricot water Salomon, the miser Mattathias, and the giant Michaël assail her with questions, offers, and performances. Mangeclous asks her about the functioning of French courts, all the while twiddling his nose hair and eating one greasy fritter after another. While scribbling clever sentences in a child's notebook, Salomon asks Aude for her opinion of Napoleon. But, as usual, the miser Mattathias is the crassest and most direct of the lot:

> Mattathias pushed [Salomon] aside and questioned Aude, looking at her suspiciously.
>
> "I am told that the Banque de France has decreased its interest rate. Is that right? (She did not respond.) Never mind. I have a first-rate sapphire. For you, it will be the *Israélite* price."†

No doubt there is much black humor in these mini-performances of the Valorous. These comic episodes provoke an underground laughter, reserved for those who possess nothing but verbal fantasy. The Valorous suffer from logorrhea, their sole point of phantasmagoric contact with the European world from which they are excluded. No doubt Solal dreads these debris of history, who weigh him down by the reminder of his origins, yet raise him up with their comic levity—heavy because they prevent his liberation from the island ghetto, light because he masochistically delights in their nonsensical banter. He almost seems to say, "You think I am so European—but look at my kin, my origin, and my self-destructive desire to regress to the scene from which I emerged and from which I cannot escape." Solal repeatedly invites the Valorous to cities where they can only undermine his position in the Gentile world, as if he has a semi-conscious, macabre death drive to undo his "painfully constructed life." In periodically inserting the Valorous into his life, he toys with the limits of his power—can he maintain himself despite the automatic dis-

*"s'abîmera. . . . je vous le garderai sur mes genoux et après le dîner je vous le rendrai, soyez tranquille." (*Solal,* 293)

†Mattathias l'écarta et interrogea Aude, l'œil méfiant.

On m'a rapporté que la Banque de France a diminué son taux d'escompte. Est-ce vrai? (Elle ne répondit pas.) Peu importe. J'ai un saphir premier choix. Pour vous, ce sera le prix israélite." (*Solal,* 296)

grace they bring to him? The most sober of the Valorous, Saltiel, wonders why, with a view to seducing Aude into Judaism, Solal would invite the Valorous, who are after all, the inferior branch of the international Solal clan? The answer to this question will soon be obvious.

The higher or more accomplished branch of the Solal clan is composed mainly of three brothers: Nadab, a professor of psychology at the University of Berlin; Reuben, a banker and financial speculator; and Saul, a possessed rabbinical mystic. Like Solal, all three are touched by insanity and must negotiate a maddening double existence. Their "normal" lives (before coming to Saint-Germain) are consonant with their existence in the Parisian underground.

Their sister, Tsillah, a tall and vivacious young woman with a mad look in her eyes, lucidly explains their madness to Aude:

> During the day, Nadab thinks and that is a geometrical coldness, the Stalactites wander in the darkness of truths, the gears turn but do not catch. At night, Nadab enters life. His frenzy detects, juxtaposes, compares, tallies with, moves about, groups, substitutes, speculates, and destroys illusory pride. During the day, Reuben, female fatty thick-blooded fecund dirty producer, calls the banks, the journalists, and the kings over the phone, he crushes, hoists himself up, cannot wait to live, persists, impassive, and swells. At night, he is pursued, cries, is afraid, fears being noticed, to take his revenge he spits, he would like to be proud, no longer smile or approve, fear distorts him, but this mud is incrusted with precious germs, he is pious and cowardly. During the day, Saul tames the Dogs of God, they become brisk and herd the sheep nations toward tomorrow and justice will be done, he rebels and hates evil, he has a hard face but his eyes flicker with tenderness. At night he smiles wearily, he loves, despises and knows that the Kingdom is proclaimed from this very day on, women understand him, a simpleton, he fits in with the children, light-hearted, his face soft, mischief sometimes draws a line across the left eye, it is the Lamb.*

*"Le jour, Nadab pense et c'est le froid géométrique, les stalactites se promènent dans le noir de vérité, les engrenages fonctionnent à vide. La nuit, Nadab entre dans la vie. Sa fureur décèle, juxtapose, compare, recoupe, déplace, regroupe, substitue, spécule et détruit des fiertés illusoires. Le jour, Reuben, femelle adipeux sang épais fécond sale producteur, téléphone aux banques, aux journalistes et aux rois, il écrase, se juche, pressé de vivre, s'obstine impassiblement et enfle. La nuit, il est poursuivi, pleure, a peur, craint qu'on ne le remarque, pour se venger il crache, il voudrait être fier, ne plus sourire ni approuver, la peur le décompose, mais cette boue est granulée de germes précieux, il est pieux et lâche. Le jour, Saül dresse les Chiens de Dieu qui deviennent vifs et conduisent les brebis nations vers demain et l'on fera justice, il se révolte et déteste le mal, il a une face dure mais ses yeux vacillent de tendresse. La nuit, il sourit avec lassitude, il aime, méprise et sait que le Royaume est proclamé dès aujourd'hui, les femmes le comprennent, un simple, il va avec les enfants, gai, son visage est doux, une malice raie parfois l'œil gauche, c'est l'Agneau." (*Solal,* 302)

These three "superior" Solals are striking insofar as they are obviously splintering into multiple tropes of self-estrangement to the point of clinical psychosis. Daily, nightly, they ascend and descend the ladder, struggling to assemble during the day that which they dismantle at night. But these struggles—going up and down the ladder—create a dissonance without any resolution. Unlike Jacob's ladder (Gen. 32: 23–33), to which all of these tropes implicitly refer, the outcome here is not life-affirming. They are just so many permutations of insanity. After the night-long struggle, these Jacobs do not become Isra-el ("one who struggles with God"), the patriarchs of nations. Morbid, circular, and endlessly repetitive, with budding delirium as the only effect, their struggles morph into the purely absurd—more like that of Sisyphus (morosely combined with Maupassant's demented Horla) than like that of Jacob.

At night, each brother decomposes into his opposite. By day, Nadab the psychologist, is Greek, geometrical, transparent. At night, Greek rationality cedes to his "frenzy [which] detects, juxtaposes, compares, tallies, moves about, groups, substitutes, speculates, and destroys illusory pride." This diurnal geometrical turn of mind refers to the nature of his scientific research, while his nocturnal forays into the ripples of Being, to perpetual interpretation at the margins of horrific history, refer to a heterogeneous Jewish turn of mind, more at home with a page of the Talmud (juxtaposition, displacement, substitution, speculation, destruction) than with a clear and distinct, rational page of Descartes. Reuben, the banker, spends his days acting as a predator, intimidating many alpha personalities in the world of business and finance, but at night, he is a tracked animal, paralyzed by fear and anxiety. Reuben and Solal are both powerful men, feared by their peers, yet once alone, their historical and ethnic memories remind them of just how fragile their power really is. Saul, the mystical rabbi, however, exhibits the greatest polarity: he is a Jew (Saul) by day and a Christian (Paul) by night. During the day, he frowns as he teaches the Law to "the Dogs of God," future rabbis, presumably, who will conduct the Jewish people toward a tomorrow when justice will be done. (In Judaism, messianic tomorrows are what George Steiner calls " 'a counter-factual optative,' a category of meaning never to be realized.")[16] But at night, he smiles, because he believes that the Messiah has already come (either in Jesus or possibly in himself), and he despises the stubborn, blind Jews ("the Dogs") who are mired in a culture of law and interpretation. At night, Saul converts to Paul: he knows that "[t]he Kingdom is proclaimed from this day." He has already passed from the world of interpretation to the world of satisfaction.[17] The rabbi's duality—diurnally Jewish, nocturnally Christian—actually inverts the pattern of daily cycles observable throughout Cohen's fiction, where Judaism is assigned to nocturnal rituals, darkness and disguise, to the underground.

All these assents and descents are not sure-footed, but wobbly, flailing, spiraling maneuvers. In their daily practices, they become chaos unto themselves. Saltiel himself describes the three to Aude as "somewhat sick in the head." Once "en famille," that is in their nocturnal mode, their behavior betrays sheer madness: "The three brothers argued ferociously, seemed to want to fight, but then one of them would say a word in the ear of the other and all three would calm down."* In the end, from Aude's point of view, the "superior" branch of the Solal clan is just as bestial as the tribal women, just as bizarre as the Valorous.

Aude's illusion is that Solal differs from his kin, that he is better at negotiating his psychosis than they are. But soon enough she realizes that he is so much like the "superior" three that his identity bleeds into theirs: "He was cheerful and passionate, as they were, bewitched. But was it he or one of the Three,"† Aude wonders, questioning her ability to distinguish her now passionate and gesticulating husband from the mad threesome.

Aude emerges into the château's visible zone distraught, all her literary and theological fantasies shattered. These creatures below are not cunning Rebecca, warriorlike Joshua, or majestic King David. Aude has the feeling of returning from "a medieval fair"; she is even sexually harassed by Reuben, while Solal remains passive. Reversing her generous Ruth-like gesture, she emphatically advises, "Sol, do not waste your life because of them. What do you have in common with these people? You are noble and handsome, unlike these *worms.* Beloved, send them away."‡ Solal himself refers to his persecuted kin as "the most magnificent dung *[fumier].*"§ When first asked where he disappears to every night, Solal already gives a zoological and psychiatric answer: he descends "[t]o the kingdom of the dead. To the land of the dreadful smile." Three key words now describe the underground and its occupants: lair/den *(antre)*, dung *(fumier)* and worms *(larves).*[18]

Solal and Aude do not have such diverging perceptions of their guests, although each interprets them differently. Whereas Aude is horrified because she fails to understand their deformation, Solal is simultaneously repulsed by and attracted to them, qualifying Jews as "the most magnificent dung," for he

*Les trois frères se disputaient férocement, semblaient vouloir se battre puis l'un disait un mot à l'oreille de l'autre et les trois s'apaisaient. (*Solal,* 302)

†Il était rieur et passionné, pareil à eux, envoûté. Mais était-ce lui ou un des Trois? (*Solal,* 300)

‡'Sol, ne manque pas ta vie à cause d'eux. Qu'y a-t-il de commun entre toi et ces gens? Tu es noble et beau, tu n'es pas comme ces *larves.* Aimé, renvoie ces gens.' (*Solal,* 306; emphasis added)

§"le plus magnifique fumier." (*Solal,* 305)

properly deciphers the signs of these "emaciated ones wandering through the centuries."* Where Aude sees only repulsive vermin, Solal sees an excessive and yet sublime people. Cohen often employs the image of the possessed King David maniacally dancing in front of the sacred ark (2 Sam. 6: 14–15) to represent the poetic "madness" of the Jews: "The crazy old people that walks alone through the storm carrying its harp immortally sounding its delirium of grandeur and persecution across the black hurricane of the centuries."†

Solal certainly hesitates. But unlike Aude, he cannot turn his back on these "emaciated ones wandering through the centuries"—he must wrestle with the demons on the ladder of history; he must be or become (which is not yet clear) this "Hebrew," this *passeur* who spans multiple dissonant identities. He has no choice, for his destiny is inscribed in his name. Solal des Solal.

A strange logical tautology of a name: Solal des Solal, for subject and predicate mirror each other. This name contains a syntactic destiny; it is a hauntingly overdetermined name, underwriting an existence that remains anything but self-evident. The narrator of *Mangeclous* explains: "And love? Why no more women? What is the point since fate had caused him to be born Solal des Solal, a man without a first name? 'A tradition in the noble family of the Solals, dear marquise. The firstborn is named Solal Solal. Impossible to make love without a first name.' "‡

It could be said that the whole drama of Solal des Solal lies in his overdetermined name, which endows him with a clear historical and mythical mission, linking him with the whole gamut of the Solals across the centuries and across continents, and deprives him of a much-coveted career as a European romantic lover, a modern individual pursuing his private interests and pleasures in secular society. Despite his name, Solal struggles to remain in the both-and logic, to carry the Solals and the Valorous with him wherever he goes, all while managing his Gentile women, vectors of his worldly ascent. The name, a verbal lure, seeks symbolically to dispense with the ambiguity with which Solal's character is fraught.[19]

The protagonist must therefore also assume his destiny as the blessed son of the old Rabbi Gamaliel and servant to his people, which jeopardizes the

*faméliques errants à travers les siècles (*Solal,* 306)

†Le vieux peuple fou qui marche seul dans la tempête portant sa harpe sonnante à travers le noir ouragan des siècles et immortellement son délire de grandeur et de persécution. (*Solal,* 305)

‡Et l'amour? Pourquoi plus de femmes? À quoi bon puisque le sort l'avait fait naître Solal des Solal, un homme sans prénom? "Une tradition dans la noble famille des Solal, chère marquise. Le premier-né s'appelle Solal Solal. Impossible de faire l'amour sans prénom." (*Mangeclous,* 584)

blessing he has received from his new father, Monsieur de Maussane, and, of course, his erotic union with Aude. Solal des Solal, then, is not identical to Aude's husband, the intimate "Sol," and when she asks him, "What do you have in common with these people *[ces gens]*?" the answer must be a categorical "Everything!" Solal cannot simply dispense with his kin, the genitive predicate that mirrors his first name. "She could not guess the pain and the distress of this man, whose heart was too fervent to be able to choose between his wife, whom he loved, and his race, which he loved; who felt guilty toward the one and the other; who no longer had the strength to stand up to life, cruel as it is to those passionate about the absolute."*

In 1930, only a sadomasochistic "vertical" juxtaposition of the oriental Jew and the European politician remains a conceptual possibility, as we see in this episode. To be in the world, the Solal of the château must clearly delineate himself from the Solal of the underground. Despite her desire to become a Swiss Ruth, Aude cannot be the joint that articulates the relationship between the two worlds—that much is all too clear: "Solal understood that it could not be otherwise."† Aude can only participate in the drama of Solal's ambivalence as the *elected victim* of her man, mirroring Solal's own status as the *elected victim* of Solal. It is worth noting that she is the only woman in Solal's career who escapes being destroyed by him (he drives the rest to suicide); she leaves Solal, marries her first love, Jacques, and raises the child she has conceived with Solal.

This perverse dynamic illuminates the surprising ending of the Saint-Germain episode. Forced by Aude to choose between her and "these worms," Solal's choice is dictated by his "original" blessing by Gamaliel and his overdetermined name. Yet he is unwilling to lose Aude. In his madness, he desires to obey the Law of the father downstairs and concurrently be the master of the Gentile woman upstairs: "With a bloody smile, he walked up to her, tore her dress and the other pieces of clothing. He admired the force and the thrust of this body. She went toward the bed, grabbed a blanket and covered up her nudity."‡

Aude struggles and shames him by appealing to his moral sense, but Solal will not let her go. Naked and isolated, she becomes captive in her own bedroom:

*Elle ne pouvait pas deviner la douleur et le désarroi de cet homme qui avait le cœur trop ardent pour pouvoir choisir entre sa femme qu'il aimait et sa race qu'il aimait, qui se sentait coupable vis-à-vis de l'une et de l'autre, qui n'avait plus le courage de rentrer dans la vie, cruelle aux passionnés d'absolu. (*Solal,* 313)

†[Solal] comprenait qu'il ne pouvait en être autrement. (*Solal,* 362)

‡Avec un sourire sanguinolent, il s'approcha d'elle, déchira sa robe et les autres étoffes. Il admira la force et le jet de ce corps. Elle s'approcha du lit, arracha une couverture et recouvrit sa nudité. (*Solal,* 307)

So that you don't leave, he sniggered, we shall leave you in the state of simple nature and we shall imprison you. I'll come back to get you soon and we'll leave with the worms for Jerusalem. . . .

See you soon, dear lady Solal. Next week in Jerusalem. You married a worm. Too bad for you. A Jewess, my dear!*

Being himself a captive of this château, Solal wants to shuttle between his captive father (and kin) and his captive wife. Obedient to his father, tyrannical toward his wife, Solal both obeys the Law of God *and* acts like Zeus—he rapes Europa, who may very well become another "misshapen" *(avachie)* woman, and therefore rejoins the animal pack on its way to Jerusalem.

The mention of Jerusalem in this diatribe recalls both the street hawker's discourse ("Go see if I am in Jerusalem") and Albert's desire for his imaginary European lover, Viviane. In many ways, as we saw in Chapter 1, the Vivianes of the world (Adrienne, Aude, Ariane) are concurrently a philo-Semitic sanctuary and the object of a great deal of aggression and resentment, because resentment of the street hawker, or de Maussane, in this instance, is always in the end directed at the infantile imaginary companion, the philo-Semitic European woman.

This combination of masochism in Solal's relationship to his father and kin and sexual sadism toward all his lovers recurs often in Cohen's fiction, from his relationship to his mother (as we shall see in Chapter 4) to its use as a fully developed theme in *Belle du Seigneur,* where Ariane becomes the full-fledged blonde captive of her despotic oriental prince. A rape, the final scene of the Saint-Germain episode, therefore suggests an important permutation in Solal's dialectics of identity. Self-dramatizing, charismatic, and irresistible, yet psychologically narcissistic and sadistic, because he wants it all and now, Solal—this constellation of dissonant desire and repulsion—forms an important identity-phantasm in which he can be both an oriental Jew *and* in possession of Europa. This persona occupies an in-between fluid zone where Cephalonia and Europe can somehow be reconciled, where the son, ever so ambivalent, shuttles between father and lover, tormenting both and all the while disgracing himself to the very core of his being. All of Cohen's romantic fiction *(Solal, Belle du Seigneur*) traffics in desire, taboo—and, above all, disgrace. And while the dialectics of desire and taboo are all too generic, the particular form

*"Pour que tu ne t'en ailles pas, ricana-t-il, nous te laisserons dans l'état de simple nature et nous t'emprisonnerons. Je reviendrai te chercher tout à l'heure et nous partirons avec les larves pour Jérusalem." . . . "À bientôt, chère dame Solal. La semaine prochaine à Jérusalem. Tu as épousé une larve. Tant pis pour toi. Juive, mon amie!" (*Solal,* 307)

that the acute consciousness of disgrace takes in Cohen's work, is a specifically Jewish experience, lodged at the center of his fiction; a haunting and recurring nightmare that is inscribed in an acute historical consciousness aware of its own mythic potential that runs the gamut of saviors from Joseph to Jesus.

After the Saint-Germain episode, Solal's life is rent apart. His wife escapes her prison, he sends away his kin, literally burns millions of francs in the fireplace, loses his political standing, and becomes an itinerant vagabond. Meanwhile, Aude, now the mother of Solal's son, reclaims the Château Saint-Germain, which Solal bought with her money, and marries her first love, the aristocratic officer Jacques de Nonne. Solal then reappears, is rebuffed by Aude, tries to kidnap his son David, dies (in the original ending), and is then miraculously resurrected (in the second edition), proudly riding his white steed, confident of the future—"Solal rode and he gazed at the sun face-to-face."[20]

Yet throughout the tortuous ending of the novel, there still remains in the Château Saint-Germain a trace of origin, for many of the original subterranean inhabitants continue to live in the secret compartments down below long after Solal has gone and after Aude has returned to live there with her husband and son: "Out of the most secret crevices of the Commanderie, where they continued living in the expectation of a miracle, the five old men, the three brothers, other old men, a few beggars, a few illuminati, and a few women contemplated Solal prostrate"*—for Saint-Germain will always have its Jewish cellar, will always also be Saint-Germain-the-Jew. Every château has its shadow; every identity its repressed origin.[21]

*Sortis des plus secrètes demeures de la Commanderie, qu'ils avaient continué d'habiter dans l'attente d'un miracle, les cinq vieillards, les trois frères, d'autres vieillards, des gueux, des illuminés et des femmes contemplaient Solal étendu. (*Solal,* 359)

4 *Kaddish and Shivah*

The true subject of poetry is the loss of the beloved.
Faiz Ahmed Faiz

In 1954, after a literary hiatus of sixteen years, Cohen published his most widely read work, *Le Livre de ma mère.* Given the fact that this autobiographical essay is Cohen's most accessible book, most often quoted, commented upon, and translated, it is useful to understand its rhetorical structure and its historical role in reestablishing Cohen's literary career. This lyrical testimony in memory of his mother inaugurates the second half of his literary life, the first part spanning from *Paroles juives* in 1921 to *Mangeclous* in 1938, and the second part stretching from *Le Livre de ma mère* to *Carnets 1978.* In the interim war period, he published numerous essays in the London-based literary review *La France libre,* including a series of essays entitled "Chant de mort," which form the rough (and sometimes more revealing) draft of *Le Livre de ma mère.*

By making his *rentrée littéraire* via the figure of his dead mother, Cohen pays impassioned tribute to the memory of Louise Cohen, who died of a heart attack on January 10, 1943, four days after 5,000 SS troops entered Marseille. But other reasons for such a *rentrée* may also be surmised. With his usual cavalier self-fashioning, Cohen dictated the book to his new bride, Bella, as a means of sharing with her his filial love of a majestic matron. This is part of the standard Cohen self-mythology—the oriental seigneur dictating the word to his *belle/mère.* His biographers claim that he did not wish immediately to tackle the rewriting of the 3,500-page *Belle du Seigneur.* The sheer task of rewriting the monumental novel after such a long hiatus no doubt seemed daunting, and the work in its original form would surely have received a reception as ambivalent as those of his previous two works. The author of *Solal* required a more manageable project to follow through on the immense literary promise universally bestowed upon him in 1930.

Cohen's previous two literary endeavors had both ended in either disaster or benign incomprehension. The one-act play *Ézéchiel* (1931–33) tells the story of Jérémie, an itinerant eastern European Jew who is entrusted with the mission of informing the noted banker Ézéchiel of the death of his only son, Solal, a minister in the British cabinet. Although at first well received, the play was soon denounced by many Jews and anti-Semites alike—a painful flop from which Cohen never fully recovered. (See Epilogue for a complete analysis of the play and its reception.)

In 1938, Cohen presented a more nuanced story with the novel *Mangeclous.* The novel *Solal* (1930) had portended such literary talent that Gallimard gave Cohen a long-term contract for eight novels, including a permanent monthly stipend. By 1938, the generous publisher had grown impatient, however, and insisted that Cohen publish something, hence *Mangeclous* was hastily extracted from the sprawling manuscript of *Belle du Seigneur.* As a stand-alone novel, it belies its fragmentary and compressed composition, and, despite certain brilliant episodes, it reads like a rough extract of a novel under construction. Although reviewers such as Marcel Pagnol, Joseph Kessel, and Arnold Mandel hailed *Mangeclous* as an unusually successful farcical novel, its reception rarely exceeded harmless indifference.[1] With Europe on the eve of World War II, Céline's hate-filled *Bagatelles pour un massacre* (1937) and *L'École des cadavres* (1938) resonated more with the reading public than a farcical Jewish self-laceration.

But leaving aside these biographical aspects, *Ézéchiel* and *Mangeclous* share the common feature of aggressive narratives that disallow productive transference on the part of even sympathetic readers. Their belligerence lies in their plots and characters; the reader is aggressively confronted with the horror of being Jewish, with all its masochistic self-deprecation, but without the real comic and romantic relief of seduction and ambition. For a typical reader, Gentile or Jew, a Mangeclous or a Jérémie does not represent a suitable object of transference, especially not in the aggressive manner in which he apostrophizes the reader. *Solal* displayed the same hostility, but it had enough sheer charismatic energy to arouse the reader's desire to continue and therefore to sustain transference with this dashing Mediterranean Estheric Joseph, notwithstanding the worms festering in the basement of Saint-Germain. Through its abundant representation of unfettered desire, *Solal* allowed an equilibrium between romantic and grotesque, enabling the reader to assimilate the narrative into existing discourses. Some saw *Solal* as a Judeo-Mediterranean take on Stendhal and the Gospels, while others understood its darker sides, but all agreed on its inherent mythopoetic dynamism. Unlike *Ézéchiel* and *Mangeclous, Solal* was thus a very successful narratological transaction. With *Le Livre de ma mère,* Cohen's "golden quill" *(plume d'or)* again achieves proper stabilization, this time with essayistic rather than novelistic rhetoric, and, given the subject matter, the balancing act proves far more delicate—a task that only the mature Albert Cohen could have handled.

The gamble worked. Cohen's *rentrée littéraire* was a resounding success in France, and the critics conveyed a sense of relief, translated into sheer euphoria. Finally, after so many aggressively grotesque jeremiads and dissonant self-mutilating autos-da-fé, Albert Cohen delivers a lyrical and tender panegyric about filial love, the most readily efficient transference machine: All men are sons, most will bury their mothers, and more than a few harbor ambivalence toward them. All expect to mourn. Indeed, one can scarcely find a more universal topic. "The great success and audacity of Albert Cohen is to have written a chef-d'œuvre on the most common of commonplaces," Marcel Pagnol declared.[2] On a similarly triumphant note, Georges Altmann asserted that "André Gide, that petit-bourgeois Lucifer, proclaimed one day that one cannot make good literature with fine sentiments. Many works, past and present, disprove this sally. *Le Livre de ma mère* is one of them."[3] While I agree that *Le Livre de ma mère* is a great literary achievement, I remain skeptical about rescuing "the most common of commonplaces" from banality and about the triumph of "fine sentiments" over the literature of suspicion and cruel redescription. I see *Le Livre de ma mère* as cut from the same cloth as the rest of Cohen's literary corpus: it remains dissonant, disturbing, and self-mutilating, and although Cohen here seduces readers into believing that they have identified with a tender, filial panegyric, they are in fact made to witness one of the most excruciatingly cruel mourning testimonies in the history of belles lettres. Why should this come as a surprise? *Le Livre de ma mère* is, after all, a book of mourning, and, except in the most propitious circumstances, dissonant ambivalence is the hallmark of incomplete mourning. That a great poet should give this searing experience its highest literary representation and insight should hardly seem surprising. What does come as a surprise, however, is the resistance on the part of most serious readers to reading the actual words on the page at the most literal level.

Incipit

The first sentence of this lyrical essay is unequivocal: "Every man is alone and no one gives a damn about anyone and our sorrows are a desert island."*[4] The phrasing of the sentence is insistent and builds into a crescendo. "Every man," the subject, by definition excludes no one, from the worst SS butcher to the author. The particular melts into the general, and vice versa. An existential state, universal and permanent, it engulfs all subjectivity and intersubjectivity. The predicate of the universal subject "every man" is the state of isolation, "alone." Solidarity is therefore excluded. Moving from the subject's state of being to its intentional action, Cohen postulates that "no one gives a damn about anyone." Notice the overdetermination and powerful symmetry of the pronouns "*tous* se fichent de *tous*": "no one" and "anyone" articulated by the strong verb, "to give a damn." Again, empathy, sympathy, passion are all merely a lure—at heart we are all encrusted in our narcissistic shells, forever aggressive and egoistic. The third term of the proposition presents pain as incommunicable, and the one who suffers as separated from all others by a sea of indifference. This is indeed a surprising incipit for a lyrical panegyric on the theme of the mother; a rather gloomy metaphysical coefficient for a book supposedly pervaded by "fine sentiments"!

I can well imagine a more sympathetic reading of this incipit. An attentive reader of Cohen could intuit here another cry of rage against death, the indifference of nature, and the supposed absurdity of life. Pervasively, such sentences typify Cohen's cavalier metaphysical gestures. True, such a generic reading echoes Cohen's morbid and nihilistic metaphysics. However, it does not do justice to its relevance here. No generic dismissal will do, for the whole narrative is a function of this epigrammatic and programmatic proposition. Reduced to its elementary particles, *Le Livre de ma mère* tells the story of a subject and a predicate: the subject, "every man," includes the narrator (son) as well as the narratee (mother) and has the metaphysical predicate of "being alone" and "not giving a damn." Period. Such is the proposition that launches this essay and that, I argue, acts as a coefficient for all its seemingly benign and nostalgic content. But this inaugural sentence is merely the first of three crucial rhetorical moves that lay the foundation for the dynamic logic of the text.

Next follows one of Albert Cohen's most often cited *beaux mots*, the poetically cadenced apostrophizing of the author's pen:

*Chaque homme est seul et tous se fichent de tous et nos douleurs sont une île déserte. (*LM,* 701)

> Magnificent, you, my golden quill, go over the page, go at random while I still have some youth, go your slow irregular way, hesitant as if in a dream, erratic but controlled wandering. Go, I love you, my sole consolation, go over the pages where sorrowfully I amuse myself and in whose cross-eye I gloomily revel.*

Writing alleviates the desolation of being. We may figuratively exist in a desert or on an isolated island; we may shut the door, cork the walls in the manner of Proust (and of the later Cohen)—writing remains our sole consolation. We can understand this in the very abstract Heideggerean sense in which poetry is the only authentic language of Being. But, more narrowly, the "golden quill" is the instrument of a literary *ruse,* an instrument of seduction. Through the revealing and hiding made possible by the protean golden quill, the painful truth of being is playfully represented. Desire abounds in this poetic playfulness: "hesitant as if in a dream, erratic but controlled wandering . . . I amuse myself . . . I gloomily revel *[morosement me délecte].*" The shattering truth of the initial metaphysical proposition must be mediated by a morosely magnificent golden quill, which both delights the author and woos the reader by pretending to speak the latter's language. And yet the disturbing truth, this time told with even greater effect, lies in the sensual folds of subtle writing.

Gone are the days of Cohen the Cynic apostrophizer. The golden quill now softens the pain of recounting the story of his mother, so that the truth of Albert and Louise Cohen may be spoken in a double language: in his own and also in that of his readers. Henceforth, the golden quill mediates between the narcissistic and masochistic desire to tell it all *here and now* and the inherent limitations of the historical and rhetorical expectations of the reading public. The reality principle gains power over Cohen and propels him to a different aesthetics. He no longer drowns his readers in grotesque dissonance but instead refines his skills of concealment and disclosure, of doubling and masking, as a self-conscious poetic of writing.[5]

Cohen frankly admits to this doubling and conceit on the very first page. There are the diurnal Cohen and the nocturnal Cohen: "And in a general way, I tell each one that each one is charming. Such are my daytime manners. But during my nights and dawns, I do not think about it any less."† Enlighten-

*Somptueuse, toi, ma plume d'or, va sur la feuille, va au hasard tandis que j'ai quelque jeunesse encore, va ton lent cheminement irrégulier, hésitant comme en rêve, cheminement gauche mais commandé. Va, je t'aime, ma seule consolation, va sur les pages où tristement je me complais et dont le strabisme morosement me délecte. (*LM,* 701–2)

†Et, d'une manière générale, je dis à chacun que chacun est charmant. Telles sont mes mœurs diurnes. Mais dans mes nuits et mes aubes je n'en pense pas moins. (*LM,* 701)

ment springs from obscurity: Light masks the necessary lies—and writing meshes truth and pretense in an eternal game of hide-and-seek. This willed doubleness and self-conscious concealment are paradigmatic to telling the truth in a rhetorically affective manner. The golden quill commands toward the end of the first chapter: "speak of your mother in *their serene manner,* whistle a bit to believe that things are not all that bad, and above all smile, don't forget to smile."* Thus a chapter that commences with a stark metaphysical proposition ends with rhetorical legerdemain. The truth will be told, but in *their* "calme manière," digestible and gratifying, a bitter pill, to be sure, but coated with enough sugar to make it seem appetizing.

Louise and Her Husband

To tell his mother's story, Cohen must start with the sordid family history. The Coens emigrated from Corfu to Marseille in 1900 when Albert was five years old. Upon their arrival, whatever money they had was lost to a fraudulent "blond businessman whose nose was not hooked" (*LM*, 712). They soon occupied a modest apartment three stories above their egg business, where Marc and Louise painfully eked out a meager existence. As an uneducated petty merchant, Cohen's father cut a shabby figure, and he soon became the object of the little boy's spite.[6] In *Le Livre de ma mère,* Cohen remains negative but circumspect about his father, dismissing him primarily as "her husband" *(son mari).* But in his *Carnets 1978,* Albert Cohen loses all pity or mercy when describing his father. This passage warrants quoting in full, because it illuminates the specific nature of the bond uniting son and mother against the tyrannical father. This passage also points to the origin of Cohen's lifelong phobia about all animal domination, the detestable natural order:

> Yes, when he entered, he was the male and the tamer with a thick mustache that he loved to obscenely curl, and his curls upset me. He asked too much of my mother, too much of this servant without pay. . . .
>
> Oh, the dreadful day when, having found that the moussaka was not authentic and not like that made by a celebrated great-aunt Rebecca, the picky gastronomist indignantly all of a sudden yanked the entire tablecloth toward himself to punish the imperfect moussaka. Oh, the verdict in the mute child's unmoving gaze. And I still see my gentle mother on her knees, pale with guilt, picking up the debris of the dishes and scattered food, and the

*Raconte ta mère *à leur calme manière,* sifflote un peu pour croire que tout ne va pas si mal que ça, et surtout souris, n'oublie pas de sourire. (*LM,* 703; emphasis added)

> pools of wine and oil, while the child silently watched the emperor of a defenseless woman.*

And even the few tender moments with the father could not be more pregnant with meaning. Albert plays the "barber" who styles and pretends to sheer the hairy male, who obscenely caresses his "thick mustaches," metonymy for his animalistic maleness and domination. This constitutes Albert's first experience of the natural order, which he later repeatedly derides as the world of baboons. Like a submissive male, the little son grooms the dominant alpha to appease him so that he may steal a few minutes with a coveted female. Albert hated Marc Coen for being "the male and the tamer *[dompteur]* with a thick mustache" and "the emperor of a defenseless woman." Cohen's lifelong obsession with the evil of the natural order, the baboonery of the Social, was thus born very early in his own family, and not, as he sometimes pretends, in the pagan and/or Christian world of European wealth, power, and erotic ideals. The family romance opposition between the autobiographical real father and the fictional Rabbi Gamaliel is striking, for Marc Coen dominates like an alpha male, whereas Rabbi Gamaliel clearly admonishes against arbitrary physical power. Moreover, Cohen's fictional identity-phantasm (Solal) endlessly oscillates between the two fathers, forever exercising alpha male power over Ariane while denouncing its use to her, as in the famous Ritz seduction scene in *Belle du Seigneur.* Marc Coen's violence frequently surfaces in Solal's imperious handling of his female captives, because the romantic protagonist remains forever caught between the father's sadism and the son's moral masochism. The ghost of the father does not easily vanish.

After his wife's death in 1943, Marc Coen escaped from Marseille and hid with relatives in the south of France for the remainder of the war. All told, between 1930 and his father's death in 1953, Cohen saw his father only once, for a few minutes, at a train station cafeteria.

*Oui, lorsqu'il entrait, il était le mâle et dompteur aux fortes moustaches qu'il aimait obscènement retrousser, et ses retroussis bravaches me déplaisaient. Il demandait trop de ma mère, trop de travail de cette servante sans gages. . . .

Ô le jour affreux où, ayant trouvé que la moussaka servie n'était pas conforme et telle que la cuisinait une célèbre grand-tante Rébecca, le pointilleux gastronome avait, d'indignation, tiré à lui, d'un seul coup, toute la nappe à titre d'amende pour moussaka imparfaite. Ô la sentence dans le regard immobile de l'enfant muet. Et je revois encore ma douce mère à genoux, pâle de culpabilité, ramassant les débris d'assiettes et les nourritures étendues, et les flaques d'huile et de vin, pendant que l'enfant en silence regardait l'empereur d'une femme sans défense. (*Carnets 1978,* 1132)

The tyrant and his *belle,* these "[t]wo escapees from the Orient,"* were completely lost in France, excluded from all social orders, Jewish or Gentile, Greek or French. They did have some distant family relations in Marseille but soon avoided them altogether. Too proud and dignified (she was the daughter of a notable), Louise Coen could not suffer her relatives' ostentatious display of wealth and hubris, which cruelly highlighted her own poverty. Marc Coen preferred evenings at a bridge club to cultivating social relationships of any sort, and so virtually no one was ever invited to the Coens' apartment. And, besides, they settled in France while the Dreyfus Affair still raged, raising pervasive anti-Semitism to a paroxysm that only the Vichy regime would match. Two significant dates bracket Louise Coen's "French" existence: in 1900, she disembarked, at a time when the Dreyfus Affair still aroused considerable passion, and in 1943, she expired, just when Vichy allowed thousands of SS to begin the "cleansing" of Marseille.

Albert spent most of his free time alone while Louise toiled in the shop from dawn to dusk, chaffing under the rule of the mustached tyrant. Every morning, the child followed a routine carefully orchestrated by her: first a long bath in a zinc basin, a careful getting dressed, then breakfast and a viewing of the daily "letter" left by Louise, usually containing drawings, such as the not too random image of "a boat carrying the little Albert, miniscule besides a giant nougat, all for him"†—substitute woman for "nougat" and you have the Solalic identity-phantasm. The mother's fantastic animal stories set the child's mind adrift. He filled her absence with . . . himself. His best friend became Albert, and he spent many hours in front of the mirror contemplating this handsome, well-groomed friend.

But the precocious Narcissus also wrote. His eyes transfixed on his own image in the mirror, he traced letters in midair with his fingers, continuation of and responses to his mother's drawings. The finger tracing letters in the air replaces the mother's language, her endless stories, with which she tried to drown her despair. Absence and suffering engendered writing, both early on in his relation to Louise and, above all, after her death. Writing became a playful game of primal language, just as the mother's drawings traced primal fantasies:

> I need some minor entertainment at once. Doesn't matter what. Yes, let's hear some absurd little singing to the tune of that French song, the church

*[c]es deux échappés d'Orient (*LM,* 716)

†un bateau transportant le petit Albert, minuscule à côté d'un gigantesque nougat tout pour lui (*LM,* 712–13)

> rooster or I don't know what. I have a depressingly good time by myself inventing cows who do strange things, and in terms that always end in "-ays." A cow in love in church lazily Bays. An Andalusian cow Dances like a good wife in sickly ways. An obese cow Plays on trapeze-trays in the most thoughtful of ways.*

This playful game of accumulation of pure signifiers, echoing the maternal morning pictograms of long ago, is the unformed magma of Cohen's Mangeclousian logorrhea. These stories are the mother's great gift to her child, and he spends the rest of his life writing both with and against and below and above his mother: "I had been placed on this earth to listen to my mother's interminable stories."† So many of her utterances are ever so slightly transposed into his writings, usually assigned to Saltiel and Mangeclous, when not directly to the prophet Solal.

The First Couple: Union unto Life

Albert's world is defined by the feminine. The father's tyrannical intrusions are nothing but that—intrusions, momentarily violating the fabric of real and imaginary femininity. Chapter 1 has alluded to Albert's early education in a convent of loving Catholic nuns, who not only taught him French but, perhaps equally important, made him conscious of his bearing; he learned to walk with studied poise, his eyes and gait all dignity and purpose. A first lesson in dandyism was thus thoroughly absorbed. But, alas, the sisters' love was not unconditional; they silently regretted his Jewishness, which made of him by definition a lost soul, albeit endearing and even seductive. We have also noted his imaginary blonde playmate Viviane, the perfect infantile *mise-en-abyme* of all the future fictional Arianes, who, like her, deflate as fantasies when Albert is undone by anti-Semitism. Only Louise's love would be real, enduring, and unconditional. An island of serenity for son and mother, this love was the only sliver of the real that both relished without any ambivalence, at least prior to Albert's tenth birthday, when he understood, humiliated and helpless, that his parents were unable to protect him.

*Il me faut un petit divertissement sur-le-champ. N'importe quoi. Oui, faire de petits chants absurdes sur l'air de cette chanson française, le coq de l'église ou je ne sais quoi. M'amuser neurasthéniquement tout seul en inventant des vaches qui font des choses étranges et d'un air qui finit toujours en if. Une vache éprise Chante dans l'église D'un air lascif. Une vache andalouse Danse en bonne épouse D'un air chétif. Une vache obèse S'élance en trapèze D'un air pensif. (*LM,* 756)

†J'ai été mis sur terre pour écouter les interminables histoires de ma mère. (*LM,* 750)

To call Albert and Louise a "couple" is hardly overreaching. (As with most complex psychological representations in Cohen's autobiographical essays, readers need not resort here to the allegorical and the symbolic—all they need do is simply read the text at its most literal level.) Albert is Louise's only friend, and she is his only friend. They form a perfectly symmetrical couple; two isolated strangers, bereft of any company except for each other. For these two awkward, oriental "simpletons" *(nigauds),* lost as they are in a world at best indifferent to their existence, the maternal-filial dimension is treated as purely incidental. An examination of a few of their outings is in order.

Louise is then (1900–1905) a ravishing young woman. Albert "remembers how [he] had found her beautiful, my young mother . . . [he] found the most beautiful mother in the world" when she came to pick him up from the convent.* In the street, Louise and Albert are now free of "her husband," free of all constraints, but oppressed by all the other people in the street, in cafes, and in theaters, for whom the strange couple, the Jews, simply do not exist. No one recognizes them, acknowledges them, speaks to them. They insinuate themselves on the sly among these others, who are utterly oblivious of these oriental phantoms who want above all to belong *(en être)* to a crowd (like Albert in the street hawker scene). The most obvious space of communion is a movie theater, where they can laugh and cry with the crowd, yet remain invisible and anonymous in the dark: "We were social nothings, isolated ones without any contact with the exterior. So, in the winter, we would go every Sunday to the movies, my mother and I, two friends, two gentle, timid ones, seeking in the obscurity of these three hours at the theater a substitute *[succédané]* for this social life that had been refused to us. How this shared misfortune, and until now unavowed, could bind me to my mother."†

I am struck by the Cohenian intratextual dimension of this text. Just transpose characters and tone, and instead of describing the autobiographical Albert and Louise circa 1902, we might be describing the fictional Solal and Ariane circa 1936, self-exiled from Geneva, in a sleazy small-town cinema in the south of France, pretending to be happy for a brief moment, a part of the Social, any Social:

*me rappelle comme [il] l'avai[t] trouvée belle, ma jeune maman . . . [il] l'avai[t] trouvée la plus belle maman du monde. ("Chant de mort," *France libre* 2 [July 15, 1943]: 189)

†On était des rien du tout sociaux, des isolés sans nul contact avec l'extérieur. Alors, en hiver, nous allions tous les dimanches au théâtre, ma mère et moi, deux amis, deux doux et timides, cherchant obscurément dans ces trois heures de théâtre un succédané de cette vie sociale qui nous était refusée. Que ce malheur partagé, et jusqu'à présent inavoué, peut m'unir à ma mère. (*LM*, 717)

> Out of the corner of his eye, he saw his unique society, so pure in profile, moving. What had they come to do in this dreadful cinema? . . . [T]he two lovers spoke about the film to escape the embarrassment of silence, spoke so artificially that a feeling of decay *[déchéance]* invaded Solal. There they were, the two of them, seated, commenting on the film in hushed voices, exceptional, elegant, disinherited among the joyous plebeians, [who] chattered fraternally and self-confidently, messily licking their Eskimo Pies. He realized that he was speaking in an ashamed voice, like a ghetto Jew fearful of drawing attention to himself. She also had become humble, whispered as he did, and he understood that the unconscious of this unhappy woman knew that they were outcasts.*

In fact, the last third of *Belle du Seigneur* portrays a tedious and comic social game where a couple that is excluded from the Social pretends to belong to it at all costs, by just sheer contiguity, just by being there, next to insiders who belong. Thus this pariahlike isolation within a hostile crowd—Cohen's signature early experience with his mother and then with the street hawker—replicates itself almost to the very details with Ariane in Agay and Nice, as it has in fact long before with Aude subsequent to Solal's demise in the first novel. (Ariane in fact becomes the Jewess that Aude resisted being at all cost.) Whatever the circumstances or rhetoric (novelistic or essayistic), the same narrative centered on "the depression of this dual solitude"† repeats itself in an intratextual web that violates chronological order and genre boundaries.

Excluded and lonely, but highly theatrical, the son and his mother play at being part of the Social, as if the social world were simply a costume ball, the right attire being the only prerequisite for admittance: "On this particular Sunday, my mother and I were ridiculously well dressed, and I reflect with pity on these two naïve people of yesteryear, so unnecessarily well dressed, for no one took any notice of them. They dressed themselves up so finely for no one."‡

*Du coin de l'œil, il regarda son unique société, si pure de profil, attendrissante. Qu'étaient-ils venus faire dans cet affreux cinéma. . . . [L]es deux amants parlèrent du film pour échapper à la gêne du silence, en parlèrent artificiellement cependant qu'un sentiment de déchéance envahissait Solal. Ils étaient là, tous deux, assis, commentant à voix basse le film, exceptionnels, élégants, déshérités parmi la plèbe joyeuse, fraternellement babillante et sûre d'elle, salement léchant ses esquimaux. Il s'aperçut qu'il parlait à voix honteuse, comme un Juif de ghetto craignant d'attirer l'attention. Elle aussi était devenue humble, chuchotait comme lui, et il comprit que l'inconscient de cette malheureuse savait qu'ils étaient des rejetés. (*BdS,* 762–63)

†la neurasthénie de cette solitude à deux (*LM,* 719)

‡En ce dimanche, ma mère et moi nous étions ridiculement bien habillés et je considère avec pitié ces deux naïfs d'antan, si inutilement bien habillés, car personne n'était avec eux, personne ne se préoccupait d'eux. Ils s'habillaient très bien pour personne. (*LM,* 717)

The social world becomes a mute theater where the two "orientals" operate as if they were invisible ghosts incapable of communicating with the living. The outside world exists only as a backdrop, or even a foil, for this *solitude à deux,* which the two pretend is an idyllic existence, despite their tacit admission of the contrary. Recall that in *Ô vous, frères humains,* Cohen refers to his childhood before the violent incident on his tenth birthday as idyllic. To be excluded tacitly is easier to bear than an explicit and violent exclusion. Even in its most hostile moment, tacit exclusion allows for hope, whereas violent exclusion, once things are publicly said and done, shuts out all possibilities. It makes the unsayable all too palpable. For Albert and Louise to continue with their happy courtship, blinders are necessary to prevent their noticing the graffiti on the walls: DEATH TO THE JEWS!

The pariah couple replaces the social world through verbal simulation, creating an "as if" society, a fiction, to chase away the demons of exclusion. Unable to speak to or with the others, they speak to each other about the others: "Simpletons *[nigauds],* yes, but who loved each other. And we talked, we talked, we made comments about the other patrons [of the café], we talked in low voices, so wise and well educated, we talked, happy. . . but with a certain hidden sadness, which perhaps came from the confused feeling that each was the other's sole social company. Why be thus isolated?"*

But talk soon turns into silence, to the passivity of gazing and listening: never recognized, the pariahs are reduced to a purely specular and auditory position. They can gaze and listen, vicariously participate in the crowd, but never be of the crowd, not even on the most abstract level. The others are literally refractory to them, their impenetrable surface reflecting back to these *nigauds* the image of their social nullity. "Seated at this green table, we observed the other patrons, we tried to listen to what they said, not because of some vulgar curiosity but because of a thirst for human companionship, to be just a little, from afar, their friends. We would really have loved to belong."†

These passages from *Le Livre de ma mère* clarify the prelude to the central episode of *Ô vous, frères humains* concerning Albert's absolute yearning to be a part of the crowd that gathers around the street hawker. His only communion

*Nigauds, oui, mais on s'aimait. Et on parlait, on parlait, on faisait des commentaires sur les autres consommateurs, on parlait à voix basse, très sages et bien élevés, on parlait, heureux, . . . mais avec quelque tristesse secrète, qui venait peut-être du sentiment confus que chacun était l'unique société de l'autre. Pourquoi ainsi isolés? (*LM,* 718)

†Assis à cette table verte, nous observions les autres consommateurs, nous tâchions d'entendre ce qu'ils disaient, non par vulgaire curiosité mais par soif de compagnie humaine, pour être un peu, de loin, leurs amis. Nous aurions tant voulu en être. (*LM,* 718–19)

with the crowd takes place when he piously kneels at his altar of the Republic, gazing upon the portraits of Corneille and Hugo, hidden and protected well in the comfort and security of his room.

Yet amid all this hate and indifference the "neurosthénique" couple stubbornly persists in the phantasm of happiness. "I see myself at the age of ten. I had a girl's wide eyes, cheeks flushed with iridescent peach, a suit in the style of La Belle Jardinière, a sailor suit with a white braid from which a whistle hung."* Already mannered and somewhat feminine, the dashing boy basks in his mother's presence, even if it is amid a sea of (as yet unspoken) hatred.[7]

Tender Interlude: Shabbath

Out in the streets, Louise and Albert were refugees—foreign, oriental, Jewish—but also free of the mustached tyrant. They were refugees twice over, as foreigners and as the son and wife of Marc Coen. Refugees as Jews and as (phantasmagorically speaking) lovers. The apartment is always potentially hostile territory, because Louise can at a moment's notice be summoned to slave in the dungeon. The "neurosthénique" couple find temporary refuge in the streets, in cafés, and in theaters, ominous and passively hostile though they are (DEATH TO THE JEWS!). These were probably the settings of Albert Cohen's happiest moments in that pre-tenth-birthday idyll. Yet there is Shabbath: a temporality when the reconciliation of the incongruent is possible.

Cohen's description of Shabbath, both during his early childhood and during the 1920s (when he occasionally visited his parents), is the most lyrically touching description of the Coens' home: all conflicts evaporate; sanctified serenity reigns, as if this singular day is exempt from the dreadful regime of the real:

> On Friday afternoon, which for the Jews marks the beginning of the holy day of Shabbath, she would make herself beautiful and ornate, my mother. She would put on her solemn black silk dress and . . . her jewelry. . . . Having finished decorating her humble apartment for the Shabbath, which was her Jewish kingdom and her poor fatherland, she would be sitting, my mother, all alone, before the ceremonial table of the Shabbath, and, ceremonious, she would be waiting for her son and for her husband. Seated and forcing a wise immobility so as not to disturb her lovely ornaments . . . moved

*Je me revois en mes dix ans. J'avais de grands yeux de fille, des joues de pêches irisée, un costume de la Belle Jardinière, costume marin pourvu d'une tresse blanche qui retenait un sifflet. ("Le Jour de mes dix ans," *France libre* 10, no. 57 [July 16, 1945]: 195)

> by the idea of soon pleasing her two loves, her husband and her son . . . moved like a small girl during an awards ceremony.*

The topos of the home as a sanctuary and rampart against ambient hostility recurs often in Diaspora Jewish fiction: the Coens' Shabbath domesticity is a highly charged variation of this. More interesting for our purposes, the paradisiacal parenthetical lull that the Shabbath represents has theological underpinnings that are highly pertinent to many strands in Cohen's thought. In brief, Jews in biblical times did not much believe in the afterlife. Hebrew Scriptures make no mention of the afterlife ("Sheol" means a dark hole more than "afterlife") and its presence in Jewish liturgy, mysticism, and postbiblical theology is mostly derived from ambient Zoroastrianism, Neoplatonism, and Christianity. In classical Judaism, as in Cohen's oft-repeated assertion, death is final, no promise can remedy its irrevocability. "Dust unto dust"; "As they came from their mother's womb, so they shall go again, naked as they came" (Eccles. 5: 15).[8] Classical Judaism focuses on the concrete *here and now*—whatever paradise there is or might be exists in this life, and principally during the Shabbath. Sparks of divine rapture occur weekly; paradise is not a posthistorical promise to come at the end of time. Unlike the Christian and Islamic postmortem heaven (or hell or postmessianic timelessness), Shabbath takes place in a real historical and psychological temporality. Mirroring the order of creation, it exists in opposition to the other six days of the week, which are characterized by agonistic toil. It is a weekly exodus from the regime of real into that of appeased, sanctified desire, sacred but only too immanent. The Shabbath is, then, a periodic suspension of the regime of necessity, suffering, and resentment. The egg shop closes, time slows down, and as the males pray, reconciled with each other in the presence of the divine, the son overcomes his categorical condemnation of his father ("Oh, the verdict in the mute child's unmoving gaze") and Louise becomes the sanctified queen of her own domain, seated between her two loves, who now face each other in the presence of Shabbath. Louise's life, most of all in the earlier period, was this Cinderella-like oscillation between humiliating work and royal sanctification, which so

*L'après-midi du vendredi, qui est chez les Juifs le commencement du saint jour de sabbat, elle se faisait belle et ornée, ma mère. Elle mettait sa solennelle robe de soie noire et . . . ses bijoux. . . . Ayant fini d'orner pour le sabbat son humble appartement qui était son juif royaume et sa pauvre patrie, elle était assise, ma mère, toute seule, devant la table cérémonieuse du sabbat et, cérémonieuse, elle attendait son fils et son mari. Assise et se forçant à une sage immobilité pour ne point déranger sa belle parure . . . émue de plaire bientôt à ses deux amours, son mari et son fils . . . émue comme une petite fille de distribution de prix. (*LM,* 703–4)

closely echoes the undulation in Cohen's main Jewish characters—be it Rachel in the underground (see Chapter 5) or Mangeclous on Cephalonia. The communion meals that are not quite eaten with the Valorous are consumed on the Shabbath eve; once a week, dissonance is suspended from sundown to sundown.

Cohen purposefully dovetails this elegy of the sabbatically sanctified Louise with a marked contrast to Ariane. Something axiomatic is at stake here. The difference between the two women is not reducible to sociological or historical categories. Rather, they point toward Cohen's moral and metaphysical themes:

> This woman, who had been young and lovely, was a daughter of the Law of Moses, of the moral law, which to her was more important than God. Therefore, it was not a loving love, not a joke à la Anna Karenina. . . . She had not married for love. She had been married and had submissively accepted. And the biblical love had been born, so different from my Western passions. The saintly love of my mother has been born in the marriage, had grown with the birth of the baby that I was, blossomed in the alliance formed with her dear husband against unhappy life. There are whirling and sunny passions. There is no greater love.*

Louise is a daughter of the Law; Ariane is a devotee of salvation through romance. Whereas Louise is constrained in many tangible ways, including religious ostracism, hard labor, and patriarchal tyranny, Ariane pretends to live beyond the constraints of time, place, or scarcity. For Louise, the Shabbath exists in contrast to the other six days; Ariane seeks to live in a perpetual Shabbath where constraints are only exercised to engender yet more desire—the Law is superseded by salvation onto desire (the religion of romance, a variation on Christian theology). This is the regime of the "loving loves" *(amours amoureuses),* the "joke à la Anna Karenina"—an endless Shabbath, orgy of will, freed from any hint of the lower functions of the body, from any reference to money and scarcity, from the tension between prose and poetry, caught in the domestic comedy of keeping things permanently and poetically magical. Cohen would satirize this ad infinitum in *Belle du Seigneur,* as demonstrated in this particularly telling satire of Ariane's perpetual denial of prose: "If, by chance, the conversation related to some prosaic subject, the

*Cette femme, qui avait été jeune et jolie, était une fille de la Loi de Moïse, de la Loi morale qui avait pour elle plus d'importance que Dieu. Donc, pas d'amours amoureuses, pas de blagues à l'Anna Karénine. . . . Elle ne s'était pas mariée par amour. On l'avait mariée et elle avait docilement accepté. Et l'amour biblique était né, si différent de mes occidentales passions. Le saint amour de ma mère était né dans le mariage, avait crû avec la naissance du bébé que je fus, s'était épanoui dans l'alliance avec son cher mari contre la vie méchante. Il y a des passions tournoyantes et ensoleillées. Il n'y a pas de plus grand amour. (*LM,* 705–6)

guardian of values [Ariane] persisted in noble language. She would say 'photograph' and never 'photo,' 'cinematograph' and never 'cinema,' and 'movie' even less. She would also call her linen underwear 'angelics,' trousers being an unutterable word."*

This Genevan mixture of salvation and spirituality coupled with pagan, albeit refined, carnal desire, this aristocratic ease in the world and sense of natural entitlement to the permanent Shabbath, is the complete antithesis of Louise's general dis-ease with everything except for her son and her home—a prosaic dis-ease illuminated perhaps by periodic sparks of sabbatical bliss, but that remains forever (under)grounded in the *agon* of estrangement, just as Louise's fictional kin (Solal's family, the Valorous, the dwarf Rachel) are under(grounded) in dis-ease in the cellars of Saint Germain and Berlin.

The Shabbath scene in particular would make highly evocative and palatable reading were it not for Cohen's "golden quill," which stains them with just enough bitterness-laced lyricism to render them unsettling. Yet even here, before it all collapsed on his tenth birthday, the reader senses in the essayist's description and attitude this hesitation between the *morality of nobility* and the *morality of resentment,* between the ridiculous and the sublime Louise, that dissonant oscillation so pervasive in the novelist's ambivalent attitude toward origin and destiny, between "the glory of Israel" and "the catastrophe of being Jewish." Such, then, is the description of the Shabbath scene, the least conflicted scene in *Le Livre de ma mère.* What follows takes a decidedly moribund turn, the signature rhetoric of an endless and ambivalent mourning.

The Second Couple: Separation

In 1914, Albert left Marseille to study law and literature in Geneva. As we have seen, he was naturalized Swiss in 1919 and married Elisabeth Brocher, daughter of a Protestant pastor. Two years later, Elisabeth gave birth to Myriam, Albert Cohen's only child. But in 1924, Elisabeth succumbed to lymphatic cancer and the three-year-old Myriam spent the following six years or so in the care of Cohen's in-laws. Cohen spent the next two years particularly active as a poet, essayist, and editor, before obtaining a post in the International Labor Organization in 1926. For the first time in his life, living in a

*Si, d'aventure, la conversation portait sur quelque sujet prosaïque, la gardienne des valeurs [Ariane] persistait dans le langage noble. C'est ainsi qu'elle disait photographie et non photo, cinématographe et non cinéma et encore moins ciné. C'est ainsi encore qu'elle appelait des angéliques ses petits sous-vêtements de linon, pantalons étant un mot indicible. (*BdS,* 819)

comfortable apartment, he was economically and socially secure and seemed to lead a dashing social life. This situation formed the background for the second series of encounters with Louise in the mid to late 1920s. Older now and suffering from a bad heart condition, she visited Albert in Geneva once a year—alone, of course.

Between roughly 1905 and 1925, Albert and Louise naturally grew apart: he was now a dashing diplomat; she remained a timid shopkeeper's wife. Being with his mother now seemed more like work than heaven, more an exercise of will than the grace of mutual complicity. Even in the best of circumstances, attachment to one's mother at age thirty differs substantially from that of early to mid childhood. Yet the gulf between Albert and Louise transcended ordinary developmental logic. It involved Cohen's newly adopted European identity, the essence of which was its opposition to the Orient, greatly compounded in this case by the fact that Louise was not simply an oriental, but a semi-literate Jew who spoke poor French. A social liability, she was decidedly unpresentable in good society.

The oriental-occidental chiasmus, with all its multifaceted connotations, now defined their relationship and acted as the arena for an elaborate identity game. The newly minted European diplomat, lover of countesses and dazzling Dianas, and the aging Sephardic Jewess, wife of the egg merchant Marc Coen, sought to relieve each other's anxiety. First, Louise attempted to disguise her orientalisms: "She is disguised as a respectable occidental lady, but it is from ancient Canaan that she comes, and she does not know it."* Albert returns the favor by orientalizing himself as much as he can: "To put her at ease, I made myself entirely oriental with her. On occasion we would perhaps even munch salted pistachios on the street surreptitiously, like two good old Mediterranean relatives."† But Louise always feared embarrassing her dashing European diplomat of a son: "Poor mother, you were so scared of upsetting me, of not being occidental enough for my liking."‡

Clearly, then, Albert Cohen had to manage his mother's presence, maneuvering around social land mines whenever she was in town. As we have seen in detail, his novels are replete with many possible permutations of "when

*Elle est déguisée en dame convenable d'Occident mais c'est d'un antique Canaan qu'elle arrive et elle ne le sait pas. (*LM,* 732)

†Pour la mettre à l'aise, je me faisais tout oriental avec elle. Il nous est même peut-être arrivé de manger subrepticement des pistaches salées dans la rue, comme deux bons frangins méditerranéens. (*LM,* 727)

‡Pauvre Maman, tu avais si peur de me déplaire, de n'être pas assez occidentale à mon gré. (*LM,* 735)

Cephalonia comes calling." Cohen's case is more subtle than the usual one in which an assimilated Jew does his best to conceal his origin, when he does not outright convert to Christianity or to secular ideology—aestheticism, republicanism, or socialism. Cohen never hid his Jewishness. He was, on the contrary, already active in significant Jewish and Zionist causes in the early 1920s, serving inter alia as the chief editor of *La Revue juive,* for which Einstein and Freud both wrote. Yet the trauma of the street hawker made it clear to Albert Cohen that, to his eternal desolation, he was neither then nor could ever be French. Neutral, decentralized, cosmopolitan Switzerland, especially Geneva, therefore suited him perfectly. No need then to constantly define himself against a universal republican ideology.

Where then did this ambivalence about Judaism originate? Conceptually, it most certainly derived from the discrepancy Cohen perceived between the ancient glory and contemporary catastrophe of Jews. Going from the biblical matriarch Rachel to her modern descendents, be it the insane fictional mother in *Solal* or Rachel the vampire, the dwarf hunchback in the Berlin cellar in *Belle du Seigneur* (see Chapter 5), Cohen cannot but bitterly reflect on this abyssal difference. Three possible paths pointed toward "normalization": assimilation into Gentile liberal democracies, socialist revolution, or Jewish nationalism. For Cohen, Zionism was the only realistic political path from the state of being pathological Jews to that of normalized Hebrews. Cohen's equation of Jewish life in the Diaspora (in eastern Europe in particular) with a form of pathology is consistent with many Jewish writers of the late nineteenth century. This context best explains Cohen's obsessive reiteration of his corrective desire to "show the glory of Israel to those who only see Jews," a desire dating back to his 1921 lyrical poetry in *Paroles juives.*

But the idiosyncratic dimension here is more interesting. Although Louise viewed her successful son as purely occidental, his own identity montage was more complex: impeccably Western and virile in appearance, he concurrently and alternatively played the oriental tyrant and the narcissistic female, hence the perfectly hybrid name for this core Cohenian phantasm—*Belle du Seigneur.* Ardently Jewish in public, he remained ambivalent in private, especially in his writings, which served as his own private linguistic game to explore this searing dissonance, whatever the consequences. This complex hybrid identity, at once Jewish and secular, oriental and occidental, feminine and masculine, generates Cohen's dynamic self-mythology, a construct that always plays *on* and *within* the difference between the fictionalized real and the realistic fiction. Thus, for example, through a classical family romance transposi-

tion in *Solal,* the egg merchant Marc Coen becomes the stately Rabbi Gamaliel, while Cohen's mother remains more or less the same. We sense the same Josephic/Estheric ambivalence in Cohen's fictional and essayistic construction. The dashing young diplomat would think to himself, "I am a Jew, but a Jew like no other; I am *in* the community but not *of* the community, as I am *of* my mother but not *like* my mother," while annually hosting his mother but keeping her away from the "blonde Dianas." Solal reflects to himself in stream-of-consciousness style about his ambivalent Judaism: "It is perhaps in order to be able to make believe that I am not a Jew like the others that I am an exceptional Jew to affirm myself to be different from the despised *[honnis]* since I make fun of them in order to make believe oh shame on me that that I am a Jew [who is] not Jewish."* Louise's arrival triggered an always renewed and acute need to negotiate two separate realities, and when these mutually exclusive realities intersected, the unspeakable was finally articulated. As he writes after her death, he pointedly wonders about the repulsion that his mother provoked in him: "[F]or what mysterious reason did I often keep away from her, avoiding the kisses and the gaze, why and what was this cruel prudery?"†

On one fateful early morning, Louise's awkward anguish intersected with Albert's suave gallantry—the anxiety of the one wounds the narcissism of the other. Cohen mines the consequences of this event in his manifest mea culpa, the heart of his shame of her and of his shame of this shame—that is, at the heart of his mourning work:

> I was malicious to her, once, and she did not deserve it. Cruelty of sons. Cruelty of this absurd scene that I made. And why? Because, worried that I had not come home, unable to sleep until her son came home, she had at four in the morning called my worldly hosts, who were certainly not worthy of her. She had called to be reassured, to be sure that nothing bad had happened to me. Upon returning, I made this dreadful scene. It is tattooed in my heart, this scene. I see her again, so humble, my saint, facing my stupid reproaches, heartbreaking in her humility, so conscious of her fault, of what she had been persuaded was her fault. So convinced of her culpability, the poor thing who had done no wrong. She sobbed, my little child. Oh,

*C'est peut-être pour croire faire croire que je ne suis pas un Juif comme les autres que je suis un Juif exceptionnel pour m'affirmer différent des honnis puisque je les moque pour faire croire ô honte sur moi que je suis un Juif pas juif. (*BdS,* 895)

†[P]ar quel mystère me suis-je tenu souvent loin d'elle, évitant les baisers et le regard, pourquoi et quelle fut cette cruelle pudeur? (*LM,* 739)

> her tears, the flow of which I shall never now be able to avoid. Oh, her small desperate hands that had begun to show blotches of blue. Darling, you see, I try to make up for it by acknowledging.*

Cohen's insistence on the uniqueness ("I was malicious to her, once") of this event reveals its symbolic importance, for the event was singular not so much in terms of what happened as of what was finally said. Up to now, his mother's exclusion from his "blond zone" had remained unarticulated. When Albert expressed his rage against his mother for "violating" their game by anxiously calling his friends at four in the morning, that which had been tacitly understood and glossed over with apparent good humor by both mother and son was finally out in the open: "She knew . . . that my life had been separated from her humble life by an abyss, which I now despise."† Complicitous silence could no longer gloss over the breach between the mother and son.

The narrative sequence and underlying logic in the autobiographical essay remarkably echo what is parsed out in detail in the fictional work. As Chapter 3 has shown, Solal counterposes his Audes and Arianes to his oriental kin and operates in between them until the situation becomes unbearable and he breaks down in lacerating cruelty toward all, including himself. Moreover, this cruel scene in *Le Livre de ma mère* repeats the essential dynamic of the street hawker scene in the autobiographical *Ô vous, frères humains,* except that Cohen himself now becomes the *camelot* and Louise the victimized ten-year-old Albert. "And why this unfounded anger?" Cohen wonders, feigning innocence, "Perhaps because her foreign accent and difficulties with the French language while calling these cultivated cretins over the phone had embarrassed me."‡ Even Cohen the mature mourner deceives himself here, for Geneva teamed with foreign accents and even occasional mistakes in French syntax.

*Je fus méchant avec elle, une fois, et elle ne le méritait pas. Cruauté des fils. Cruauté de cette absurde scène que je fis. Et pourquoi? Parce que, inquiète de ne pas me voir rentrer, ne pouvant jamais s'endormir avant que son fils ne fût rentré, elle avait téléphoné, à quatre heures du matin, à mes mondains inviteurs qui ne la valaient certes pas. Elle avait téléphoné pour être rassurée, pour être sûre que rien de mal ne m'était arrivé. De retour chez moi, je lui avais fait cette affreuse scène. Elle est tatouée dans mon cœur, cette scène. Je la revois, si humble, ma sainte, devant mes stupides reproches, bouleversante d'humilité, si consciente de sa faute, de ce qu'elle était persuadée être une faute. Si convaincue de sa culpabilité, la pauvre qui n'avait rien fait de mal. Elle sanglotait, ma petite enfant. Oh, ses pleurs que je ne pourrai jamais n'avoir pas fait couler. Oh, ses petites mains désespérées où des taches bleues étaient apparues. Chérie, tu vois, je tâche de me racheter en avouant. (*LM,* 730)

†Elle savait . . . que ma vie était séparée de son humble vie par un abîme que je hais maintenant. (*LM,* 745)

‡Et pourquoi cette indigne colère? Peut-être parce que son accent étranger et ses fautes de français en téléphonant à ces crétins cultivés m'avaient gêné. (*LM,* 730)

Surely, if Louise had been an English countess, and not a Jewish shopkeeper, her imperfect French would hardly have mattered. Rather, what was at stake was Albert's myth of origin, the integral part of his exquisite Jew identity montage, the misunderstanding of which lay at the root of his visceral hostility to his mother. That charismatic public persona—the predatory hunter armed with "dazzling sharp teeth"*—could not possibly have originated from the womb of Louise Coen, whose voice as it came across the telephone to the ears of a countess certainly quivered with the memory of pogroms, fear, submission, and humiliation, even if defiant. There simply was no room for Louise in this montage.

This theme is a very raw nerve in Cohen's fiction: Solal is haunted by the specter of the hysterical Jewess, most notably the maternal figure in *Solal* and the dwarf Rachel in *Belle du Seigneur.* But, as "Chant de mort," the earlier version of *Le Livre de ma mère,* makes amply clear, the essayist Cohen was haunted by the identical specter. Writing about Louise, he frankly admits that "her watchful eyes on my health and on my worries bothered me or, cruelly, indisposed me. Obscurely, I blamed her for watching and guessing too much. Which proves that one can be almost anti-Semitic even with one's own mother."† This revealing "glitch" of being "almost anti-Semitic" was cleaned up by 1953, when he wrote the final version of *Le Livre de ma mère:* "Obscurely, I blamed her for watching and guessing too much."‡ Full stop! And again, thinking about her death, he is relieved that "she was no longer a Jew with eternally hunted eyes, with eyes animally set on the defensive, in carnal denial, frightening denial of culpability, a Jew with her mouth half-open in an obscure stupefaction inherited from fear and waiting."§ In this case, biography hardly illuminates fiction; on the contrary, the fictional stands on its own, but the autobiographical essays become much more penetrating when read against it, much like adding color, volume, and tone to a flat line drawing.

Unlike the Valorous in general, the mother cannot remain a collapsed metaphor, a figure brushed against, handled, managed, but never really unpacked.[9] There is no escape from the mother. The urgent necessity palpable

*d'éblouissantes dents acérées (*LM,* 704)

†ses yeux guetteurs de ma santé et de mes soucis me gênaient ou, cruel, m'indisposaient. Obscurément, je lui en voulais de trop surveiller et deviner. Comme quoi on peut être presque antisémite même avec sa mère. ("Chant de mort," *France libre* 1 [June 15, 1943]: 103)

‡Obscurément, je lui en voulais de trop surveiller et deviner. (*LM,* 707)

§elle n'est plus une Juive aux yeux éternellement traqués, aux yeux animalement sur la défensive, charnellement dénégateurs, effrayamment dénégateurs de culpabilité, une Juive à la bouche entr'ouverte par une obscure stupéfaction héritée de peur et d'attente. ("Chant de mort," *France libre* 1 [June 15, 1943]: 105)

throughout *Le Livre de ma mère* is to finally write the mother; to unpack the maternal figure, so omnipresent in his fiction, but always obliquely. Whereas Gamaliel often recurs in Cohen's novels, the maternal figure receives only one scene in *Solal.* As we saw in the metaphysical bar mitzvah, her solitary appearance takes the form of a caricature of the hysterical Jewess, after which her affect and her discourse disappear altogether as those of a maternal figure per se, but reappear intermittently in the guise of other characters, such as the physical person of the dwarf Rachel and the ramblings of Uncle Saltiel.

Thus no easy management of Louise is possible. The tongue-lashing at five in the morning, the verbal breach, that moment when the definitive rupture with the idealized "first couple" made up of the boy and his beautiful young mother takes place, was not only remarkable in its trenchant cruelty, but also a primal scene of estrangement that would haunt the novelist as much as the mourner: "I am haunted by this scene that I inflicted on her. 'I'm so sorry,' sobbed my darling. She was so terrified by her sin of having dared to call the countess. . . . 'I won't do it again,' sobbed my darling."* But at five in the morning, the imperious son stood unmoved, towering over his panicked and exhausted mother, spite in his eyes, and lashed her with words that could never be taken back—"Which proves that one can be almost anti-Semitic even with one's own mother." In his rage, he told her that she was unworthy of phoning respectable people, that, in sum, she was to remain a pariah forever. But then came that familiar Cohenian moment when tenderness follows cruelty, when narcissism recognizes its depravity and recoils from it: "When I saw the blue spots on her hands, the tears came to me and I knelt, and I kissed her small hands madly and she kissed my hands and we looked at each other, son and mother forever. She took me on her knees and comforted me."† Louise's eloquence lay not in verbal platitudes—those made the son even more spiteful—but rather in her figuratively bleeding flesh, the somatic eloquence of the "blue stains" on her small quivering hands. Overcome with emotion, Albert begged forgiveness at her feet, exactly as his fictional protagonist does in *Solal* after humiliating Gamaliel by crossing himself in public. Yet despite the momentary reconciliation—the momentary lucidity of the

*Je suis hanté par cette scène que je lui fis. 'Je demande pardon', sanglotait mon adorable. Elle était si épouvantée par son péché d'avoir osé téléphoner à cette comtesse. . . . 'Je ne le ferai plus', sanglotait mon adorable. (*LM,* 733–34)

†Lorsque je vis les taches bleues sur ses mains, les larmes me vinrent et je m'agenouillai et je baisai follement ses petites mains et elle baisa mes mains et nous nous regardâmes, fils et mère à jamais. Elle me prit sur ses genoux et elle me consola. (*LM,* 734)

narcissist—the next day reverts to the familiar pattern: "But then, the following evening, I attended another grand reception, and I did not take my mother along with me."* Contrition is followed by brief reunion with the carnal and maternal calling-reminding of origin, although further estrangement lies close at hand. Again, this trajectory of hard rejection, remorseful recognition, followed by soft rejection forms the repetitive procedure in Solal's and Cohen's dealings with "Cephalonia."

The inscription of the truth in the flesh occurs even more dramatically in "Chant de mort," where the mother's presence becomes an almost palpable part of the very movement of Cohen's somatic life, of his rhythmic inhalation and exhalation. He painfully imagines his mother's reproaches for abandoning her in Marseille, alone with her husband, the Vichy police, and the Gestapo:

> What I know is that my suffering does not lie in my feelings but in my throat and my organs and above all in this breathing which is difficult but sadly wants to live on and that, between inspiration and expiration, always contains my mother coming heavily toward me and telling me that it is not true and that she is alive or smiling weakly at me and saying that her darling whom she trusted could have saved her *[aurait pu la sauver]* and taken her from Europe and that, far from the Germans, she would have lived and we would have gone to the movies together in Leicester Square and strolled around Piccadilly.†

It seems very improbable that Cohen could have rescued his parents from Marseille, especially after June 1940, but only his somatization of this guilt is relevant here. Breathing is a struggle because the desire to die correlates with writing about his mother. Every inhalation and exhalation contains this hesitation between the desire to expire of sorrow and this sad longing to endure so that the penitent can further wound himself with his golden quill. "[H]er darling whom she trusted" certainly lets her down, and in spirit the mother comes back to exact her revenge. Such a failure recalls the repeated collapse of the Josephic Savior phantasm in *Solal* and *Belle du Seigneur.* Savior he is not—

*Mais lorsque, le lendemain soir, je m'en fus à une autre brillante réception, je n'emmenai pas ma mère avec moi. (*LM,* 734)

†Ce que je sais, c'est que ma souffrance n'est pas dans mes sentiments mais dans ma gorge et mes organes et surtout dans cette respiration difficile mais qui veut tristement vivre et qui, entre l'inspiration et l'expiration, contient toujours ma mère venant lourdement vers moi et me disant que ce n'est pas vrai et qu'elle est vivante ou me souriant faiblement que son chéri en qui elle avait confiance aurait pu la sauver et la sortir d'Europe et que, loin des Allemands, elle aurait vécu et nous serions allés ensemble aux cinémas de Leicester Square et nous aurions badaudé dans Piccadilly. ("Chant de mort," *France libre* 2 [July 15, 1943]: 198)

not even of his mother, let alone of the Jewish people. But this Josephic failure is secondary in the context of the work of mourning. So the question remains: What does the maternal specter want? And why does it have this morbid effect on her son? The key to these questions lies in the banal train station scenes of the late 1920s where the mother's departure from Geneva is festive for the son and solemn for the mother. It is a funeral where the son's delight in the departure of the mother is all too conscious, all too Solalic in its sadism.

Here we finally arrive at the core chronotope in this mourning narrative: the *train as coffin.* To unpack the maternal figure, Cohen the mature writer can no longer give his mother the slip. The young poet, diplomat, and seducer turns his back on the train, but as a sober mourner he must—at last!—turn toward the train and follow it as if it were a funeral procession, which ends only in writing about it. The feelings of the departing mother could not contrast with those of her son more starkley:

> Her tears at the station in Geneva, the night of her departure for Marseille. . . . At the coach door, she observed me so tenderly, with madness and unhappiness *[malheur]*. . . . Oh, her benediction in tears in the doorway, of her watching me so intently . . . somewhat mad with unhappiness, a bit inane with unhappiness *[malheur].**

Yet Albert experiences only relief and even euphoric joy and triumph—at last she is gone, departed! As the train pulls away, he rushes off to see "the blonde demon named Diana."† As the train carries away the old Louise, whom Cohen now, at the time of writing, views as "exposed, crestfallen, miserable, defeated, pariah,"‡ Albert, happy beyond measure to finally be rid of Louise, the dead weight that has collared him for weeks, "laughs with love in the taxi getting nearer to Diana."§ Albert consciously dismisses himself as a libidinous socialite, a bit cruel to his mother, but not wanting her definitive departure. Yet he cannot but admit this disturbing truth: "Strange that I hadn't noticed to this day that my mother was a human being, a being different from myself and with genuine sufferings."|| And in a later observation, almost clin-

*Ses larmes à la gare de Genève, le soir du départ pour Marseille. . . . À la portière du wagon, elle me considérait si tendrement, avec folie et malheur. . . . Oh, la bénédiction en larmes d'elle à la portière, d'elle me regardant tellement . . . un peu folle de malheur, un peu imbécile de malheur. (*LM,* 744–45)

†la blonde démone qui avait nom Diane (*LM,* 746)

‡exposée, déconfite, misérable, vaincue, paria (*LM,* 745)

§riait d'amour dans le taxi qui le rapprochait de Diane. (*LM,* 745)

||Étrange que je ne m'aperçoive que maintenant que ma mère était un être humain, un être autre que moi et avec de vraies souffrances. (*LM,* 745)

ical in its acuity: "And this desperate lover who sobs in front of the tomb, beneath his pain there is perhaps a dreadful and involuntary joy, a sinful joy to still be alive, him, an unconscious joy, an organic joy of which he is not the master, an involuntary joy of contrast between this dead [woman] and this living [man] who speaks his pain in truth, all the same. To feel pain, is to live, is to still belong *[en être],* is to still be here."*

Surely the mother's identity with the child, her lack of otherness, was a by-product of their early two-against-all bond; but, now in the late 1920s, his inability to imagine Louise's suffering suggests precisely the opposite, namely, that they were now so deeply split that only drawing on the amorous capital of their first "couplehood" could still make their incongruity bearable. Absorbed in his ambition, the affect of the other/mother is now invisible, inaudible.

Louise was imprisoned in Albert's apartment, safely (for Albert) tucked away from the elegant world—especially from the elegant, sunny Dianas—just as, by way of simple transposition, Gamaliel is hidden in *Mangeclous* by Solal in a suburban house, completely isolated from the outer world, except for semi-clandestine nightly visits from his diplomat son.[10] The hiding place where the unpresentable pariah is kept becomes, for Louise, a "sabbatical" sanctuary, a sanctified domain, a space in memoriam of her first union with her son. However, her predicament is now much more confusing, for it is her son himself who exiles her from blond Gentiles and condemns her yet again to a sabbatical prison where the old oriental Jew is confined but crowned.

But as the train pulls away, the son promptly defiles even this sabbatical sanctuary: "The night of my mother's departure. . . . Diana accompanied me home, and in the apartment that my mother had blessed before leaving, I dared to undress the impatient Diana."† Against the mother stands Diana. Against sanctification stands nudity. And, above all, against the benediction of the quivering mother stands the denuding of the quivering Diana, impatient to be undressed and taken in a space that only a few hours before was saturated by the presence of that other lover, his first lover, Louise Coen. The two women, who were most likely cleverly separated from each other, intersect now on the son's bed through his transgressive daring, his sadistic desire to defile and thus cleanse the apartment of his mother's presence. The nudity of the

*Et cet amant désespéré qui sanglote devant la tombe, sous sa douleur il y a peut-être une affreuse involontaire joie, une pécheresse joie à vivre encore, lui, une inconsciente joie, une organique joie dont il n'est pas le maître, une involontaire joie de contraste entre cette morte et ce vivant qui dit sa douleur pourtant vraie. Avoir de la douleur, c'est vivre, c'est en être, c'est y être encore. (*LM,* 759)

†Cette nuit du départ de ma mère. . . . Diane me raccompagna chez moi, et dans l'appartement que ma mère avait béni avant de partir, j'osai dénuder Diane impatiente. (*LM,* 746)

one erases the presence of the other. Something very urgent is at work here, something stronger than pent-up desire. This defiling is not far from a post-funeral orgy fantasy. And as Cohen comes closer to articulating this fantasy, the text's cohesion splinters under the weight of such an insight.

Faced with the recognition of this desire for the permanent departure, the death of the mother, the first person narrative can no longer bear the pressure of such an avowal, and it splinters into a listening first person to whom another and distant son is speaking, or rather, pleading:

> A son said to me, and it is he who speaks now. Me also, this son with dark circles under his eyes told me, I have lost my mother. Me also, I lived far away from her and she came to see me each year for a few weeks that were also the poor fairytales of her life. Me also, said this son, on the very night of her departure, instead of crying all night for my incomparable, I went, sad but quickly comforted, toward a comparable, one of the exquisite she-devils of my life and who was named Diana, Diana priestess of love.*

The hidden death wish eliminates any chance of identification with the earlier self. Cohen can no longer bear the first person narration even if the earlier "Albert" is understood to have been replaced by the mature Cohen, the actual narrator. The narrator becomes downright hostile toward his subject: "I hate him, this son."†

The shift from "I" to "this son" displaces moral responsibility from Albert Cohen the individual to a generic son, any son of any mother, as if Albert and Louise had simply experienced the universal mother/son conflict. Cohen repeatedly exploits this subtle shift, first in interjections in this scene: "Oh, shame. Sons and daughters, accursed bread . . . oh, cruelty of youth";‡ followed by more sustained exhortations toward the end of the book, which start with: "Sons of mothers who are still alive, never again forget that your mothers are mortal."§

To shift the onus to a universal son can diffuse Cohen's anguish, but cannot account for the cruelty in terms of the specific narrative in this essay. After all, however ambivalent sons may feel about their mothers, these mothers do *not* represent an automatic social death sentence if and when introduced to

*Un fils m'a dit, et c'est lui qui parle maintenant. Moi aussi, m'a dit ce fils aux yeux cernés, j'ai perdu ma mère. Moi aussi, je vivais loin d'elle et elle venait me voir chaque année pour quelques semaines qui étaient aussi la pauvre féerie de sa vie. Moi aussi, dit ce fils, le soir même de son départ, au lieu de pleurer toute la nuit mon incomparable, j'allais, triste mais vite consolé, vers une comparable, une des exquises diablesses de ma vie et qui avait nom Diane, Diane religieuse d'amour. (*LM*, 745)

†Je le hais, ce fils." (*LM*, 735)

‡Ô honte. Fils et filles, maudite engeance. . . . Ô cruauté de jeunesse. (*LM*, 746)

§Fils des mères encore vivantes, n'oubliez plus que vos mères sont mortelles. (*LM*, 771)

good company. But Louise Coen *does* represent that death sentence for Albert Cohen in Geneva of the interwar period. In his fiction, Cohen faces this truth directly; he endlessly conjugates and declines this psychological and social (inner) reality. In his essays, however, he recoils from explicitly articulating his ambivalent horror and fascination with his Jewish origin, which remains always in Cohen the privileged domain of the novel, and within the novel the deepest levels of the ambivalence are reserved for the recesses of long streams of consciousness.[11] But even this rhetorical slippage (from the first person "I" to the universal subject "mothers' sons") fails to constitute a convincing apology. Cohen may spin the narrative toward a benign interpretation; Cohen may program the reader toward a universal transference of affect into the text-screen, yet beneath the narration of events and situations, lies a discourse on the precise nature of his transgression, which constitutes the rawest nerve in the fiction, namely, his ambivalence about his origins, experienced as shame and guilt, and, above all, his shame of shame. This is why his mourning for his mother never ended, either in 1943, when she died and he wrote "Chant de mort," or in 1953, when he produced the final edition of *Le Livre de ma mère,* or even in his final *Carnets 1978.*

Forever, he mourns his mother; forever, he is condemned to walk behind that train carrying Louise Coen away. Toward the very end of the book the metaphor that predominates remains that of the train/coffin/hearse: "[A]nd me I go behind the moving train . . . behind the moving train, bearing my dead and blessing mother."* Mourning becomes the creative principle; writing, in its deepest level of discourse, echoes the rhythm of the funerary procession and the Sephardic shivah,[12] and it will unite him with his mother in their third "couplehood."

The Third Couple: Mourning, Writing, and Dying

Having stripped the text of its most obvious and deceptive layers, we can mine the matrix metaphor that relentlessly recurs throughout it—marching behind the mother's iron coffin and moaning regrets in a shivahlike stream of consciousness. Cohen endlessly lacerates himself with this cruel scene, whose symbolism seems to engulf him.[13]

Albert Cohen could not walk alongside Louise Coen's actual coffin, because her funeral took place in German-occupied Vichy France. He thus could not

*[E]t moi je vais derrière le train qui va . . . derrière le train qui va, emportant ma mère morte et bénissante. (*LM,* 773)

vocalize his grief or lower her into death's dark pit and had to settle for writing these acts, transposing the physical into the scriptural. But even if circumstances had permitted the traditional burial, kaddish, and shivah, the self-creating charismatic poet would not have performed the year-long mourning ritual (with all its salutary rites); for him, this act belongs to the interminable realm of writing.[14]

The writer's point of view fixes on the train's movement, charging ever forward. Haltingly, he tries to accompany his mother, his gaze seeking to capture the fleeting funeral procession that will soon disappear forever beyond the horizon: "Thus, scanning the axles of the long train, always scanning, this train, my pain, always carrying away, this funeral train, my disheveled dead at the carriage door, and me, I follow behind the receding train, and I run out of breath, so utterly pale and perspiring and obsequious, behind the receding train, taking away my dead and blessing mother."*

The blessing corpse is none other than Louise, who showered her son with the blessings at the Geneva train station, leaving him indifferent at best, joyful about her departure (death) at worst. Likewise, the cadaver's disheveled hair at the carriage door as the death train pulls away toward Sheol recalls the tousled, panicky Louise as the train to Marseille pulls away from Geneva. And as the corpse fades away from the mourner, Cohen—now in postmortem writing—chases it almost to the point of fainting. But the train rolls ever faster, and neither in dreams nor in inarticulate remorse will Cohen ever catch up with it. He can do so only in repeatedly rewriting the events, so that what had already been lost in reality might be restored and perhaps relived in stylized fantasy. But however he relives it, however he tries to restore Louise into his inner self, the funerary train reappears, like a ghostly apparition tracking a psychotic. Now only words redeem past acts and restore the lost mother to her rightful place.

Cohen saunters behind the coffin—mumbling reproaches, evocative memories, daydreams, and nightmares. The repetitive semantic and syntactic nature of the dreams holds far more relevance than their content, for the dreams fashion the text into a rhythmic incantation, as if it were a stream of mourning, a mumbling to oneself that the trauma of burial and mourning allows. Dwelling upon lost moments, he repeats "never again . . . never again"; recognizing the impossibility of reliving the past, he begins many successive para-

*Ainsi scandent les essieux du long train, toujours scandant, ce train, ma douleur, toujours emportant, ce train de funérailles, ma morte décoiffée à la portière, et moi je vais derrière le train qui va, et je m'essouffle, tout pâle et transpirant et obséquieux, derrière le train qui va, emportant ma mère morte et bénissante. (*LM,* 772–73)

graphs with: "Finished . . . finished"; unable to escape his mother's affectionate gaze, he belatedly acknowledges the uniqueness of Louise's love: "love of my mother . . . love of my mother." The lamentation climbs to its apex when the mother's love is compared to all other past and present loves: "Love of my mother, comparable to no other . . . Love of my mother, comparable to no other";*[15] incapable of remaining in the depressed mourning position, he lacerates himself for the sinfulness of small joys he experiences while his mother turns to dust: "Sinfulness of life . . . sinfulness of life." Finally, comes the inevitable recognition—whatever his thoughts, regrets, promises, or poetic genius might be—she is irremediably departed: "She is dead . . . she is dead." On the penultimate page, despite all his repeated protestations, he strives to bring Louise back to life (or to an afterlife) by the sheer power of thought: "I don't want her to be dead. I want hope, I demand hope."† Cohen finally lacerates the truth into his consciousness: "My mother is dead, dead, dead, my dead mother is dead, dead."‡ These repetitions replace the comforting yearlong, daily repetition of the kaddish prayer (seven to ten times a day) that Judaism requires of the mourner. The golden quill replaces the rhythm of traditional mourning, if not its efficacy.

But soon enough the mourner reaches the edge of the dark pit where the corpse, already in rigor mortis, will decompose, become a skeleton and turn to dust, while future corpses pursue their petty ambitions and indulge in their foolish sorrows, indifferent to the dead and thus to their future nonselves. Death for Cohen is very palpable, concrete, even overwhelming in its materiality: "And you, mother, so white and yellow that I dare, in a blink of the eye, look into your already rotten coffin, my thin abandoned one . . . you so gloomy now and laconic in your soil-tinged melancholy, asleep in the black silence of the tomb, in the heavy wet soil-silence of the ground of the tomb . . . where only roots live and joyless and obscure creatures of the dark with incomprehensible going abouts and always silent though frightenedly busy?"§

"God, how absurd it all is,"|| he says toward the end of *Le Livre de ma mère,*

*Amour de ma mère, à nul autre pareil . . . Amour de ma mère, à nul autre pareil (*LM,* 743–44)

†Je ne veux pas qu'elle soit morte. Je veux un espoir, je demande un espoir (*LM,* 763),

‡Ma mère est morte, morte, morte, ma mère morte est morte, morte. (*LM,* 772)

§Et toi, mère si blanche et jaune que j'ose, en un battement de paupières, regarder dans ta caisse déjà pourrie, mon amaigrie abandonnée . . . toi si morose maintenant et laconique en ta terreuse mélancolie, couchée en ce silence noir de la tombe, en ce lourd humide silence de terre de la tombe . . . où ne vivent que des racines, des radicelles sans joie et de mornes créatures d'obscurité aux incompréhensibles démarches et toujours silencieuses quoique effrayamment affairées? (*LM,* 766)

||Dieu, que tout cela est absurde (*LM,* 765)

but he could have repeated this lament at the end of every paragraph. Now that the funeral is over, only a morbid retreat to the writing self can constitute a justified existence. The blue stains that blotted the hands of the aging mother bleed into the ink blots on the page—early signs of the mother's aging that made Cohen break down in theatrical remorse during the horrific "late-night phone call scene." Writing as entombment constitutes Cohen's mourning ritual. He writes himself onto death, drowning himself in inkblots, just as Louise slowly liquefies into nothingness. Both traffic now in the liquids of death, blots of existence and nonexistence.

To write the death of the beloved (and one's own death, if one completely identifies with the beloved) is then the task at hand. This funerary meditation therefore supplants all the letters that were not written due to the writer's cruel ego ("[this book] is my last letter"). But this writing requires a major displacement from the *vita activa* (diplomat, activist) to the *vita contemplativa* (writer, mourner). Cohen hints at that dislocation in his 1943 "Chant de mort," but in 1953, after his career shifts completely from international diplomacy to writing, this retreat becomes an essential correlative for this funerary meditation. Like Proust in his cork-lined apartment, Cohen permanently retreats into an isolated and insolent tomb of writing—an *écritoire morbide*—where son and mother, although one of them is dead, exist in analogous postures. "Enough, enough, no more mourning, ever. We are both quite alone, you in your soil, me in my room. Me, slightly dead among the living, you, slightly living among the dead."* The apartment door locked thrice over, shades drawn down, the *écritoire morbide* resembles a dark, quiet crypt. While worms consume his mother, the vermin of regret and remorse, secreted through the poison of writing that he savors above all else, consume him. Writing distills memories, just as worms reprocess the rotting flesh of cadavers. The golden quill becomes the death quill; Cohen now desires to embroider his death with the golden threads of Louise's presence, "I was put on earth to listen to my mother's interminable stories."† A symmetry thus forms between the two, for both are entombed, both listen and recount to each other, even in absentia, the same stories—and the mother's claim to life, even in dead letters, is a function of the son's self-execution through writing. Here at last we come to a deeper understanding of Cohen's likening of his mother to a parasite *(ma mère était mon gui)*.

*Fini, fini, plus de Maman, jamais. Nous sommes bien seuls tous les deux, toi dans ta terre, moi dans ma chambre. Moi, un peu mort parmi les vivants, toi, un peu vivante parmi les morts. (*LM*, 711)

†J'ai été mis sur terre pour écouter les interminables histoires de ma mère. (*LM*, 750)

But there is more. The morbid entombment for the purpose of writing the mother represents just another repetition of the cellar nightmares of Saint-Germain and Berlin. All are symbolic spaces of exclusion, where laceration, whether inflicted by the *méchants* or self-inflicted, is the rule. To return to the mother, to the womb, is to slither through the crevices of memory and writing the way worms slither into the grave, feasting on the corpse. In writing his mother, Cohen places himself in an identical position to that of the Valorous and Rachel, prolonging life by bleeding oneself ever so slowly, and sometimes not without some perverse delectation:

> Ever since her death, I've loved living alone, sometimes, for days and days, far from the absurdly busy living, alone just as she was alone in her apartment in Marseille, alone and the telephone unplugged so that the outside does not enter my home just as it did not enter hers, alone in this residence that has the perfection of death and where I ceaselessly set things in order to believe that all is well, alone in my room deliciously locked up, too well-ordered and too clean, mad with symmetry, pencils arranged by size on the small shining cemetery of the table.*

To be like his mother, Cohen must break with the world and make giving voice to Louise in writing his sole occupation. Everything in the room—papers, books, pencils—must be controlled, immaculate, symmetrical, exactly as in a mausoleum. The shining surface of the writing desk is explicitly equated with a cemetery. Once isolated in his *écritoire morbide,* he obsessively arranges and rearranges his room "to believe that all is well"—like an encased future mummy who perfectly arranges his dark sepulture to make believe that all is well. But all is not well. His days are spent daydreaming and writing, dreaming and awakening to his nightmares, all alone with his golden quill and, for sole companion, his mirror. Is this not identical to the world of the lonely child in Marseille who led a solitary imaginative life above the inferno of his father's detestable egg shop? Again, he is alone, lamenting his mother's absence, tracing letters in front of the mirror, letters that are inspired by her inventive pictograms and endless stories. This is Cohen's *Fort! Da!* game, supplanting his mother's pictures by tracing letters in the air and then wiping

*Depuis sa mort, j'aime vivre seul, parfois, pendant des jours et des jours, loin des vivants absurdement occupés, seul comme elle était seule dans son appartement de Marseille, seul et le téléphone décroché pour que le dehors n'entre pas chez moi comme il n'entrait pas chez elle, seul dans cette demeure qui a la perfection de la mort et où je fais sans cesse de l'ordre pour croire que tout va bien, seul dans ma chambre délicieusement fermée à clef, trop rangée et trop propre, folle de symétrie, crayons allongés par ordre de grandeur sur le petit cimetière luisant de la table. (*LM,* 767)

them away to cope with her absence. Childhood rejoins old age, except that as a mature artist, this game of *Fort! Da!* occasions an ever more complex identification with his mother, followed by fantasies of regression, only to be reversed at the end with yet another cruel betrayal. But before that last betrayal, the most cruel, the identification with Louise will become visceral.

"And unable to do anything else for you, mother, *I kiss my hand that came from you.*"* Taken literally, this is a fantasized regression to the earliest infantile stages where the newborn makes no distinction between his own and his mother's flesh.[16] *Baiser*: in this context, to kiss, to lick, to suck . . . to swallow and penetrate the other that I am, or that I now fantasize being—such is Cohen's desire as he lovingly contemplates his own hands, now stained with blue veins, just like the trembling hands of his mother pleading for mercy at four in the morning. And then the identification becomes sacred, devotional: "O you, the only one, mother, my mother and the mother of all men, you alone, our mother, deserve our confidence and our love. All the rest, wives, brothers, sisters, children, friends, all the rest is nothing but misery and a leaf carried away by the wind."† Cohen deifies the (m)other: She exists above and beyond all others. The alibi of devotion to the Madonna allows the world to be cast aside in good conscience, thus directing all energy toward the conjuring up of this deity. Specular identification follows: "I look at myself in the mirror, but it is my mother who is in the mirror."‡ And when he wants even more company than just himself and himself-as-Louise, he physically presses on his eye in order to double the image in the mirror. Now two mothers stare at him from within the glass, and he is with himself thrice over (himself and his two doubles in the mirror). Cohen's mirror stage reverses the classical scheme where the child learns to see himself as other; instead, he sees the (m)other as himself, and vice versa.[17] This regression to the maternal whole is experienced through the narcissistic gaze and the lips that kiss the hand, one's hand, given to one by the absent (m)other.

That immaculate *écritoire morbide* admits no lovers, friends, or family; only the golden quill to inscribe sin onto the flesh and the mirror accompany the author. Writing as dying. Writing as suicide:

*Et ne pouvant rien faire d'autre pour toi, Maman, *je baise ma main qui vient de toi.* (*LM*, 721; emphasis added)

†Ô toi, la seule, mère, ma mère et de tous les hommes, toi seule, notre mère, mérites notre confiance et notre amour. Tout le reste, femmes, frères, sœurs, enfants, amis, tout le reste n'est que misère et feuille emportée par le vent. (*LM*, 742–43)

‡Je me regarde dans la glace, mais c'est ma mère qui est dans la glace. (*LM*, 754)

> Sometimes, at night, having once again checked the dear lock of the door, I sit, hands flat on my knees and, the lamp turned off, I look in the mirror. Surrounded by various minotaurs of melancholy, I wait in front of the mirror, while on the floor slither shadows, like rats—the malicious of my life among men—while sudden glances also flash, noble glances . . . in front of the mirror, seated with the pharaonic hands lain flat, I wait for my mother, beneath the moon that is her message, to appear perhaps. But only memories come. Memories, this terrible life that is not life and that hurts.*

The mirror is the screen for the drama of mourning. Isolated in a room, lit only by the radiant moon, Cohen awaits the apparition of Louise. She does not appear; only phantoms move about, first the haunting silhouettes of street hawkers, then a few rays of warmth, followed by a stream of "[m]emories, this terrible life that is not life and that hurts." No magic can bring back Louise, and no rhetorical chicanery or wishful thought can resolve the pain that she represents. The son's memories resemble the act of writing: a substitute for presence that can neither revive the deceased nor restore her into an "unambivalent" inner object, but that can playfully (some games are masochistic) rework Ur-scenes, traumas suffered and inflicted. At present, writing (and mourning) the pain constitutes Cohen's sole pleasure: that of dying after his own fashion, committing suicide by concentrating his whole existence on the inscription of his mother. Connecting writing, dying, and pleasure requires no "uncontrolled" metonymical conjectures of the "ceci n'est pas un cigar" variety. As usual, Cohen plainly articulates this complex psychoanalytical concept: "'Tired of living,' I write with my finger in the air. Then, I write the word 'catalepsy.' It's a word that I read in a book, and I learned from the dictionary that it means that one does not move anymore, that one is like the dead."† The *écritoire morbide* is Cohen's "penal colony," and the golden quill, his exquisite "execution instrument." Writing the pain becomes a delectable pleasure, akin to the ecstasy experienced by the officer in Kafka's *In the Penal Colony,* tortured by and for the Law, just as Cohen feels tortured by Louise who also stands for the Law.

*Parfois, la nuit, après avoir une fois de plus vérifié la chère fermeture de la porte, je m'assieds, les mains à plat sur les genoux et, la lampe éteinte, je regarde dans la glace. Entouré de certains minotaures de mélancolie, j'attends devant la glace, tandis que filent sur le plancher, comme des rats, des ombres qui furent les méchants de ma vie parmi les hommes, tandis que luisent aussi des regards subits, nobles regards . . . devant la glace, assis et les mains pharaoniques à plat, j'attends que ma mère, sous la lune qui est son message, apparaisse peut-être. Mais seuls les souvenirs arrivent. Les souvenirs, cette terrible vie qui n'est pas de la vie et qui fait mal. (*LM,* 768)

†"Fatigué de vivre", écris-je avec mon doigt sur de l'air. Ensuite, j'écris le mot "catalepsie". C'est un mot que j'ai lu dans un livre, et j'ai appris par le dictionnaire qu'il signifie qu'on ne bouge plus, qu'on est comme mort. (*Carnets 1978,* 1129)

Then, deep into the night of mourning, he falls asleep, wakes up abruptly, and recalls fragments of dreams:

> Why did I take out of my pocket an enormous false cardboard nose? . . . Mom's bizarre fur hat is now a crown, but cardboard too, and a sick horse follows us. . . . An antique coach, golden and inlaid with small mirrors . . . behind the gentle tubercular horse that falls and stands up again and pulls the courtly carriage nodding wisely. . . . the laughing crowd throws rotten eggs at us while my mother shows them the sacred rolls of the Ten Commandments. . . . and I awake and I am terrified by my solitude.*

The dreams condense the most archaic and disturbing montage of Cohen's rich imagery. The enormous fake nose both signifies the evil Haman in the Purim carnival and disguises Solal as an old eastern European Jew. Cohen wonders upon awakening: "Why did I take out of my pocket an enormous false cardboard nose?" Having worked through the various metamorphoses of estrangement, we can hazard a well-grounded answer: to be with his mother (or the Valorous and Rachel), Cohen had to disguise himself as either a persecutor or a deformed Jew—either as victimizer or victim. Either way, his sleep in the *écritoire morbide* remains perturbed by these fragments of dreams, which he here in *Le Livre de ma mère* pretends not to understand, but that he fully develops in his fiction, especially in the dwarf Rachel episode in *Belle du Seigneur,* the subject of the next chapter. Louise's cylindrical fur hat metamorphoses into a crown, just as Rachel's hunchback metamorphoses into a crown; and just as with the dwarf Rachel, son and mother ride in a mirror-studded carriage pulled by sickly horses; the crowd derides them, but they hold fast to the Torah, notwithstanding the horse's repeated falls. This is the matrix chronotope in all of Cohen's fiction.

Cohen's question—which he never answers, at least in his essays—might be now specified as: "How is it that I could not imagine being with my mother face-to-face? How is it that I need these props? And to what end?" Cohen asks exactly the right question; in a dialectic of blindness and insight, he connects his mourning dream work with the most archaic and disturbing symbolic montage of his fiction—but leaves it to us to either turn away from its mean-

*Pourquoi ai-je sorti de ma poche un énorme faux nez de carton? . . . La bizarre toque de Maman est maintenant une couronne, mais de carton aussi, et un cheval malade nous suit. . . . Un antique carrosse, dédoré et incrusté de petits miroirs . . . derrière le doux cheval poitrinaire qui tombe et se relève et tire le carrosse de cour avec des hochements sages. . . . la foule nous lance des œufs pourris tandis que ma mère lui montre les rouleaux sacrés des Dix Commandements. . . . et je me réveille et je m'épouvante de ma solitude. (*LM,* 748)

ing or face it. He invites us to connect the dots, while offering yet another regressive fantasy. Only in fantasies can he be reconciled with his mother, just as his protagonist Solal can reconcile himself with his kin and the dwarf Rachel only by playing Joseph or Purim.

But the ultimate identification comes through regressive fantasies. What is most appealing about Louise's love is its absolute unconditionality. This is important, because every woman that Cohen writes of falls short in this respect. "My mother was my mistletoe"*—in other words, a parasite, dependent on its host. His mother would stick by him even if he were to become a quadruple amputee *(un homme tronc),* but Ariane wouldn't. No wonder, then, that normal women would fall short of this infantile demand. Other women's desire is contingent; his mother's is absolute, parasitical in all respects. Yet Cohen knows that there is no return to childhood, even in fantasy. "Your child," he laments to his mother, "died at the same time that you did. Through your death, I was suddenly passed from childhood to old age."† In place of the dead child, the moribund old man, entombed in writing, fancies a new sisterly existence with Louise, which leads us to one of the most delirious hallucinations in Cohen's work of mourning:

> Wide awake, I dream and speak to myself of what it would be like if she were still alive. I would live with her, *in a little way [petitement],* in solitude. A *little* house, beside the sea, far from men. The two of us, she and I, a *little* house a bit crooked, and no one else. A very quiet *little* life without talent. I would make myself a new soul, a *little* old lady's soul like hers so that she should not be bothered by me and so should be completely happy. . . . Two old sisters, she and I . . . two real *little* old ladies. . . . And this is how I imagine paradise.‡

At last, far away from the father and from Europe, the two old women will live in harmony. Gone, therefore, is the Oedipal drama, the tension between Europe and Asia, and, of course, the tension between Judaism and assimilation. The two old sisters will speak in Judeo-Venetian, leaving aside all the awk-

*Ma mère était mon gui. (*LM,* 743)

†Ton enfant est mort en même temps que toi. Par ta mort, me voici soudain de l'enfance à la vieillesse passé. (*LM,* 721)

‡Tout éveillé, je rêve et je me raconte comment ce serait si elle était en vie. Je vivrais avec elle, *petitement,* dans la solitude. Une *petite* maison, au bord de la mer, loin des hommes. Nous deux, elle et moi, une *petite* maison un peu tordue, et personne d'autre. Une *petite* vie très tranquille et sans talent. Je me ferais une âme nouvelle, une âme de *petite* vieille comme elle pour qu'elle ne soit pas gênée par moi et qu'elle soit tout à fait heureuse. . . . Deux vieilles sœurs, elle et moi. . . . deux vraies *petites* vieilles. . . . Et c'est ainsi que j'imagine le paradis. (*LM,* 751–52; emphasis added)

wardness of French. They will unconditionally nurse each other unto death. This bliss is made possible because the differences between them end; identities contract to the asexual feminine of the mother culture. The male-son becomes a woman-sister; the European intellectual trades his aggressive, skeptical masculine soul for that of a naïve old woman. Away from males and their phallic order—the rule of nature, as Cohen terms it—all aggression evaporates and sisterly bliss reigns, whence the repetition of the plural feminine adjective "little" *(petites)* five times. In a world free from the phallic gorilla, everything is lived "petitement." Gone are the aggressive teeth of the castrating father; Louise is described as "an [unweaned] infant, all gums, childish and articulating poorly without her false teeth."* This is finally the total emptying of the Solalic ego.

I am compelled to digress here to the essential and highlight (and foreshadow) the crucial link between this maternal-sisterly fantasy in *Le Livre de ma mère* and Solal's true, but secret, desire in *Belle du Seigneur.* The chiseled, tall, powerful Solal, undersecretary-general of the League of Nations, seduces Ariane, the wife of an underling. Their liaison starts with a sexual frenzy. Yet even during the famous seduction scene at the Ritz, Solal is lucidly eloquent about his disdain of male sexuality: "All these gorilleries," he thinks to himself, "while I would have loved [Ariane] to come sit beside my bed, she in an armchair, and I lying down and holding her hand or the bottom of her dress, and she singing me a lullaby."† And much later in the novel, when sexual infatuation exhausts itself, the narrator confides in us that "[Solal] wanted to kiss her on the cheek. But no, they were lovers, condemned to the lips."‡ Solal does not want to penetrate and devour Ariane. Rather, he wants to be with her in a sisterly and maternal manner, more like a cat, but feels himself condemned to play the part of a male gorilla. In other words, Solal wants to be with Ariane just as Cohen fantasizes about being with Louise: two older women, liberated from the phallic regime, nursing each toward death. Indeed, Solal would like to love Ariane the way she loved her first lover Varvara, whom she tenderly nursed toward a premature death. This is the one absolutely dignified death scene in Cohen's writings. It is also the only true, and covert, love affair in *Belle du Seigneur,* and that feminine love is precisely what Cohen desired for

*un nourrisson tout en gencives, enfantine et prononçant mal sans ses fausses dents (*LM,* 744)

†"Toutes ces gorilleries, alors que j'aurais tant aimé qu'elle [Ariane] vienne s'asseoir auprès de mon lit, elle dans un fauteuil, moi couché et lui tenant la main ou le bas de la jupe, et elle me chantant une berceuse." (*BdS,* 364)

‡[Solal] eut envie de la baiser sur la joue. Mais non, ils étaient des amants, condamnés aux lèvres. (*BdS,* 735)

Louise and himself, had she been among the living—and had the world not been what it was. Cohen's fantasy in *Le Livre de ma mère* is in fact achieved by Ariane in *Belle du Seigneur,* except that the "regime of the real" condemns Solal and Ariane to act out a tragicomic drama where each desires at heart the identical feminine existence but feels compelled to pretend the opposite—condemned to play their respective roles in *The Beauty and the Beast* when each really would like it to be *The Beauty and the Beauty.*

We thus see the dissonant oscillation between two desires: either become his mother's twin sister—a feminized male—or excel in the phallic order of domination and power. At the end of *Le Livre de ma mère,* Cohen seems to opt for the feminine and maternal, even if purely in fantasy. These senior sorority dreams parade deep into the night in his imagination, yet at dawn the specter of repetition comes knocking on the door. What is particularly striking here is Cohen's figurative self-understanding in terms of the Passion, where, in a reversal of the classical typology (so typical of his procedure), the mother is Jesus and the Son, Israel:

> The hours have passed and it is morning, another morning without her. A knock at the door. I rose hastily and looked through the peephole *[le judas].* But it was merely nothing more than a dreadful old woman collecting for charity, notebook in hand. I did not open the door, to punish her. I went back to my table and took up my pen. It ran and I have blue blotches on my hand. She wept, and she asked my forgiveness. "I'll never do it again," she sobbed. Her little hands stained with blue. A woman old and so kind, crying like a little girl, overcome with sobs, is a dreadful thing. I imagine, for a few seconds, that I never caused this scene, that just before beginning my reproaches I took pity on her terrified eyes, and that there were no blue blotches. Alas. And yet I loved her. But I was a son. Sons do not know that their mothers are mortal.*

On the penultimate page of the book, Cohen betrays Louise yet again. He sees the old supplicant woman through the "Judas" in the door. Despite the gentle

*Les heures ont passé et c'est le matin, un autre matin sans elle. On a sonné à la porte. Je me suis levé en hâte et j'ai regardé par le judas. Mais ce n'était qu'une affreuse vieille de bienfaisance, avec son calepin à la main. Je ne lui ai pas ouvert, pour la punir. Je suis revenu à ma table et j'ai repris mon stylo. Il a coulé et j'ai des taches bleues sur la main. Elle pleurait, elle me demandait pardon. "Je ne le ferai plus," sanglotait-elle. Ses petites mains tachées de bleu. Une femme âgée et si bonne, qui pleure comme une petite fille, toute secouée de sanglots, c'est affreux. J'imagine, pendant quelques secondes, que je n'ai pas fait cette scène, que juste avant de commencer mes reproches j'ai eu pitié de ses yeux effrayés, et qu'il n'y a pas eu les taches bleues. Hélas. Et pourtant je l'aimais. Mais j'étais un fils. Les fils ne savent pas que leurs mères sont mortelles. (*LM,* 770; emphasis added)

knocking, his door (heart) remains shut, insolent; he means to punish the supplicant not just avoid her. Meanwhile, on the *écritoire* his quill—instrument of truth and torture—is leaking, and when Cohen picks up the bleeding quill, it drips blue stains onto his hands, which are now tattooed blue just like his mother's. The identity between the respective blue stains *(taches bleues)* imposes itself. And then comes the inner monologue: I (Israel) loved Louise (Jesus), and yet I was simply a rebellious son (stiff-necked people) and did not know that my mother (Savior) was mortal; I looked at her through the Judas, that is, I betrayed her; I could have prevented her humiliation (his crucifixion), but I did not—and, since then, blue ink (red blood) is dripping on me, condemning me to an endless death by writing. *Le Livre de ma mère* concludes with this Christian typology, just like *Solal* and *Belle du Seigneur.*[18]

The only fitting conclusion to this is the first sentence of the book: "Every man is alone and no one gives a damn about anyone and our sorrows are a desert island." Perhaps there are good books built on fine sentiments, but *Le Livre de ma mère* is not one of them.

5 Purim in Berlin

Ambivalent, ambivalent are my sentiments!
Albert Cohen, Belle du Seigneur

The passage quoted just below opens a grotesque novella (chapter 54) placed exactly in the center of *Belle du Seigneur* (pp. 500 to 515 in the 1,000-page Pléiade edition). Up to this point in the novel, Solal, undersecretary-general of the League of Nations, has seduced Ariane, the wife of a lowly subordinate, and rather successfully managed another burlesque intrusion by the Valorous into his glamorous life in the penthouse of the Geneva Ritz Hotel and in the Palace of the League of Nations. The novel also contains hundreds of pages of highly comic and minute descriptions of the political inanity and subtle cruelty of the League of Nations' bureaucracy and the ridiculous mores and affectations of the Swiss bourgeoisie. But what takes place in chapter 54 has nothing to do with any character, place, or situation mentioned previously in the narrative; and, after this chapter, there will be no reference to it for another 360 pages, after which the importance of this episode becomes apparent, though in a very subtle way. Nothing, in short, would have prepared readers when they turn the page to chapter 54 and read the following introductory description:

> Perched on a ladder with a lantern in one hand, the tiny creature examined herself in the mirror on the wall, made faces at her reflection, then rouged her lips, powdered her square face, smoothed her large soot-black eyebrows, licked her finger and with it wet her beauty spot, smiled to herself, finally climbed down, and ran toward the far end of the underground, along walls

> oozing with dampness and bristling with long nails. When she reached the prone man, she struck an elegant pose with one hand on her hip and, smiling clever smiles, hummed a tune. He shuddered, sat up, leaned against a wall, and passed one hand over his blood-soaked forehead.*[1]

Once again, as he has with the Valorous and Ariane, Solal has been playing Purim; this time, however, the identity-as-multiple-disguises game turns violent. While on a diplomatic mission, Solal strolls the streets of Berlin circa 1936 dressed in orthodox Jewish garb. Nazi youths beat him senseless, lacerate a swastika into his chest, and leave him for dead in the street. When Solal regains consciousness, he finds himself in a strange basement, where an articulate but neckless hunchback addresses him—the dwarf Rachel, most haunting of Cohen's characters. What follows in the next fifteen pages is a paroxysm of Cohen's tortured inner dissonance, a narrative that juxtaposes the historical tragedy of the Jewish people with the erotic madness of a repellant dwarf.

This episode is also tightly connected to the crucial last "Purim" dream in *Le Livre de ma mère* and to the expository logic of Ariane's introduction at the beginning of *Belle du Seigneur.* In other words, this Purim in Berlin episode is the fulcrum text in Albert Cohen's work, where the relationship among Louise Coen, Rachel Silberstein, and Ariane Cassandre Corisande d'Auble becomes apparent in all its psychotic dissonance.

In contrast to this Purim in *Belle du Seigneur,* the 1930 Château Saint-Germain episode in *Solal* is represented as a highly stylized dramatic allegory where religious and tribal origins comically clash with political and social ascendancy; where the Jewish subtext of all things Christian and modern finds its perfect architectural and temporal chronotope. With Solal's ultimate resurrection from death, the novel *Solal* leaves open the possibility of a positive historical outcome. But here in Berlin in 1936, this hope dies. Cohen's Berlin underground might be a chilling commentary on Kafka's observation: "There is abundant hope. But there is none for us." The pliability of identities that we have been following runs up against the brutal concreteness of history. Dread is now the absolute real, and there is no longer any room for figurative metamorphosis. Solal's space for identity maneuvers, so playfully portrayed in the

*Juchée sur une échelle et une lanterne à la main, la petite créature s'examina avec des mines dans le miroir pendu au mur, puis rougit ses lèvres, enfarina son visage carré, lissa ses gros sourcils charbonneux, lécha son index pour en humecter son grain de beauté, se sourit, descendit enfin et courut vers l'autre bout de la cave, le long des murs suintants, hérissés de longs clous. Arrivée devant l'homme étendu, elle se mit en posture gracieuse, un poing sur la hanche, fredonna avec des sourires spirituels. Il tressaillit, se souleva, s'adossa au mur, passa la main sur son front ensanglanté. (*BdS,* 500)

seriocomic scenes, slips away. Here in the Berlin basement, the metaphysical, historical, and sexual dimensions should at last morph into a cohesive conscious existence; here, at last, the tortured stranger should once and for all unambiguously embrace his estrangement. *But he does not.* Instead, we have another surprising dichotomy: the absolute assertion of Solal's public solidarity is juxtaposed to inner erotic repulsion.

In order to avoid Nazi persecution, Rachel and her family, the Silbersteins, have moved from the visible part of their Berlin home down into its hidden basement. For all intents and purposes, they have become invisible. Bereft of father and mother, Rachel lives with two uncles; the first is a pious man of learning, the second, a wealthy businessman ("uncle-in-majesty and uncle-in-business"). She also shares the basement with her sister, who is strikingly tall, erect, and beautiful, in contrast to Rachel, as well as altogether "brainless" *(sans cervelle).*

Through her basement window, the dwarf Rachel sees Solal, disguised as an orthodox Jew, beaten senseless by Nazi Brownshirts, and persuades her uncles to drag him into the basement. Her uncles having departed, Rachel puts on a bizarre seduction scene when Solal regains consciousness. The dire situation notwithstanding, the dwarf still pursues her matrimonial quest for "a great doctor." Solal's rescue turns into entrapment at the hands of a sexually predatory woman. He may be just the man Rachel is looking for; the man who can see beyond her repulsive physical deformations and love her for her intelligence and verve, or at least for her wealth. Thus unfold concurrently the drama of hiding from the Nazis and that of handling Rachel's marital and sexual fantasies. All these elements seem allegorical, but history, as we shall see below, collapses the symbolic into the all too real.

The subterranean space where this double drama unfolds resembles a cross among Kafkaesque allegory, Balzacian descriptive plethora (notably as in *La Peau du chagrin*), and Bergmanian mise-en-scène (the Jew's house in *Fanny and Alexander*). When Solal regains consciousness, he notices nails protruding from humid walls, as if there has been much tearing and weeping—they are "weeping walls" *(murs en pleurs).* Divining Solal's perplexity, Rachel explains: "Beautiful, our dark underground, full of nails, our underground! Nails everywhere! Big nails for big tribulations and small nails for small tribulations! They were put there by my uncle-in-business! Fingernails torn out, one nail! An ear sliced off, one nail! It's a pastime, a consolation! There are lots of them, maybe

a hundred! We shall count them together! It's just that you have got to entertain yourself, you have to forget!"*

The nails are there to wound and therefore to remind the underground's inhabitants of the reason for their hiding. Rachel insists that these nails were planted by the "uncle-in-business," grounded in the real, rather than by the "uncle-in-majesty," grounded in the symbolic. And the real must pragmatically inscribe onto flesh the physical truth, which no "majesty" can neutralize by abstraction. Rachel harkens to this ancient truth by reciting a prayer that seeks to explain—and why not outright justify!—all the pains undergone in the history of Israel, at present, most palpably, the swastika slashed onto Solal's chest by the Brownshirts and the omnipresence of the protruding nails. History cuts and bleeds: "Praise to thee, O lord who hath chosen us above all peoples to be the recipients of Thy Holy Law! And so, on every morning of mischief and every evening of despair, we say how joyful we are, how beautiful our lot and how pleasant our fate!"† To stud the walls with sharp nails is to remind the "uncle-in-majesty" that blood is real, that the symbolic difference of which Israel is the depositary extracts a high price. In so doing, the "uncle-in-business" resembles the captain in Kafka's *In the Penal Colony* who insists that for the law to hold true, the executing torture machine must continue churning, punishment and sacrifice must go on. But the dialectic between the two uncles, literally between prayers and nails, is also perverse: the nails, planted deliberately, are masochistic fetishes of the sensual and symbolic kind. Each nail has a specific function: this one is good at cutting ears, the other, good at tearing nails—and all are extremely efficient in reminding those who are "the receptacle of Thy Holy Law" to pay their tribute by the repeated "mischief of each morning" and "despair of each evening." The absurd price of election! In this underground engorged with Christian art, the nails also refer to the heavy studs that nailed Jesus to the cross, except that the victim here is, not a singular subject sacrificed "once and for all," but rather the sacrifice-in-potential of every Jew in each generation. The christological nails studding the Wailing

*Belle, notre cave sombre, pleine de clous, notre cave! Des clous partout! Les grands pour les grands malheurs et les petits pour les petits malheurs! C'est mon oncle de commerce qui les a plantés! Des ongles arrachés, un clou! Une oreille coupée, un clou! C'est un passe-temps, une consolation! Il y en a beaucoup, peut-être cent! Nous les compterons ensemble! Que veux-tu, il faut se divertir, il faut oublier! (*BdS,* 502)

†"Sois loué, Éternel qui nous as choisis entre tous les peuples pour dépositaires de Ta sainte Loi! C'est pourquoi, à chaque matin de malheur et à chaque soir d'angoisse, nous disons combien nous sommes heureux, combien notre part est belle et notre sort agréable!" (*BdS,* 502)

Wall ("weeping walls") thus become the object of a perverse counting ritual: "We shall count them together," Rachel promises Solal with some relish. Knowing the function of each nail, as well as the total number of nails, is a probing symbolic activity, correlating with the piercing of the difference between the human and the divine for which prayers strive. A single and definitive tally is not possible or sufficient. Prayer to God complements the counting of misery. Each nail stands for an event to be known and to be relived, which echoes the imperative of the Passover *Haggadah:* "In every generation each individual is bound to regard himself as if he had personally gone forth from Egypt." Ritual is reiteration. Some reiterations are symbolic, bread for flesh, wine for blood. The nails, however, are cruel and bloody rituals of commemoration that have not yet had the "privilege" of slipping from the event to its symbol. Their sense is not "thrown together" (sym-bol) into a symbolic ritual (the Mass) but rather remains forever all too real in its historical *thereness,* which exacts blood for election—in this case, Solal's blood for his Josephic election (phantasm). In Christianity, the stigmata of martyrs, inflicted by nails, constitute a historical phase limited in time. The stigmata inflicted on the Jews, however, are seemingly eternal.

But the nails also become objects of diversion, venues for forgetting. Again the perversity is layered. On the one hand, the nails constitute a macabre response to the consolatory prayers; they represent objects of deep knowledge and reexperience. On the other hand, however, they also aid the act of forgetting, because they themselves become objects of masochistic and sadistic desire! There is a certain pleasure to be drawn from counting the deeds and preserving the memory of martyrs. This almost sensual aspect of the nightmare (along with the "weeping" walls) is yet another ironic reiteration of iconographic Christian representations of the Passion, with all their inherent aesthetic and erotic ambiguities. The nails, beyond their obvious function in the real, assume their full symbolic weight as instruments of torture and secret delectation. They extend into lived reality the Passion images that hang on the walls of the plethoric underground.

Rachel's father had dealt in art, antiques, and antiquities. When the family descended to the underground, they took their goods with them and continued dealing from the underground. This was a condition for survival, since the landlord kept quiet only as long as his desire for American dollars exceeded his hatred of the Jew. Fabrics, furniture, paintings, statues, and mummies gorge the dark underground. Silent and horrified, Solal follows Rachel on a guided tour of her father's prized possessions. Besides being a depository of the Law

of Moses, the family functions as guardian of multiple symbolic objects (whence the mutually complementary nature of the two uncles); guardians of the very sacred objects of a culture that forced them into the grotto and therefore made them grotesque.

Like Raphael de Valentin in the beginning of *La Peau de chagrin,* Solal is stunned and numbed by what he sees:

> Then she took him by the hand and they walked along the paintings hanging from the weeping walls, she holding the lantern up, naming the artists, and at each picture ordering him with a dig of her heel to admire. But when he stretched out his hand to lift the veil that covered the last painting, she started and grabbed him by the arm. "It's not allowed," she screamed, "You're not allowed to look at She with the Child! You could go to the stake for it!" Drawing him closer to her, she led him past the antique bric-à-brac, suits of armor, mounds of fabrics, ancient dresses, globes of the world, glassware, rugs and statues, making faces as she prattled on about them, giving their prices. All at once, she stopped in front of a tall iron statue, and scratched herself furiously.
>
> "The German Virgin, the Virgin of Nuremberg!" she announced grandiloquently. "It's hollow, my dear!" . . . His mind reeling, she leading him on, periodically turning and leering at him, he walked past chests, armchairs, cabinets and grounded chandeliers, meekly following her while the clocks ticked at different times and while the wax figures smiled, watching over them in the dark. . . . and then raised her lantern over a sarcophagus where a mummy lay.
>
> "Pharaoh too!" she said. "He destroyed us, to the very last one. They destroy us, and then they die!"*

Silent and shaken, Solal accompanies Rachel on her gory tour of the subterranean gallery. She first stops at the covered painting of "She with the Child." For Rachel, this is a taboo painting, a disturbing and threatening representa-

*Puis elle le prit par la main et ils allèrent le long des tableaux suspendus aux murs en pleurs, elle tenant haut la lanterne, nommant les peintres, et à chaque tableau lui ordonnant d'admirer, avec des coups de talon. Mais lorsqu'il avança la main pour soulever le voile qui recouvrait le dernier tableau, elle tressaillit, le saisit par le bras. "Défendu, cria-t-elle, défendu de regarder Celle avec l'Enfant! Danger de bûcher!" Le tirant à elle, elle le promena le long des vieilleries, armures, piles d'étoffes, robes anciennes, mappemondes, verreries, tapis, statues, les commentant avec des moues et en disant les prix. Soudain, elle s'arrêta devant une haute statue de fer, se gratta furieusement.

"La Vierge allemande, la Vierge de Nuremberg! annonça-t-elle avec grandiloquence. Elle est creuse, mon cher!" . . . La tête confuse, mené par elle qui parfois se retournait pour une œillade, il alla le long des coffres, des bergères, des bahuts et des lustres gisant à terre, docilement la suivant cependant que les pendules battaient à contretemps et que les mannequins de cire souriaient, les surveillant dans l'ombre. . . . puis elle approcha sa lanterne d'un sarcophage où reposait une momie.

"Pharaon aussi! dit-elle. Il nous a détruits jusqu'au dernier! Ils nous détruisent jusqu'au dernier et ensuite ils crèvent!" (*BdS,* 509–10)

tion, since she associates the Madonna and Child with autos-da-fé, recalling the long history of forced conversions at the foot of the stake. The veil covering the painting signifies the taboo; unveiling it would be an act of transgression. The painting is so tabooed that it becomes the painting of the unnameable ("she" *[celle]*), yet it is owned and trafficked in by those whom her son long ago supposedly superseded. We cannot overstress the irony here: the "superseded," invisible and Auschwitz-bound, collect and preserve the prized totems of their executioners; totems that are for the most part images of their own ancestors.[2] And yet, the veiled painting is uncannily for Rachel the most desired of images. The painting of the Madonna and Child, after all, depicts a Jewish mother holding a circumcised Jewish infant, and Rachel desires nothing more than to hold in her hands a Jewish baby of her own, just like the Holy Mother.

The disquieting guide and her captive next come up to another figure of the virgin, an unveiled, tall iron statue—the German virgin of Nuremberg, hard yet hollow, unthreatening to Rachel because of its obvious foreignness. Its pointed hollowness is of little use to this woman, who desires marriage and fertility. Thus this statue could never become an object of identification and transference for her. No need therefore to veil it. In a more macabre tone, she explains that the iron virgin was in fact an instrument of torture: "It's hollow, my dear! They used to lock us up inside and the long blades on the door would sink into the Jew!"*

Finally, the two stop before the mummy of a pharaoh, symbol of ancient persecutions. But this archaic Hitler is here reduced to the status of a collectible objet d'art, trafficked in by these same Hebrews he had wished to extinguish and who have outlived him and his culture by over twenty-five centuries. Although cadavers and exhumation are taboo objects in many cultures, the mummy, in a curious reversal, is the least disturbing object here. After all, his case was long ago decided, and at best he deserves a dismissive and triumphal comment. Standing above the preserved cadaver, Rachel comments on Pharaoh (and Hitler): "He destroyed us, to the very last one. They destroy us, and then they die!" Walking through this weeping grotto is akin to touring a museum of Jewish history, although the sanitized surroundings of a normative museum experience cede here to the uncannily grotesque.

This grotto is the stage where Rachel acts out her fantasies. Beyond the apparent chaos of these objets d'art, there is a clear narrative. Her deformation is itself a by-product of history, for, as we now learn, her body and conduct are

*"Elle est creuse, mon cher! Ils nous enfermaient dedans et les longs couteaux de la porte entraient dans le Juif!" (*BdS,* 509)

products of a concrete transmission of violence and resentment. In Rachel's body, the distinction between flesh and history disappears, and all attributes, both physical and psychological, flow from the same blood-stained source. Like Solal's mother, Rachel's mother was raped in a pogrom. It is not clear whether she was raped when she was already pregnant with Rachel or whether she became pregnant as a result of the rape. The latter makes more sense, since it explains the mother's overt hostility toward the fetus. Taking her revenge on this seed of rape implanted in her, the mother imprints her suffering upon the daughter, making her deformed and deranged.[3] First, Rachel declares almost casually, as if it were a matter of archetypal fairytale mother-daughter conflict, "It's my mother who made me small to get revenge."* But then the motives for the cruel vengeance are explained: "In Lodz, there was the pogrom when she was pregnant with me, and so she took her revenge, and I was born small."† Born of violence and blood, Rachel is not only misshapen physically but shows constant potential for violence in her language and gestures. From Solal's point of view, the dwarf Rachel will soon become a fearsome castrating vampire. (It is worth remembering here that this scenario of deformation through anti-Semitic violence repeats in almost identical terms the story of Solal's mother in *Solal.* Both Rachels bear the scars of their violation and subsequent insanity.)

Rachel bears, both in form and gesture, the traces of a collective history, transmitted through the hostile mother. The Berlin grotto forms a perfect setting for the enactment of this deformation because the subterranean bazaar is in itself the message, because memory is objects, thrown together. The pathological joins the macabre when Rachel shows Solal an ear floating in a jar. It is her mother's ear, sliced off by beasts screaming "*Heil* and the name of their German who barks! It's the authentically guaranteed *[garantie]* ear of my dear mother! I keep it ceremoniously in eau-de-vie [clear brandy]."‡ Ironically, the ear is preserved in eau-de-vie, water-of-life—liquid of memory—which reasserts the presence of the hostile mother in every drop of blood in Rachel's veins. The narrator cannot resist a jab at Rachel's shopkeepers' language: it is the "guaranteed" ear of her mother, the way the provenance of a Persian rug might be guaranteed. If the mother took revenge on Rachel by deforming her,

*"C'est ma mère qui m'a faite petite par vengeance!" (*BdS,* 506)

†"À Lodz, il y a eu le pogrome lorsqu'elle était enceinte de moi, et alors elle s'est vengée, et je suis née petite" (*BdS,* 511)

‡"*Heil* et le nom de leur Allemand qui aboie! L'oreille garantie de ma chère maman! Je la conserve cérémonieusement dans l'eau-de-vie" (*BdS,* 505–6)

Rachel returns the favor by making the violated and violating mother ever-present in the jar.

But this mutilated ear also points to a possible typological interpretation. "Suddenly, one of those with Jesus put his hand on his sword, drew it, and struck the slave of the high priest, cutting off his ear. Then Jesus said to him, 'Put your sword back into its place; for all those who take the sword will perish by the sword'" (Matt. 26: 51–53). For Rachel, the mutilated ear is a totem of the history of continual suffering. For Jesus, on the other hand, the mutilated ear, or the violence it results from, is no longer relevant, since his messianic self-sacrifice shepherds humanity from history to utopia: "But how then would the scriptures be fulfilled, which say it must happen in this way?" (Matt. 26: 54).[4] The recalcitrant Jews do not accept this theoretical utopia, and are for better or worse *in* history and *of* history. The suspended ear stands in opposition to the doll that Rachel's sister carries in her arms, most likely a figurine of the Madonna and thus a utopian symbol of procreation without penetration, of sex without violence—of history without the sword. Rachel's doll, on the other hand, is her mother's bloody ear, suspended in the liquid of this "catastrophe of being a Jew." The ear also recalls the symbolism of Purim, where cookies shaped like Haman's ears are eaten by the festive Jews, thus consuming the body of their archenemy in an act of final triumph and vengeance, an act of macabre cannibalism, of which the mother's ear suspended in the jar is a perverse echo.

The Vampire

This nightmarish promenade underground is so overwhelming for Solal that he refuses to speak; during the entire scene, he utters words to Rachel only three times: first, he ritually wishes her a good week *(bonne semaine)* when Rachel pretends that it is the Shabbath. Then, when she demands that he reveal his name, he responds, "Solal Solal," and finally, toward the end of the chapter, once they are both masked and engaged in a Purim ritual, Solal tells her freely that she is beautiful. Otherwise, Solal is encased in silence, if not stupor. From the beginning, Solal perceives Rachel as a vampire. Throughout the scene, she makes explicit references to attacking, biting, and dismembering. "If the person is nice I pounce on him a bit to kiss him, but it's mischievous cuddling,"* she says playfully, and then proclaims euphorically: "I'm

*"si la personne est sympathique je lui saute un peu dessus pour l'embrasser, mais c'est mutin câlin!" (*BdS*, 504)

so proud [to be Jewish] I could bite you!"* She then commands him: "Speak also in praise! Hurry up, or else I'll bite!"† And she adds: "Dwarfs are very dangerous! And beware of their bite!"‡ and later, "[a]nd so I say that I like them ripe or else that I'll bite you."§ The vampire's standards of mutilation worthy of note are so high that she dismisses Solal's bleeding swastika stigmata as "'marks, nothing really! Nothing worth a jar !' (She held her nose . . .)."||

Ever perceptive and vigilant, Solal notes these blatant warnings and constantly remains on guard against a possible assault: "He stood back and let her walk ahead, realizing all of a sudden that if she stayed at his rear she would be tempted by the nape of his neck, would start screaming with fear, pounce at his neck, bite him perhaps."# Solal is so terrified that he walks behind her, lest he also become an object in an exhibit suspended in a jar in this grotesque museum. Solal is obviously torn apart here, in a figurative sense this time. His persona, his main life-narrative, his political fantasy, is that of a Joseph-like savior of the Jewish people. For him, Rachel would then be a heroine of survival and dignity, potential subject of his political guile. He would like to identify with her for her sense of difference vis-à-vis the bloodthirsty "beasts" who march above. He would like to see through and beyond Rachel's madness and ugliness, to forget the disfigurements, to suffer them with her, to pretend that only the eyes count: "Well, what do you think?" . . . "After all, only the eyes count! And don't mock my hunchback! It's a crown in my back"** When Rachel stands over the mummy in triumph, Solal shares with her the collective, tribal pride of having survived: "Saying nothing his head still throbbing, he smiled out of pride, became like her, [he] knew it."†† In the abstract, the identification is full. But in the very next sentence, Rachel inspires disgust in Solal: "Suddenly, her damp little hand revolted him, but he did not dare brush it away, lest she retaliate."‡‡ The Jew-to-Jew identification, or more precisely

*"J'ai envie de mordre tellement je suis fière!" (*BdS*, 510)

†"Dis aussi louange! Vite, sinon je mords!" (*BdS*, 505)

‡"Les naines sont terribles et gare à la morsure!" (*BdS*, 506)

§"Alors je dis que je les aime à point ou bien que je te mordrai" (*BdS*, 512)

||"mais des marques, c'est peu de chose! Rien pour un bocal!" (Elle se pinça les narines . . .) (*BdS*, 507)

#Il la laissa passer devant lui, sachant tout à coup que si elle restait derrière lui elle aurait la tentation de la nuque, se mettrait à hurler de peur, lui sauterait au cou, le mordrait peut-être. (*BdS*, 510–11)

**"Qu'en dis-tu?" . . . "Après tout, seuls les yeux comptent! Et ne te moque pas de ma bosse! Elle est une couronne dans mon dos!" (*BdS*, 509)

††Muet, le crâne en douleur, il souriait d'orgueil, devenait comme elle, le savait. (*BdS*, 510)

‡‡Soudain la petite main humide le dégoûta, mais il n'osa pas s'en détacher, craignant une lubie de représailles. (*BdS*, 510)

here, that of Jewish savior to Jewish victim, persists only so long as it remains abstract. The mirrors hanging all around the walls of the underground call Solal into total identification and transference with the Rachels of the world. The mirror is a calling and a reminder; a calling for the archetypal face-to-face encounter, as well as for the answerability to the call: "Here I am"—present with you in this mirror. "'Take a look at yourself!' she cried in a wild frenzy, once more holding out her mirror to him. 'That's what living outside can do to you, idiot! Now, down to the underground, Jew! You'll like it with me around.'"* But Solal recoils from this identification, from transferring his desire onto Rachel, from actual physical contact with her. Only the fear of Rachel's castrating vampirism deters him from fleeing at once. Juxtaposed here in the most concrete sense are the two fundamental drives in Solal: the first toward identification with his kin as a collective whole (note that Solal is dressed in Orthodox Jewish garb), the second toward aesthetic and libidinous desires for individuated Aryan women. The narrator, however, will now bring the two women together: "Then from the shadows she appeared, tall and marvelous of face, sovereign Virgin, living Jerusalem, beauty of Israel, hope in the night, a sweet mad creature with extinguished eyes, moving slowly on, an old doll in her arms, which she rocked and from time to time looked down upon."†

Rachel's sister is laconic in language and passive in nature; she is instead mute and blind. Is she, like her sister, an allegory for yet another permutation of Jewish madness or rather a thinly veiled allegory for a sister religion . . . Christianity? The latter seems more likely. All her features are symbolically laden with theological double entendres: she is a "sovereign virgin," the "living Jerusalem made flesh—as opposed to the "ossified Jerusalem"—and she cuddles an old doll, most likely a representation of the Virgin Mary. Seeing this, Rachel explains, "She's wrong . . . she believes that it's the Law."‡ Rachel knows the Law but is deprived of a desirable body: "As for me, I am hunchbacked and yet I am a daughter of man!"§ Her sister mistakes an idol for God, but possesses a desirable body. Contemplating both sisters, Solal experiences

*"'Regarde-toi!', cria-t-elle avec une farouche frénésie, et de nouveau elle lui tendit son miroir. 'Voilà ce que c'est de vivre dehors, écervelé! Dans la cave, Juif! Tu seras bien avec moi.'" (*BdS,* 511)

†Alors, sortie de l'ombre, elle apparut, haute et merveilleuse de visage, vierge souveraine, Jérusalem vivante, beauté d'Israël, espoir dans la nuit, douce folle aux yeux éteints, lentement allant, une ancienne poupée dans ses bras, la berçant et parfois sur elle se penchant. (*BdS,* 514)

‡"Elle s'est trompée . . . elle croit que c'est la Loi." (*BdS,* 514)

§"Moi j'ai une bosse, mais je suis fille humaine!" (*BdS,* 503)

attraction to and repulsion from each of them. Does Rachel's sister refer in fact to the blonde, Aryan, Christian Ariane, the real *Belle du Seigneur*?[5] After all, this is a chapter central to a novel whose title is *Belle du Seigneur.* And titles are not gratuitous. Is Rachel the real *Belle du Seigneur,* not of the narcissistic and dissonant Solal-as-Seigneur, but of the real Seigneur? But the blind blonde quickly fades into the grotto and a dramatic deus ex machina will temporarily resolve Solal's ambivalence. It is time for the grotesque carnival!

Purim

As noted in Chapter 2, Purim (*La fête des Sorts* in Cohen) is the Jewish carnival. It contains all the elements typical of carnivals as described by Mikhail Bakhtin, but with an important difference. Whereas in all other cultures the carnival serves a homeostatic normative function (inversions of hierarchies and gender, temporary decrowning, etc.), in the Jewish context, it is also, if not principally, an annual reenactment of a survival narrative, a narrative of collective fate, first and foremost a ritualistic celebration of *Holocaust avoidance.* At least three times (Sarai, Joseph, Esther), the nation of Israel has avoided extinction thanks to the actions of seductive, charismatic court Jews. Purim simply reiterates in carnivalesque performance what these narratives signify in words.

But here in the Berlin underground circa 1936, this particular narrative-performance is exhausted. No Jewess is about to seduce Hitler into letting her people go. In Germany, the Jews will be burnt—fate(s) is not plural, not open to possibilities; here in Berlin, as Rachel asserts, fate has already been decided. The future will be a repetition of the past, and the present is just an agonizing wait for the seemingly inevitable: "They burnt us in the thirteenth century! They will burn us in the twentieth! There is no salvation for us, understand this, my dear! They love their nasty leader, the barking one with the moustache!"* Stripped of any redeeming historical value, this Purim act simply provides the carnivalesque scene for yet another of Solal's doublings, masqueradings, and desperate acts of reconciliation—all of which are impotent gestures en route to suicide. At the beginning of the nightmare, Solal is already in the customary Purim orthodox Jewish garb, which leads to his being beaten and then his convalescence in Rachel's grotto. Now, despite his being horrified and revolted by Rachel, he nevertheless finds a ritual narrative that will unite the two, thereby finally joining her desire and his. Such is the purpose of the

*"Ils nous ont brûlés au treizième siècle! Ils nous brûleront au vingtième siècle! Il n'y a pas de salut pour nous, sache-le, mon cher! Ils adorent leur méchant chef, l'aboyeur avec la moustache!" (*BdS,* 509–10)

Purim act here, and the text certifies that Purim functions as a deus ex machina. Solal and Rachel act in pure symbolic time, a carnivalesque suspension of historical time. Rachel invites Solal to play Shabbath for its holiness and later to play Purim for its historical irony—and this is in fact the first suggestion made by Rachel to which Solal freely assents. Solal's prior actions and words were coerced by the vampire. Notice the predatory, castrating verbs in the two sentences, which immediately precede the explicit introduction of Purim: "She opened the sparkling door, with many mirrors, *shoved him in with both hands, forced* him into the seat, *climbed up* beside him, and in turn sat down. For pleasure *she swung* her little legs, [then] stopped suddenly and *motioned him to be quiet.*"*

Solal is terrorized by two things: first by the vampire dwarf, then by what takes place above the underground in the streets of Berlin, where the Nazi youth march to the martial beat of drums and trumpets, singing "Wenn Judenblut unter'm Messer spritzt" (When Jewish blood gushes from under the knife). Rachel and Solal hear and feel the pulsating presence of the bloodthirsty beasts above, as reality physically beats down upon the underground outcasts, as real-time Nazi history is closing in on the symbolic time of Shabbath and Purim. In these extreme circumstances, Purim truly constitutes this "temporary liberation from the prevailing truth and from the established order" that Bakhtin emphasizes—only, alas, on a much darker note.[6]

> "Can you hear them outside? They are happy to march to music, the idiots. Whereas we in a royal coach! Oh, my beautiful underground, oh, high destiny, oh, dearest nails! Now will you please enjoy yourself? We have masks for the feast of Lots [Purim], masks bought before I was born! Imagine how young I must be! You want a good laugh? We have games for the feast of Lots! Look!" she cried in a vibrant voice, and, bending down, produced from under the seat a cardboard crown decorated with fake rubies and put it on her head. "On the feast of Lots, I have always been Queen Esther, I was thankful to my father's delight! And for you, here, a false nose for you to rejoice! In what, do you know, ignorant? in the death of Haman, understand it! . . . Come on, put your false nose on!"
>
> He obeyed and she clapped as he stroked the grotesque cardboard appendage, gloriously, he stroked it.†

*Elle ouvrit la portière étincelante de nombreux miroirs, *le poussa à deux mains,* le *força* à s'asseoir sur la banquette, *se hissa* auprès de lui, s'assit à son tour. D'aise, elle balança ses petites jambes, s'arrêta soudain, *lui fit signe de se taire.* (*BdS,* 512; emphasis added)

†"Tu les entends dehors? Ils sont contents de marcher derrière une musique, les imbéciles! Tandis que nous, en carrosse royal! Ô ma cave belle, ô grand destin, ô clous chéris! Maintenant veux-tu être gai?

In all carnivals, the mask allows temporary detachment from the real. In Rachel's case, it is a liberation from both her image in the mirror and Nazi time. The mask allows one to assume a more transitive identity or even to proceed to an ironic reversal of identities. We have already studied the extensive deployment of masks in Cohen's fiction, where they facilitate a comic transition from identity to identity; insider to outsider, beauty to ugliness and vice versa. Thus, the deformed dwarf Rachel becomes the seductive concubine Esther, and Solal, the charismatic seducer, wears the long, disgraceful nose of Haman. Once engaged in this decrowning and role reversal, with respect both to the Nazi beasts aboveground and to Rachel, Solal finally surrenders himself to his mask: "He stroked the grotesque cardboard appendage, gloriously, he stroked it." Solal then is finally at ease with Rachel. Not, however, as Solal and Rachel, the real individuated beings, but masked as the evil Haman and the gorgeous Esther. Only then can she entice him into accepting himself as a Jew with her and caress his grotesque appendage.

And so, holding each other by the hand, "queen and king of sad carnival" (*reine et roi de triste carnaval* [513]) looking toward the nail-studded walls of the underground and feeling the pulsating presence of the Nazi youth marching above, they mount a royal carriage to which are harnessed two old white horses. Not surprisingly, the door of the royal carriage is inlaid with many mirrors, lest Solal forget. The mirror forces vigilance! This is the precise moment when the narrator shifts the focalization of the narrative from a surreal, but detached, perspective to an emphatic point of view.

> Seated beside him once more in the coach, in sober mood, Rachel the midget was plucking the strings of another guitar, from which she drew sad strains, and from time to time glanced at him shrewdly. Him, he watched her and felt pity, pity for this small deformed one with the large eyes, beautiful eyes of her people, pity for the crazed little one, heiress of age-old fears and the misshapen fruit of those fears, pity for this hump, and in his soul he revered the hump, hump of fears and sweats of fear, sweats through the ages and expectations of sorrow, sweats and anxieties of a hunted people, his

---

Nous avons des masques pour la fête des Sorts, des masques achetés avant ma naissance! Pense si je suis jeune! Veux-tu rire? Nous avons des jeux pour la fête des Sorts! Regarde!" cria-t-elle d'une voix vibrante, et elle se pencha, ramassa sous la banquette une couronne de carton, ornée de faux rubis, se la posa sur sa tête. "À la fête des Sorts, je faisais toujours la reine Esther, j'étais gracieuse, délice de mon père! Et pour toi, voilà, un faux nez pour te réjouir! Sais-tu de quoi, ignorant? De la mort d'Aman, apprends-le! . . . Allons, mets ton faux nez!"

Il obéit, et elle battit des mains tandis qu'il caressait le grotesque appendice de carton, glorieusement le caressait. (*BdS,* 512)

> people and his love, the ancient people marked by genius, crowned with grief, with regal knowledge and disillusionment, his mad old king walking alone in the storm and bearing its Law, a harp resounding through the dark hurricane of the centuries, and immortally its madness for grandeur and persecution.*

As Solal detaches Rachel's deformity from its concrete reality in the world of individuated desire and understands her as an abstraction, a masked actor in a carnival, an allegory of the Jewish disfigurement resulting from millennia of persecutions, he finally unambiguously embraces his Jewish identity ("unflagging son of his people"). He identifies with Rachel the Jew and transfers onto her the pity that he also harbors for himself, because of this mutual "catastrophe of being a Jew." Another key narrative shift happens on this climactic page when the author's voice overtakes that of the narrator and refers directly to the "chant of *my* king David." Here again, as was the case with the Château Saint-Germain in *Solal,* we have a significant intersection of perspectives, where the discourses of author, narrator, and character are juxtaposed in a hybridized and dissonant narrative.

But if there is reconciliation here between Solal and Rachel, it is only on the abstract, collective level. Solal does not sit with Rachel in the carriage as a man would with a woman. Instead, they are united as brother and sister, siblings, and thus subject to a Father: "[T]hey sat holding hands in the ancient coach, he with his false nose, she with her cardboard crown, *brother and sister,* holding each other tightly by the hand, queen and king of some sad carnival. . . . And look the dwarf removed her crown and puts it on the head of *her brother* whose eyes were closed."† Their union is decidedly unerotic; what allows it to happen is the play-acting warranted by the carnival, warranted by the shift from "sister and brother" to "queen and king." The masks allow Solal to detach himself from his own narcissism, thus enabling him to overcome his

*De nouveau assise auprès de lui dans le carrosse, sérieuse, la naine Rachel promenait ses doigts sur une autre guitare, en tirait des mélancolies, avec parfois vers lui un regard perspicace. Lui, il la considérait et il avait pitié, pitié de cette petite difforme aux grands yeux, beaux yeux de son peuple, pitié de cette petite insensée, héritière de peurs séculaires, et de ces peurs le fruit contrefait, pitié de cette bosse, et en son âme il révérait cette bosse, bosse des peurs et des sueurs de peur, sueurs d'âge en âge et attentes de malheurs, sueurs et angoisses d'un peuple traqué, son peuple et son amour, le vieux peuple de génie, couronné de malheur, de royale science et de désenchantement, son vieux roi fou allant seul dans la tempête et portant sa Loi, harpe sonnante à travers le noir ouragan des siècles, et immortellement son délire de grandeur et de persécution. (*BdS,* 513)

†[I]ls se tinrent par la main dans l'antique carrosse, lui avec son faux nez, elle avec sa couronne de carton, *frère et sœur,* se tinrent fort par la main, reine et roi de triste carnaval. . . . Et voici, la naine ôta sa couronne et la posa sur la tête de *son frère* aux yeux clos (*BdS,* 513; emphasis added)

revulsion from Rachel as a woman, as a potential erotic object, and to participate with her in a collective carnivalesque reenactment of a ritual narrative. It is toward God the Father that their union is aimed and definitely not toward each other as desiring individuals.[7]

Once this gesture of sibling reconciliation is made and the deafening sound of the marching Nazi youth merges into the supplicating chant of the Jews praying in the nearby underground, Rachel crowns the wounded, bleeding Solal with her cardboard Esther-crown. Again, notice the ironical telescoping of all these archetypal figures: Solal as the wounded and bleeding Jesus of the Passion (same as at the end of *Solal*) and a feminine cardboard crown (of a "queen") as a crown of thorns. Rachel then covers Solal's shoulders with a blue-and-white prayer shawl *(talit)* and places the Torah in his hands. In other words, the bleeding evil Haman, whom we recognize by his long nose, is crowned like Jesus and is then covered by the *talit* and given the Torah to hold. And there, from the belly of the underground, after play-acting Purim with the dwarf Rachel, Solal, silently and majestically, hoists the Torah scrolls into the air. But the Torah is hoisted in the underground while above, in the streets, those who worship force parade in martial cadence. This gesture is at once majestic and impotent: majestic in its affirmation of the Law, impotent in its acknowledgement of hopelessness, for the miracle of Purim is not to be reenacted in Berlin. And Solal, the Mediterranean sun man, must now hide in the dark underground and participate in grotesque parodies with the dwarf Rachel, stalling for a time the inevitable banging on the door of the Brownshirts.

But here is the crux of the matter: this mocking scene, this Via Dolorosa writ large, this defiant parade in a royal carriage drawn by sickly horses, seated next to a woman one does not desire, while hoisting the Torah to a jeering crowd of Jew haters is the *core and often repeated montage* in Solal's series of identity phantasms. This montage, for example, recalls in precise terms and tone the scenario that haunts Cohen's dreams as he mourns his mother, Louise Coen. Only now, having understood all the mythological and historical dynamics (Joseph and Esther), as well as Cohen's core ambivalence about his mission and his people—only now in the repetition of this scenario at the heart of *Belle du Seigneur,* can we appreciate in full the import of this nightmare crowning *Le Livre de ma mère.* This repetition is so striking that it warrants requoting in full:

> Why did I take out of my pocket an enormous false cardboard nose? . . . Mom's bizarre fur hat is now a crown, but of cardboard also, and a sick horse follows us. . . . An antique coach, golden and inlaid with small mir-

> rors . . . behind the gentle tubercular horse that falls and stands up again and pulls the courtly carriage nodding wisely . . . the crowd that throws rotten eggs while my mother shows them the sacred rolls of the Ten Commandments . . . and I awake and I am terrified by my solitude.*

I have always suspected that the dwarf Rachel bears a relationship to Louise Coen (as is also the case with the wormlike mother named Rachel in *Solal*), that the visit to the Berlin Jews and to the dwarf is not unrelated to visits by Cohen, imaginary or real, desired or dreaded, to his parents, if not during the 1930s then perhaps during the early 1940s, when Marseille was under the Franco-German fascist boot.[8] At any rate, the astonishing repetition of the identical Purim scenarios at the most painful moment in Cohen's autobiography-as-mourning and at the heart of *Belle du Seigneur* should clue us into a very fundamental dynamic in Cohen's works. But let us return to *Belle du Seigneur.*

Our Purim play now ends. Grotesque stage, baffling actors, macabre plot, and carnivalesque dénouement all merge into one horrific montage where the historical real subsumes textual desire for infinite metamorphic play; a montage where the sun (Solal) sets in the Berlin underground. Such is the power of this montage that brings Solal's successive metamorphoses of estrangement to a catastrophic end. In the end, comic relief can negotiate hard reality only partially; in the end, and especially in extreme situations, identity is either embraced by the subject or tattooed onto him by the Brownshirts; in the end, Berlin, 1936, puts an end to Solal's phantasm of *being of the Jews but otherwise.*

This face-to-face becomes a hand-in-hand, because the faces of both Solal and Rachel are turned toward God, ironically turned upward, from the underground toward the Nazi boots pounding above. In the hand-in-hand, Solal accepts Rachel's essence as a Jew, leaving aside the contingent factors of her deformity and homicidal insanity. As an individual, she becomes an abstraction: as kin-in-covenant, she occupies her rightful place beside him facing up toward the Lord, but, also, simultaneously facing up toward the marching

*Pourquoi ai-je sorti de ma poche un énorme faux nez de carton?. . . . La bizarre toque de Maman est maintenant une couronne, mais de carton aussi, et un cheval malade nous suit. . . . Un antique carrosse, dédoré et incrusté de petits miroirs . . . derrière le doux cheval poitrinaire qui tombe et se relève et tire le carrosse de cour avec des hochements sages. . . . la foule nous lance des œufs pourris tandis que ma mère lui montre les rouleaux sacrés des Dix Commandements . . . et je me réveille et je m'épouvante de ma solitude. (*LM,* 748)

Brownshirts. The scene is modulated by Solal's revulsion, Rachel's vampirism and delirium and, most important, by their ritualistic reconciliation through the mask of Purim. The hand-in-hand mediated through the carnival allows their identities, foreign but finally not mutually exclusive, to unite in a carnivalesque affirmation of the Law in the most physical sense, that is, in the hoisting of the Torah scrolls. Thus they are engaged together in an activity that transcends erotic differences. To allow this reconciliation, a shift from the *eye* to the *hand* had to occur. To hold is less of an engagement than to gaze directly into someone's eyes. The eye-to-eye is a crucial moment in Hebrew Scripture: in the *panim el panim,* the full weight of *alterity* is upon us. And that eye-to-eye was impossible for Solal until the very end: "Ambivalent, ambivalent are my sentiments!" Rachel says, but echoed by Solal all along.

This Berlin underground signals the end of a cycle in Cohen's fiction, which began with his childhood fantasies about hiding with his imaginary playmate Viviane and now ends just before the Shoah. This last underground, full of pathos and devoid of comedy and irony, points to a certain poetic limit where the chronotope meets its concrete analog in the nightmare of the real. Cohen's text struggles with a poetic representation of this lived torment. In the Berlin underground, the textual utopia, a world of signs pointing toward infinite permutations, is defeated by historical necessity: the playfulness of multiple identities butts against the real pressure of history.[9] Whereas the Château Saint-Germain drama in *Solal* ends in his Jesus-like resurrection, *Belle du Seigneur* ends in a double suicide. After the Berlin underground, the novel drifts toward the inevitable suicide, as the utopia of the text cedes to the dystopia of the historical and the textual tension among all these dissonant voices—the messianic, the erotic, the burlesque—finally comes to naught faced with the unthinkable.

Rachel and Ariane

Critics have asserted with reason that the episode of the Berlin underground is the counterpart of the Château Saint-Germain underground in the earlier novel *Solal.*[10] But the Berlin underground has another, more pertinent and much more revealing counterpart, namely, the very first scene of *Belle du Seigneur* in which Solal endeavors to seduce Ariane through a series of burlesqueries. Solal fell in love with Ariane at first sight at a diplomatic reception. He begins to spy on her at the villa on the chic outskirts of Geneva where she lives with her husband, Adrien Deume (a Class B bureaucrat at the League of Nations), and his parents. The first page of the novel contains a picaresque scene in which Solal rides his steed toward the villa, intending to win Ariane's heart and then carry her away on a horse. But first a moral experiment must be carried out to ascertain whether this woman is in fact the elected one or not, whether she is the one woman who will make his life worthwhile and thus allow him to cancel or at least postpone his suicide. This experiment consists in disguising himself as a hunchbacked old Hassidic Jew with a heavily accented, raspy voice, then breaking in through Ariane's bedroom window to catch her unawares—and finally attempting to seduce her as an old Jew representing the glory of Israel! And if she is seduced by the grotesque old man, she will then be worthy of election, of being the princess of humanity instead of a princess of baboonery. That is Solal's wager, the moral experiment to which Ariane is subjected.

This first scene of *Belle du Seigneur* is of interest to us because, despite what may appear as obvious differences, it mirrors the exact expository and ethical logic of the Berlin underground. In both episodes, Solal disguises himself three times and penetrates a woman's space, bringing about a grotesque seduction scene in which the mirror finally acts as the place of ultimate truth. Solal, for whom Purim's customs, masks, and self-dramatization constitute the fundamental phenomenology of his being, is first introduced in *Belle du Seigneur* as a Don Juan riding high in the saddle, stripped to the waist, "a towering seigneur with high boots" (*haut seigneur aux longues bottes* [7]), accompanied by a footman carrying a suitcase in one hand and leading a horse with the other. (This is also an exact reprise of Solal riding away on horseback in the last scene of the novel *Solal.*) So Don Juan is the first costume. Next, once in the house, he opens the suitcase and takes out his second costume—that of the Hassidic Jew, a "dilapidated old coat and a hat of moth-eaten fur, white beard" (*vieux manteau délabré et une toque de fourrure mitée* [8–9]). However, Solal still manages to include the honorific diplomatic necktie *(cravate de commandeur)* in his Hassidic costume, sign of his high political station, which is also his third disguise—that of Solal the "gros poisson," undersecretary-general of the League of Nations. Now, returning to the episode with Rachel, we recall that Solal arrives in Berlin as a diplomat (he often refers to his position as phony role-playing, Solal as the "under-buffoon general");[11] he then disguises himself as a Hassidic Jew who wanders the streets of Berlin, and finally, once he is in the underground, Rachel disguises Solal as the evil Haman. He is thus triply disguised in both scenes.

But the similarities go much deeper. Solal disguises himself and then breaks into the villa and attempts to seduce Ariane for the openly stated purpose of ascertaining whether she can morally and aesthetically overcome her repulsion from ugliness and yield to repulsive Israel in the guise of Solal in his Purim costume. Solal wants to know whether Ariane can become the Madonna who will absolve *(racheter)* the sins of men, which consist of the adoration of beauty, which is nothing else but adoration of power, and, ultimately, of the power to kill. Were she to yield to Solal in his hideous disguise, she would indeed become the elected one. She would then make life worthy of living. Should she succeed, Solal, who contemplates suicide from the first page, will indefinitely postpone killing himself, while should she fail, and therefore force the routine machinery of seduction, Ariane will only serve to postpone the inevitable suicide. Ariane "fails" her test; she throws a glass at Solal's face. The seduction will therefore be banal and the suicide certain.

But flip this scene around and you have the precise logic of the Berlin underground. In Berlin, Solal is the "idiotic" Ariane who is horrified by Rachel's ugliness and deformity; Solal experiences Ariane's inability to desire the hunchback. In brief, Solal disgusts Ariane just as the dwarf Rachel disgusts Solal. Just like Ariane later on, Solal will need the pretext of Purim to surrender to Rachel in the underground carriage covered with mirrors. In Berlin, Solal is put to the test as Ariane was at the beginning of *Belle du Seigneur.* The Berlin episode is thus a nightmarish version of the picaresque parody of the first Geneva episode. The two are but a single montage with variable elements, in which identity and difference morph into opposites—but the same logic operates throughout.

On the formal level, both Ariane and Rachel are respectively narcissistic and masochistic doubles of Solal. This accounts for the fundamental differences between the two scenes, notwithstanding their formal symmetry. From his first encounter with Ariane, Solal drowns in her image, while Rachel repels him until the very last moment where, in a ceremonial carriage under the shadow of the Torah, and in costume for this sad Purim carnival, she becomes tolerable as a tribal abstraction, tolerable as a simulated sacramental name (Esther), tolerable in this incessant dialectic of calling and reminding. As for Ariane, she is loved for what she is on the most individuated level, Solal's sensual double. With the vampire Rachel, Solal always fears being bitten and bled, while, from the first moment with Ariane, he desires to suck the marrow of her subjectivity, in which he sees a feminine version of himself. Upon entering Ariane's bedroom window, he looks in the mirror at himself and sees a man good-looking enough to make one vomit. A few pages later, Ariane looks in the mirror and sees "the most beautiful woman in the world" *(la plus belle femme du monde).** No need here for the mediation of the Torah: subjective narcissism largely suffices. The identification in the mirror is complete, spontaneous . . . natural—and therefore, alas, the true one—or, at least, the consciously desired one. The very syntax of the passage describing their encounter shows how Solal spontaneously melts into Ariane, dives within himself. Note all the terms of equivalence; note how pronouns, markers of difference, slip into ontological identity, most obviously through the reiteration of "like me."

> That night at the Ritz, night of destiny, she appeared before me, appeared noble among the ignoble, frighteningly beautiful, she and I and no one else in this mob of ambitious social climbers *[réussisseurs]* . . . the two of us the only exiles, she alone like me, and like me unhappy and scorning and speaking to no one, a friend only to herself, and with the first beat of her eyelids I knew her. It was her, the unexpected and the expected, at once elected during this evening of destiny, elected with the first beat of her long curved eyelashes.†

> And even more explicitly, repeating the myth of Narcissus:

> Voluntarily banished like me, and she did not know that from behind the curtains I was watching her. Then, listen, she drew close to the mirror of the parlor, because she is obsessed with mirrors like me . . . and then . . . she drew close to the mirror and kissed her lips on the mirror. Our first kiss, my love. O my mad sister. Loved on the spot, my beloved on the spot by this kiss she gave to herself.‡

In her implied narcissism, Ariane already loves Solal, without knowing it.[12] In her narcissism, she is at once loved and condemned—victim, as it were, of Solal's ambivalence about his very self. The struggle with Ariane, detailed *in fine*

*beau à vomir (*BdS,* 9); "[l]a plus belle femme du monde" (*BdS,* 34)

†"En ce soir du Ritz, soir de destin, elle m'est apparue, noble parmi les ignobles apparue, redoutable de beauté, elle et moi et nul autre en la cohue des réussisseurs . . . nous deux seuls exilés, elle seule comme moi, et comme moi triste et méprisante et ne parlant à personne, seule amie d'elle-même, et au premier battement de ses paupières je l'ai connue. C'était elle, l'inattendue et l'attendue, aussitôt élue en ce soir de destin, élue au premier battement de ses longs cils recourbés." (*BdS,* 38)

‡Volontaire bannie comme moi, et elle ne savait pas que derrière les rideaux je la regardais. Alors, écoutez, elle s'est approchée de la glace du petit salon, car elle a la manie des glaces comme moi . . . et alors . . . elle s'est approchée de la glace et elle a baisé ses lèvres sur la glace. Notre premier baiser, mon amour. Ô ma sœur folle, aussitôt aimée, aussitôt mon aimée par ce baiser à elle-même donné. (*BdS,* 38–39)

for hundreds of pages, delineates intimate differences between Solal and Ariane, while the short and abrupt struggle with Rachel, on the contrary, locates an abstract grounding for identity and for political action—but that is it. Ariane is an erotic and narcissistic doubling phantasm—Rachel, a nightmarish one. And in the body of Solal, the two will be united, in a searing dissonance, the outcome of which can only be death.

Joseph the Pariah

In chapter 94, some 360 pages after the Berlin episode (chapter 54), we finally learn the details of what happened to Solal subsequent to his stay in the Silbersteins' underground in Berlin. Solal is here in deep meditation, delving into delirious streams of consciousness, commencing with the story of his political demise, while watching Ariane stitching hems that he deliberately undid in order to give her a purpose in life (*un but de vie* [872]):

> but even so some day I'll confess to you [Ariane] perhaps all about the Silbersteins' cellar, I wanted to stay on with them but they asked me to save them so on the fourth day I left only to fail in each and every capital failed in London failed in Washington failed in the Council of their damned L of N when I asked the self-important clowns to take in my Germans Jews to divide them among themselves, they said my plan was utopian that if they took them all there would be an upsurge of anti-Semitism in the countries that accepted them in other words they threw them to their butchers because they loathe anti-Semitism for which I arraigned both them and their love-thy-neighbor cant O great Christ betrayed whereupon ructions and to put it simply I was turfed out as the Forbes woman put it ignominiously instant dismissal for conduct prejudicial to the interests of the League of Nations said the letter Old Cheyne wrote to me and then followed the decree rescinding my nationality on grounds of procedural irregularity*

*mais une fois tout de même je t'avouerai peut-être la cave Silberstein, je voulais rester longtemps avec eux mais ils m'ont demandé de les sauver alors je suis parti le quatrième jour j'ai échoué dans les capitales échoué à Londres échoué à Washington échoué devant le Conseil de leur Essdéenne quand j'ai demandé aux importants bouffons d'accueillir mes Juifs allemands de se les répartir, ils ont dit que mon projet était utopique que si on les acceptait tous il y aurait une montée d'antisémitisme dans les pays d'accueil bref c'est par horreur de l'antisémitisme qu'ils les ont abandonnés à leurs bourreaux, alors je les ai mis en accusation eux et leur amour du prochain ô grand Christ trahi alors scandale et bref chassé ignominieusement comme a dit la Forbes renvoi sans préavis pour conduite préjudiciable aux intérêts de la Société des Nations a précisé la lettre du vieux Cheyne ensuite le décret annulant ma naturalisation pour cause d'irrégularités (*BdS,* 873)

Everything in the seemingly baroque plotline of *Belle du Seigneur* becomes at once historically and politically coherent, ironically through the most incoherent of literary devices—the stream of consciousness. Of course, from the beginning Solal knew that the League of Nations was a charade, a cynical bureaucracy serving its own interests, when not outright those of the colonial powers. But this pompous institution served his own purpose of escaping the ghetto of his kin and belonging to the Social, the coveted world of the European Gentiles *(en être),* and even his burning desire to exercise power, notwithstanding all of his protestations to the contrary. Succeed and lie low was the motto; wait for the "myself later on" *(moi de plus tard),* promised to us in the earlier novel *Solal,* to come forward and succor his kin. Having risen so far so fast, there was no one better qualified than he to assess the true nature of this institution, which explains in part why he is so distraught, even suicidal, from the very beginning of the novel. Although at the apex of his power, a true "under-buffoon general" of the world government of sorts, a true Joseph-like viceroy—viceroy, yes, but of the "house of memos" *(la maison du papier)*—his power was limited to palace intrigue and various other hierarchical babooneries, and never employed in effective diplomacy. In other words, he was bound to be a failed Joseph, his pharaohs being impotent golf-playing clowns, interested more in securing their retirements than in fashioning an effective role on the stage of world diplomacy.

But as soon as he steps out of bounds, as soon as he is transformed by his experience in the Berlin underground from a marginal, cagey, exquisite Jew, always performing a coy "high-wire act and without a safety net,"* as soon as he becomes categorical about the imperative necessity for the League of Nations to actually carry out its mission, he ceases to be a "trustworthy" court Jew and becomes an embarrassment to the cynical bureaucracy, a liability that must be immediately neutralized. He is then fired on the spot. He once again becomes an itinerant Jewish Greek immigrant in France, an illegal immigrant, a pariah, a leper, a stateless person *(apatride),* a "chemically pure Jew"—exactly where Cohen's own estrangement had begun on that fateful day of his tenth birthday in 1905 when, walking away from the street hawker berating him with anti-Semitic libel and slurs, he first recognized the ineluctable fate awaiting him.

Now absolutely undesirable in Geneva, a social zero rather than the social alpha he had been, Solal proposes to Ariane that she leave her husband and accompany him to the south of France (Ariane is ignorant and will not be ap-

*[u]ne réussite sur corde raide et sans filet. (*BdS,* 846)

prised for months of the fact that she is no longer with the great Solal, under-secretary-general of the League of Nations, but only with a clever pariah who has to speculate in the stock market to finance his lavish lifestyle). In other words, the Berlin underground, which at first seems to be an entirely gratuitous macabre reverie in the unfolding of a seemingly romantic plot, in fact constitutes its linchpin—it articulates the entire logic of the narrative both historically and psychologically, a logic unrevealed for almost forty chapters.

Indeed, chapter 93, which depicts Solal's desperate final attempts to reestablish himself, and chapter 94, which contains his searing stream of consciousness as he watches the vainly stitching Ariane, constitute Cohen's most accomplished, and most maddening, almost psychotic, meditation on anti-Semitism and his own ambivalence about the "catastrophe of being a Jew." These two chapters are much more powerful in depicting this catastrophe than the long, cohesive autobiographical essay *Ô vous, frères humains.*

His dismissal from his high perch without prior notice throws Solal back to square one in his trajectory, reminding us yet again of the tone and themes of the autobiographic violent bar mitzvah at the hand of the street hawker in *Ô vous, frères humains* (see Chapter 1, "Bar Mitzvah II"). Again, he becomes the ten-year-old Albert, but this time a hunchbacked pariah with a solicitous and frightened smile, who walks the streets terrified to the core of his being by every obvious and more or less subtle sign of anti-Semitism, abounding on that fateful day of his Parisian promenade, Monday, September 10, 1936. Graffiti on walls proclaim "Mort aux Juifs" (Death to the Jews); more charitable ones only demand their suppression: "À bas les Juifs" (Down with the Jews). Every political conversation engaged in or overheard, whatever the milieu of the speakers, tails off with "It's the fault of the Jews." And in short: "Nothing but wishes of death for the Jews in these cities of love-thy-neighbor."* Solal is avid to reintegrate himself into the Social, and at the end of *Belle du Seigneur,* there is an exact reprise of the pivotal crowd scene that precipitated the violent bar mitzvah. He experiences a desperate desire to belong, not to be ontologically guilty, to commune with the others, however obliquely:

> Streets and streets. Suddenly, two cars in a crash, a policeman writing an accident report, onlookers arguing about the incident. He listens, joins in, ashamed for falling so low, but it's a good feeling. A group is anonymous, it's not like an individual whom you try to decipher and who makes your blood run cold. Besides, it puts you in touch with the social. You are part of it, you

*Que de souhaits de mort aux Juifs dans ces villes de l'amour du prochain. (*BdS,* 852)

> belong, you can say your peace, you can agree about the cause of the accident, you can smile at the others, you are all equal, you rub shoulders, you can criticize the driver who is to blame, you love one another.
>
> The group breaks up. Goodbye love.*

The happiness of the crowd consists in witnessing the accident, the blood and the twisted metal, and then finding fault, assigning culpability—loving one another through the blood spilt and the designation of guilt, just like the crowd in Marseille in 1905 fraternizing through its hatred of the "kike." Here, Solal, anonymous, just a passerby can participate in the passion of the crowd. Rather than always being designated as the guilty one, he can now, a member of the crowd, unstained by any universal condemnation, joyfully assign blame with the crowd, "love-thy-neighbor" through the passion of assigning fault, an ecstatically organic member of an accusatory crowd. Finally, he has a fleeting sensation of belonging.

Unable to commune with real Christians, except, as we have just seen, in the most fleeting and anonymous fashion, he buys himself some "Christian" comforters in the shape of chocolate truffles and takes them back to his private ghetto, his luxurious apartment at the Hotel George V.

> Place de la Madeleine. A bakery. He goes in, buys six chocolate truffles. . . . Six truffles, gentlemen, there'll be a crowd. Six friendly little Christians in the ghetto. . . . That's it, go back to the hotel, get into bed, get into bed with himself, with his good friend Solal, and while away the time reading anti-Semitic obscenities and scoffing truffles. Oh yes, back in the ghetto is a whole suitcaseful of anti-Semitic obscenities, and suddenly in the night he gets out of bed, feverishly opens the case, and begins reading their obscenities standing up, avidly, continues through the night, goes on reading their obscenities, each one read with interest, a dead man's interest. No, men are not good.†

*Rues et rues. Soudain, deux autos fracassées, un agent de police dressant un constat, des badauds discutant de l'accident. Il écoute, il se mêle à la discussion, honteux de sa déchéance, mais c'est bon. Un groupe est anonyme, n'est pas un individu qu'on devine et qui vous glace. Et puis, c'est du social. On en est, on appartient, on dit la sienne, on est d'accord sur la cause de l'accident, on se sourit, on est des égaux, on fraternise, on dit du mal du chauffeur responsable, on s'aime.

Le groupe se défait. Fini, l'amour. (*BdS,* 855)

†Place de la Madeleine. Une pâtisserie. Il entre, achète six truffes aux chocolat. . . . Six truffes, messieurs, on aura de la compagnie. Six petites amies chrétiennes au ghetto. . . . Oui, rentrer à l'hôtel, se coucher, se coucher avec lui, avec son ami Solal, et passer le temps en lisant des méchancetés antisémites tout en mangeant des truffes. Oui, au ghetto il y a une valise pleine de méchancetés antisémites, et tout à coup la nuit il sort de son lit, il ouvre vite la valise, et il se met à lire leurs méchancetés, debout, avec avidité, continue tout au long de la nuit, continue à lire leurs méchancetés, toutes lues avec intérêt, un intérêt de mort. Non, les hommes ne sont pas bons. (*BdS,* 862–63)

Solal (Cohen) is reliving down to the last detail the core trauma of the day of his tenth birthday, the day when he "was driven from human communion."* This is the moment of memory relived, that is, of trauma reexperienced; the Cohenian moment of bitter-sweet herbs rudely regurgitated, the moment of thorns that draw blood once again, and not the Proustian moment of the sweet Madeleine, soaked in tea, sucked on softly, evoking lyrical reminiscences. No wonder then that it is on the place de la Madeleine, and not any other place, that Solal buys his Christian truffles, just after a series of images flowing straight out of the day of his banishment at the hands of the street hawker. Here, though, the somatic recovery of the sensation bears no trace of nostalgia, of a lost paradise: it is, in fact, hell regained. And, not being able to be with Christians, except anonymously and in passing, but loving them all the same, he will take them in the form of little truffles back to his ghetto, keep them as company for a while, arrange them on a table, have them watch him, pay him attention, keep him from his frightening solitude, keep him from just defenestrating himself—and then eat his companions out of boredom and despair, ultimate communion with those who wish him banishment or death. And in this chic five-star ghetto of a hotel room, he turns also to his ambulatory altar, not his promising *Israélite* altar in Marseille prior to his tenth birthday (an altar to the French Republic, with flags, statuettes, portraits of Corneille, Napoleon, and Hugo, before which he dreamed of becoming an army colonel), but a masochistic Jewish altar consisting of a collection of anti-Semitic tracts, carried in a suitcase—so many ways of declining and conjugating the street hawker's diatribe, of spewing the hatred of the anti-Semites, the Drumonts, the Célines, the scribes of the popular daily *L'Antijuif* (The anti-Jew), with horror, but also not without a certain pleasure. Madeleine of bitter-sweet herbs, the chocolate he loves, but that hates him; the consumption of those he loves in front of a satanic altar composed of the Pantheon scribes of hate. A Proustian moment but poisoned. The mass of bitter herbs. A Passover seder with no deliverance from Egypt, but with self-crucifixion.

We also learn something astounding in these pages. The narrator refers to two "gaffes" committed by Solal and makes an astonishing revelation about one of them: "And then he'd made his blunder *[gaffe]* at the meeting of the Council of their League of Nations and had come a cropper. And the very next day he'd made an even more serious blunder *[gaffe]*: *he'd sent an anonymous letter dis-*

*. . . jour de mes dix ans, jour où je fus chassé de l'humaine communion. (*Ô vous,* 1119)

closing the irregularity in his naturalization papers."* One is struck first by the very use of the word gaffe, normally connoting an unintentional blooper or blunder that is regretted after the fact. But Solal's intervention on behalf of German Jewry was intentional and repeated. Does he regret it now? Is it just a tactical regret for the "gaffe" of using the figure of Christ in his final pleas to the governing board? But the second use of "gaffe" is even more surprising. After the fateful meeting, we learn, Solal himself sent an anonymous letter to the French Interior Ministry informing it of an irregularity in his naturalization papers. He then promptly loses his French nationality, becomes undocumented, illegal, a refugee of sorts. This willed, highly intentional act of self-destruction, self-fashioning social death, could never be described as an unintentional "gaffe." If anything, it is exactly the contrary. It is as if Solal desired his own total dissolution, not a partial one, limited to politics, but a final and decisive dissolution. "Call off the whole charade," he seems to be saying, "let me lose it all, rank, nationality, and everything, so that I can at last become again a *chemically pure Jew,* stateless, nomadic. King of nothing instead of viceroy of the world." Or as Cohen puts it himself: "Pariah forever and walled alive in love."† Solal seems to either swallow the world or vomit it, with the beloved (Gentile) woman as a sanctuary phantasm of last refuge.

This willed self-destruction begs the question again. Is there pleasure for Solal in this self-induced dissolution? Does he "reduce" himself to a pariah as an act of pure masochism, regressing to the ten-year-old Albert's earliest phantasm about hiding with Viviane in an underground cave, safe from all the evil lurking on the outside, where his secret identification lies not with, or exclusively with, his kin—for whom he sees himself always as a sacrificial lamb—but rather with the anti-Semites? In chapters 93 and 94, the definite summit of Cohen's often repeated introspective hara-kiri, he wonders about it himself: "A born suspect. Will they turn him into an anti-Semite? Is he one already? Is his pride merely a cover for shame, loathing? Is he proud because there is nothing else he can be?"‡[13]

*Et alors sa gaffe à la réunion du Conseil de leur Société des Nations, et il s'est cassé les reins. Et le lendemain, la gaffe plus terrible *d'avoir envoyé la lettre anonyme révélant l'irrégularité de sa naturalisation.* (*BdS,* 847; emphasis added)

†[P]aria à jamais et muré vivant dans de l'amour. (*BdS,* 744)

‡Un suspect de naissance. Vont-ils faire de lui un antisémite? L'est-il déjà? Et sa fierté recouvre-t-elle une honte, une détestation? Fier, faute de mieux? (*BdS,* 857)

But nowhere can this question be better asked, and again with the same self-consciousness, than in chapter 94's first person stream of consciousness. First, Solal explains the details of his downfall, quoted above, and then he dives into a nightmarish vision of a visit by the Rosenfeld family, whom he has never really encountered, but which distills in its crassness all the Jewish stereotypes. Solal catalogs their awfulness in a dense six-page stream of consciousness that could rival any anti-Semitic caricature contained in his famous ambulatory altar, the essence of which could be paraphrased as follows: You invite Mr. Rosenfeld to your house; he comes too early with the whole family in tow: wife, son, daughters, grandmother. Rosenfeld is a Romanian Jew with a thick accent. Everything about him is crass; his manners, pushy. His children are prodigious. They speak so many languages and play so many instruments and would like to exercise such and such professions. They snoop in your medicine cabinets, compare medications, give you advice on constipation. They open your cabinets and Frigidaire and criticize your stock of provisions, insist on giving you the best recipes for salted cucumbers, gefilte fish, apple strudel, tzibbele, kugel, hashed liver; they show you how to drink tea correctly. They leaf through books in your library, dispute everything: if you prefer Racine to Corneille, they take the opposite view. They criticize your apartment, what you paid for it, its location; they wonder aloud whether you pay your taxes in full; they suggest an excellent surgeon, a professor they personally know, for an operation you might need, according to them; they declare your authentic personal effects fake; their daughters, gangly and silly, giggle awkwardly, eyeing you as a possible match, and so on and so forth.

And then Solal in the midst of this nightmare catches himself in midair (Cohen uses a comma to set the following reflection apart in a stream of consciousness), and wonders:

> but why why have I told myself this ridiculous made-up tale that has no basis in reality why because I've never met any such crowd of grotesques nor have I ever been present at any such masquerade on the contrary it has always been among my Jewish brethren that I have encountered human beings with the noblest hearts and the most courteous manners, why so fascinated the minor eccentricities of the handful of Rosenfelds who do exist why did I exaggerate inflate give them such a free rein why did I join so willingly in the festivities oh yes it's because I'm unhappy that I said all those horrible things that aren't true its perhaps because I want to convince myself convince other people that I'm not a Jew like other Jews that I am an exceptional Jew to make it absolutely clear that I am different from those who

> are reviled because I mock them to let it be known oh shame on me that I am not a very Jewish Jew and that it's quite all right for you [Ariane] to like me maybe there is in me some terrible wish to disown the greatest people on earth some terrible wish to be free of them*

Solal then switches to a torrid three-page defense of Jews as survivors of persecutions, deniers of nature, lovers of the Law, real princes of humanity. Yet he cannot but return to his original question: why does he take such obvious pleasure in deriding them, and in front of his beloved, Ariane? And here by way of an apology, Cohen has Solal make a terrible analogy, but a revealing one all the same: "If I exaggerated them [the Rosenfelds] and multiplied their little eccentricities it was perhaps for love of them and to enjoy the taste of them, just as a man who likes spices will sprinkle on enough to take the skin off his tongue, so that he gets the full benefit."† But the fine connoisseur, the true aficionado of spices, never indulges in such excess. The true aficionado savors the finesse, the accent, the rarity, the suggestion, the hinted contrasts in very small doses—and *never* the overdoses. The intoxicating, overwhelming pleasure of the overdose belongs to the domain of the insane, the drug addict, the suicidal—the masochist, to be precise here, who must overwhelm his senses, flagellate them, pierce them, incise them . . . to assuage his desire for punishment to the point of delirious self-mutilation, and not his desire for a sublime taste.

But beyond the bad analogy, Cohen returns to the explicit truth of his conscious *will,* his existential *inability* to unambiguously love Jews. His syntax is categorical: "*I want to love* everything in my people and even the large and lovely ridiculed noses of my people noses tormented by angst noses so keen in scenting danger and *I want to love* the bent backs of my people."‡[14] Notice

*mais pourquoi pourquoi me suis-je raconté cette histoire fausse absurde sans aucun fondement dans la réalité pourquoi alors que je n'ai jamais rencontré pareille grotesque horde alors que je n'ai jamais assisté à une telle mascarade alors que c'est parmi mes frères juifs que j'ai rencontré les êtres les plus nobles de cœur et de manières, pourquoi les menus travers des quelques rares Rosenfeld de la réalité pourquoi les avoir grossis exagérés à plaisir pourquoi m'être complu à ce festival oui c'est le malheur qui m'a fait dire ces horreurs pas vraies c'est peut-être pour croire faire croire que je ne suis pas un Juif comme les autres que je suis un Juif exceptionnel pour m'affirmer différent des honnis puisque je les moque pour faire croire ô honte sur moi que je suis un Juif pas juif et que tu peux m'aimer c'est peut-être un horrible vouloir caché de renier le plus grand peuple de la terre un horrible vouloir peut-être d'en sortir (*BdS,* 895)

†si j'ai grossi et multiplié leurs menus travers c'est peut-être par amour et pour en jouir davantage tel l'amateur d'épices qui en met beaucoup qui en met trop et à s'en emporter la bouche pour les savourer davantage (*BdS,* 899)

‡je veux tout aimer de mon peuple et même les chers grands nez moqués de mon peuple nez tourmentés par les angoisses nez flaireurs des dangers et je veux aimer les dos voûtés de mon peuple (*BdS,* 900)

that the accent is on the volition: "je veux + infinitive" carries in French a very strong (and impolite) volitional aspect, an act of pure *will* and in no way natural state of mind. Contrast this volitional syntax with the syntax employed when his stream of consciousness focalizes (again, after a long interval) on Ariane, his Gentile lover: "yes my love I love you more and more and silently I shout it to you while you quietly restitch the hems that I undid to give your life a brief purpose I worship you while you sew swallowing a little saliva as do all sewers intent on the task in hand I love the even rhythm of your breathing as you sew I love your serene and demur face as you sew."* Solal does not *want to love* Ariane—he loves her *still.* It is a present love that continues from the past, projected into the future. It flows from the core of his being. Between Solal and Ariane, there is spontaneous interior fusion. Ariane is the Penelope to whom Odysseus returns as a matter of *natural* fact and not as a matter of moral, ethnic, or metaphysical *will.* The verbs relating to her do not need willful auxiliary modifiers; they just state that which is the case: subject, conjugated verb, present indicative. Period. Solal is able to love the Gentile naturally. But again this is a love of narcissistic ambivalence. He sees himself in Ariane and despises her snobbery, her femininity, and so forth. In the end, Solal cannot manage either world, either part of himself.

At the very moment here in chapters 93 and 94 where Solal suffers the consequences of his actions on behalf of the dwarf Rachel and her kin, you would expect that he would overcome his ambivalence, or at least "manage" it more constructively. But, no, he simply repeats yet again the same scenario of the Berlin underground. First, the repulsion from the dwarf Rachel (and here of the Rosenfelds) as real existential individuals and then, as a counterpoint, strong identification with these repulsive ones, never as individuals but as part of a collective for whom, he, Solal, their messiah, is responsible, and for whom he sacrifices himself. In both instances, Cohen repeats the same dialectic of repulsion, then reconciliation followed by a withdrawal. Yet with the dwarf Rachel, Purim functions as the occasion for an abstract eulogy for the nation of Israel, while at the end of the Rosenfeld nightmare here, Solal precisely and emphatically articulates his praise of Israel without the pretext of ritual. But at heart they are both exactly the same montage. Likewise, the *will* to love the

*oui mon amour je t'aime toujours plus et en moi-même je te le crie pendant que tu couds gentiment les ourlets que j'ai défaits pour te donner un intérêt à vivre je te chéris pendant que tu couds en aspirant un peu de salive comme les couseuses attentives je chéris ta respiration régulière pendant que tu couds je chéris ton visage paisible et modeste pendant que tu couds (*BdS,* 906)

Rosenfelds contrasted with the naturalness of his love for Ariane repeats the precise attraction-repulsion logic discussed above in comparing the similarities and inversions between the beginning of the novel and the Berlin underground. These scenes telescope into each other; the same logic, the same dynamics, replayed in so many registers. This is the identity impasse that Solal forever repeats, as a madman haunted by the repetition of the same symptoms, despite his conscious *will* to the contrary.

This chapter ends on the most dissonant note in Cohen's fiction. With the dwarf Rachel and the Rosenfelds, Cohen's ambivalence about Judaism could not be more pronounced. And if Cohen had stayed suspended there, suspended in an ambivalence bordering psychosis, the great novel *Belle du Seigneur* would have been ruined. The searing identity impasse can only be (fatally) bridged by another synthetic phantasm, in which Solal's antagonist, Ariane, is but an ideal projection of himself. Because of his failure to save his children (the people of Israel), Solal constitutes himself as an *Ariane who commits suicide because she is Jewish,* a suicide nevertheless officiated over by the deformed projection of himself, the weeping Rachel.

6 Ariane-Solal

Ariane, she is just as much Albert Cohen as Solal.
Jean-Pierre Winter, Les Errants de la chair

Before *Belle du Seigneur,* Cohen did not particularly distinguish himself in endowing female heroines with a rich interiority. From Adrienne and Aude in *Solal* to Ariane's first sketch in *Mangeclous,* these women function as foils to Solal's epic. While they are not cartoon characters à la Voltaire, and their subjectivity does seep through at times, they never occupy the foreground of the narrative. But for her to succeed in *Belle du Seigneur,* Cohen had to endow Ariane with a strong inner voice and a singular inner lucidity. Hence the necessity to front-load Ariane and back-load Solal in the order of narrative exposition. Ariane's notes for an autobiographical novel, her first autonomous streams of consciousness, and various other inner monologues dominate the first half of the novel, whereas Solal's interiority becomes more prominent as the novel nears its end. Thus the whole novel hinges on Cohen's ability to fashion a feminine complement to Solal. Cohen needed to balance the *Belle* with the *Seigneur* so that their genitive grammatical relationship would convey all the power of Solal's inner dissonance.

Solal falls in love with Ariane at first sight. He knows nothing about her, except that she is just like him—his feminine other. Following the night on which he chooses her, Solal spies on the Deumes' villa and finally gathers the courage to break in and make his famous moral experiment in the guise of seduction. Once in the villa, as he nears Ariane, he comes upon a school notebook where, with the view of becoming a "romancière de talent," Ariane has outlined her life. Solal reads these notes, quoted in full in the novel. From a narratival perspective, the Who, What, When, How, and Why of the main

Genevan characters are quickly and efficiently disposed of—and, more important, the reader gains an insight into Ariane's state of mind. Our sole interest here concerns Ariane's self-understanding and, correlatively, Solal's apparent inability to grasp that self-understanding.[1]

Our heroine was born "Ariane Cassandre Corisande d'Auble" to a noble Protestant family that traces its Genevan roots back to the middle of the sixteenth century. Her immediate family history is as tragic as her extended family history is noble: her mother died while giving birth to her sister Eliane; her father, a professor of theology, died five years later; and her brother Jacques and Eliane were killed in a car accident shortly thereafter. The lone orphan was brought up by her Aunt Tantlérie, a very devout Calvinist, rich but pious beyond measure. Puritanism is de rigueur: almost never a tender word uttered, and kisses on the forehead are rare. So palpable is the omnipresence of original sin that the bathroom towels are arranged according to body parts, lest those destined for the middle of the body sinfully soil the others.

At eighteen, Ariane begins her studies in literature at the university, where she meets a young Russian immigrant named Varvara Ivanovna: "Soon we became friends. I found her very beautiful. I loved to kiss her hands, her pinkish palms, her heavy braids. I thought about her all the time. In sum, it was love."* Tantlérie is not thrilled, especially when she discovers that Varvara is a socialist revolutionary. Ariane rebels against the Calvinist aunt and moves out into a small student apartment with Varvara, where she spends the happiest moments of her life. "Happy, she and I. . . . a life of coeds. The little restaurants. I started powdering myself a little. . . . I started learning Russian, to be able to speak it with her, to be more intimate. We slept together. Yes, it was love, but pure, well almost."† And later in the novel, in her second stream of consciousness, striking a distinctly more sensual note: "I never loved kissing except with Varvara I liked touching her breasts and I believed that it was affection oh! what a lay *[quelle couche].*"‡ This is clearly an enduring lesbian love affair, not a passing sorority infatuation.[2] But paradise comes to an end when Varvara admits to being severely ill with tuberculosis. She has a year to live. Ariane drops out of school and nurses her lover until she dies. Yet at times

*"Bientôt nous devînmes amies. Je la trouvais très belle. J'aimais baiser ses mains, ses paumes rosées, ses tresses lourdes. Je pensais à elle tout le temps. En somme, c'était de l'amour." (*BdS,* 18)

†"Heureuses, elle et moi. . . . Une vie d'étudiantes. Les petits restaurants. Je commençai à me poudrer un peu. . . . Je commençai à apprendre le russe, pour pouvoir le parler avec elle, pour être plus intimes. Nous dormions ensemble. Oui, c'était de l'amour, mais pur, enfin presque." (*BdS,* 19)

‡[J]e n'ai jamais aimé les baisers qu'avec Varvara j'aimais toucher sa poitrine je croyais que c'était de l'affection quelle couche oh (*BdS,* 184)

she cannot resist the temptation of a guilt-ridden evening out, from which the dying Varvara is necessarily excluded. In a scene eerily reminiscent of *Le Livre de ma mère,* Ariane reflects on her cruelty to the dying Varvara: "One night, however, returning from a ball at two in the morning, as I was telling her I don't know what to justify myself, she calmly responded: 'Right, as for myself, I am going to die.' I shall never forget that look fixed on me."* This is the answer that Louise Cohen never gave her son when he came back at four o'clock in the morning from a party from which the mother was excluded, but it looms, self-evident, in the air. Varvara voices what Louise kept silent. In Cohen, transpositions and projections are more revealing than direct personal recollections.

Varvara dies; Ariane moves into a small hotel. Desperate and depressed, she swallows a large quantity of sleeping pills, but by chance another hotel guest, the young international civil servant Adrien Deume, finds her unconscious and patiently nurses her back to life. When Adrien asks her to marry him, Ariane—who is utterly alone in Geneva, her aunt being in Scotland and her uncle in Africa—consents. She soon realizes that it was a colossal blunder, for besides being of the wrong gender, Adrien is a mediocre and pretentious upstart in all respects; and he suffers from the worst sin in the Gallic world—that of being ridiculous. Ariane has nothing but contempt for him; his only redeeming quality is servile patience. "[He was] the only being in the world who paid me any heed," she explains defensively. "I was numb. The poison had damaged my head."† Adrien is compassionate when Ariane tells him of her fear of male intimacy. She promptly becomes "neurosthénique" and one evening sends him away in a rage because Varvara is not there, that is, because he is not Varvara.

Disregarding the obvious meaning of these personal notes, Solal, who carefully reads them before confronting Ariane, quixotically clings to his idées fixes that Ariane desires men and adores patriarchal domination, something he asserts repeatedly throughout the novel. Although something in Ariane touches Solal's inner core, he fails to appreciate her visceral hatred of the phallic order, her phobia about the phallus itself, her homosexuality, and above all, her desire for death.[3] Solal must be partly blind to the obvious, since the whole novel

*Un soir pourtant, rentrée d'un bal à deux heures du matin, comme je lui disais je ne sais quoi pour me justifier, elle me répondit calmement: "Oui, mais moi je vais mourir." Je n'oublierai jamais ce regard fixé sur moi. (*BdS,* 20)

†[Il était le] seul être au monde qui s'occupait de moi. J'étais engourdie. L'empoisonnement avait abîmé ma tête. (*BdS,* 21)

would not be narratable, would implode, did Solal not cling to these misconceptions. Likewise, my own critical reading of Cohen's novel would lose its own narratability if I were to disregard Cohen's fictional antagonism with respect to Solal and Ariane. The identity between the two would merely become tautological and therefore unnarratable; to exist novelistically, their identities must be in a dynamic relationship of differences through gender, time, geography, social class, religious and historical consciousness, and personal stories.

The most obvious plot structure of *Belle du Seigneur* revolves around suicides. The first suicide is botched (Ariane) or deferred (Solal), but suicidal themes continue to hover over virtually every page and culminate in the final double suicide. Ariane tries to commit suicide; she is subject to suicidal depressions and assures herself that "one could at a pinch always commit suicide."* Solal mirrors this existential option in almost the exactly the same terms when he wonders whether it would not be better to "put an end right away to this drudgery [of life]."† These two fleeting thoughts could serve as the thematic coefficients to every page of the novel, a direct continuation of the morbid themes of *Solal* and *Le Livre de ma mère.* "He knows that in a year, or later, or earlier, it will be suicide, and yet he eats his croissants with tranquility, with a lot of butter and marmalade."‡ Solal desires death because he cannot be an effective palace Jew. That is the overarching Josephic-Estheric dimension of his suicide; but folded within this failure are more interior and intimate states, these suicidal leitmotifs so well articulated by his Genevan feminine double. Without the Josephic-Estheric historical dimension, Solal's love story loses its epic dimension; and the epic would lose its proper novelistic depth without Solal's interior struggle as a descendent of Aaron (founder of the priestly tribe, the Cohens) in love with his own feminine projection.

The following paragraph, as macabre as they come, represents Solal's thoughts as he breaks in and enters Ariane's second-floor bedroom just prior to reading Ariane's autobiographical notes:

> He stopped to consider this small, squat companion, always ready to be of service. The bullet was already there that later, yes, later. No, not the temple, risk of staying alive and blind. The heart, yes, but must not shoot too low. The right place was at the angle formed by the edge of the sternum and the third space between the ribs. With a pen left on a pedestal table, close to a

*on pourra toujours se suicider à la rigueur (*BdS,*188)

†[s]e débarrasser dès à présent de cette corvée? (*BdS,* 9)

‡Il sait que dans un an, ou plus tard, ou plus tôt, ce sera le suicide, et pourtant il mange tranquillement ses croissants, avec beaucoup de beurre et de marmelade. (*BdS,* 848)

flask of cologne, he marked the proper place and smiled. There would be the small starry hole, surrounded by black grains, within a few centimeters of the nipple that so many nymphs had kissed. Put an end right away to this drudgery? Finish with the human gang, always ready to hate, to slander. Just bathed and shaved, he would make a presentable cadaver, commanding even. No, first try this unheard-of enterprise.*

Solal's choice seems clear—suicide or redemption. But he does not really believe in redemption in and through Ariane's virtue; it is, then, only a question of relative postponement. The dramatic resolution, "No, first try this unheard-of enterprise," is balanced by the initial certitude voiced just above: "The bullet was already there that later, yes, later." All means have been deployed toward a successful suicide: the gun, the targeted organ, the entry angle of the bullet, even the shape of the wound, and the aesthetic and social appropriateness of the cadaver. Ariane has the same desire for death and the same fear of botching her suicide: "I feel ill at ease in my skin it is too tight . . . try my trick from the wall no rather the jumping trick so I am thus high above on the seventh I jump out of the window I have jumped, that's it, fallen on the hard hard cement thump I didn't break anything but it hurts all over."† So for both Solal and Ariane—from the very beginning of the novel—it is simply a story of aestheticized despair, postponement of and stalling the suicide that both know to be inevitable and necessary.

In this state of mind, Solal reads Ariane's suicidal autobiographical notes. He should recognize the state of deferred suicide as Ariane's permanent existential state, her loathing of the phallic order, and her lucid and articulate sense of imprisonment and violation in marriage, but he is too absorbed in his own fantasies to recognize the specific attributes of Ariane's persona. This distortion leads us, however, to an important general point about Albert Cohen as a novelist and about the standard interpretation of the novel. By having So-

*Il s'arrêta pour considérer le petit compagnon trapu, toujours prêt à rendre service. La balle s'y trouvait déjà qui plus tard, oui, plus tard. Non, pas la tempe, risque de rester vivant et aveugle. Le cœur, oui, mais ne pas tirer trop bas. La bonne place était à l'angle formé par le bord du sternum et le troisième espace intercostal. Avec le stylo qui traînait sur un guéridon, près d'un flacon d'eau de Cologne, il marqua l'endroit propice, sourit. Là serait le petit trou étoilé, entouré de grains noirs, à quelques centimètres du mamelon que tant de nymphes avaient baisé. Se débarrasser dès à présent de cette corvée? En finir avec le gang humain, toujours prêt à haïr, à médire? Fraîchement baigné et rasé, il ferait un cadavre présentable, et commandeur de surcroît. Non, tenter d'abord l'entreprise inouïe. (*BdS,* 9)

†je suis mal dans ma peau elle est trop étroite. . . . essayer mon truc du mur non plutôt le truc de sauter je suis donc tout en haut au septième je saute par la fenêtre voilà j'ai sauté ça y est tombée sur le ciment dur dur plouf je me suis rien cassé mais mal partout. (*BdS,* 183)

lal be the first misreader of Ariane, and therefore of *Belle du Seigneur,* one senses that Cohen willfully programmed this misreading. The reader, after all, identifies with the protagonist and therefore perceives Ariane through Solal regardless of what Ariane explicitly says about herself. Solal recognizes their mutual singularity, but resists articulating the reasons for it, except for their shared disdain for others and their correlative loneliness in crowds. Yet, despite misdirecting our reading of Ariana, Cohen's multiple streams of consciousness allow Ariane to articulate all these themes in detail in her unmistakable voice.

The Stream of Truth

Ariane's first extended autonomous monologue, which takes up all fourteen pages (616 lines) of chapter 18, with neither paragraphs nor punctuation, occurs at a crucial moment in the narrative.[4] Adrien has finally gathered the courage to invite Solal over to dinner. The whole family is consumed by the preparations, except for Ariane who feigns indifference yet is the only one who knows why the undersecretary-general would even consider such an undistinguished invitation. Solal has fallen in love with her, has been spying on her, has broken into her bedroom, has disguised himself as an old and particularly repulsive Hassidic Jew in a gambit to see whether she, by letting herself be seduced by a grotesque old man, will redeem the "sinfulness of women" and become the first "[female] human" *(la première humaine)* (*BS,* 41). She does not live up to this hope. Instead, she throws a glass at Solal, wounding him just above the eye. Mistaking her for a common romantic dupe, Solal spitefully promises to seduce her with the usual fare of alpha male aggression mixed with just enough saccharine sentimentality. Repelled by Solal's aggressive tactics and perhaps also by his disguise, Ariane nevertheless begins to visit the Palace of the League of Nations and seems to encourage her husband to respond to Solal's sudden interest in this heretofore undistinguished and lazy class B bureaucrat. Now the great moment is at hand: the undersecretary-general is about to knock on the door (Solal actually never shows up that night) and the class B bureaucrat's wife remains locked in her steamy bathroom, gazing into a mirror, indifferent to repeated appeals to come down and prepare for his eminence's arrival.

Solal accepts the Deumes' dinner invitation for the sole purpose of seducing Ariane. Male-female sexual tension should therefore be flowing. But Ariane's stream of "gratuitous verbal agitation without communicative aim"[5] could not be more hostile to heterosexual romantic myth, men, their hairy bodies and intrusive penises—at least at first, as the stream of consciousness, after a long detour, does end up all the same in a sustained Joycian orgasmic "yes." Ariane holds male sexuality in contempt; she abhors her submission to her husband's assaults: "he is going to do his gymnastics on me and at the same time I want to laugh."* Ariane suffers her husband's ridiculous campaigns on and in her body: "oh, dreadful his canine haha on me how can that captivate him so much and at the same time want to laugh when he moves on top of me so red busy so occupied concerned the wrinkled eyebrows then this canine haha so self-serving is it so palpitating this to and fro it is it is comic and then this lack of dignity oh he injures me this imbecile."† Adrien's orgasms would be purely comical were it not for the physical and psychological pain they cause Ariane: "he pushes cannibalistic cries on me because it is the end and how much he seems to love it and then he falls close to me very winded and it is finished just until the next time."‡

Ariane's visceral free-associative stream of consciousness articulates a cogent opposition to the specific cultural contexts of heterosexual romantic ideology: "beautiful now isn't it the pleasures of the novelists are there really women idiotic enough to like this crap,"§ thusly mirroring Cohen's obsessive indictment of the romance and his repeated equation of Ariane, the Western woman, and romantic heroines, these "idiotes" led astray by romantic mystification. Ten pages later, Ariane becomes much more specific in her indictment of "the typists with polished nails and three millimeters of filth underneath and then their conversations about how they all love *Madame Bovary* because it's a beautiful film and also *Anna Karenina* also because it was with Greta Garbo."|| Far from being a foolish consumer of romantic ideology, Ariane articulates the connection between high and popular culture with her somatic phobia about the masculine. In fact, the masculine and the crass are intertwined by their very nature. Her lucidity is exemplary. It is in her deepest, most "transparent"

*il va faire sa gymnastique sur moi et en même temps j'ai envie de rire (*BdS*, 176)

†oh affreux son haha canin sur moi comment est-ce que ça peut le captiver tellement et en même temps envie de rire quand il bouge sur moi tellement rouge affairé si occupé soucieux les sourcils froncés puis ce haha canin si intéressé est-ce que c'est si palpitant ce va-et-vient c'est c'est comique et puis ça manque de dignité oh il me fait mal cet imbécile. (*BdS*, 176)

‡il pousse des cris de cannibale sur moi parce que c'est la fin et que ça a l'air de lui plaire beaucoup et puis il tombe près de moi tout essoufflé c'est fini jusqu'à la prochaine fois (*BdS*, 177)

§c'est du joli les voluptés des romanciers est-ce qu'il y a vraiment des idiotes qui aiment cette horreur (*BdS*, 176)

||les dactylos avec ongles vernis et trois millimètres de crasse dessous et puis leurs conversations qu'elles aiment bien *Madame Bovary* parce que c'est un joli film et puis *Anna Karénine* aussi parce que c'était avec Greta Garbo (*BdS*, 186)

moments, that she is the closest to the Aaronite Solal, her ideological nemesis according to the manifest plot of the novel. Here, Solal, at the end of the novel, contemplates Ariane eating leftovers off the floor like a beaten but grateful dog after a violent scene of jealousy: "Some beauty, the passion called love. If not jealousy, ennui. If jealousy, bestial hell. She a slave and he a brute. Wretched novelists, band of liars who embellish passion, making male and female idiots desire it. Wretched novelists, suppliers and sycophants of the ruling class. And the idiots loved these dirty lies, these swindles, they fed on them."* At their deepest, the protagonist and antagonist mirror each other's thoughts, down to the very nuance. All else is plot and alibi—a foil masking identity and repetition.

Ariane views any phallic-based sexuality as bestial due to the asymmetry between the penetrating male and the violated female: "he will climb on top of me *an animal above an animal below*" *(une bête dessus une bête dessous).*† Bestialness and repulsiveness also define male anatomy: "that women should be attracted by men *in general* that is beyond me these hairs on the arms and then each monsieur knows better than the other men have these little teats that serve no purpose at all."‡ Although she hates the bestial male rapist, the bourgeois spouse resigns herself to periodical violation. Adrien Deume may force himself upon his wife from time to time, but the lesbian aristocrat keeps her subjectivity intact, her own stream of thoughts, her irony and laughter just as he inflates and deflates into his repulsive epilepsy. The very concept of penetration, by custom or by violence, sears her mind as much as her vagina: "what right has this stranger what right has he to hurt me hurts me especially at the beginning like a red iron oh I don't like men and then what a funny idea what imbecility wanting to introduce this this this this *[ce cette ce cette]* thing in someone else in another's place who does not want it and whom it hurts."§ In a particularly apt metaphorical juxtaposition, Ariane shows the similarities be-

*Du joli, la passion dite amour. Si pas de jalousie, ennui. Si jalousie, enfer bestial. Elle une esclave, et lui une brute. Ignobles romanciers, bande de menteurs qui embellissaient la passion, en donnaient l'envie aux idiotes et aux idiots. Ignobles romanciers, fournisseurs et flagorneurs de la classe possédante. Et les idiotes aimaient ces sales mensonges, ces escroqueries, s'en nourrissaient. (*BdS,* 962)

†il va monter sur moi *une bête dessus une bête dessous* (*BdS,* 176; emphasis added)

‡que les femmes soient attirées par les hommes *en général* ça me dépasse ces poils sur les bras et puis chaque monsieur sait mieux que l'autre les hommes ont des mamelles petites qui ne servent à rien (*BdS,* 188; emphasis added)

§de quel droit cet étranger de quel droit il me fait mal me fait-il mal surtout au début comme un fer rouge oh j'aime pas les hommes ne ne et puis quelle drôle d'idée quelle imbécillité de vouloir introduire ce cette ce cette chose chez quelqu'un d'autre chez quelqu'un qui n'en veut pas à qui ça fait mal. (*BdS,* 176)

tween her situation and that of colonial subjects: "The funny epilepsy of monsieur who deals with territories under [colonial] mandate."* This metaphor plays on the fluid boundaries between the political hypocrisy of the League of Nations with respect to colonial subjects (it actually only represents the interests of England, France, and the international bureaucracy and not those of the indigenous populations) and the sexual hypocrisy of marriage with respect to women—institutionalized rape under the guise of propriety (in Ariane's deep interiority). Ariane describes her civic, political, and physical states as subject to a mandate beneath which she squirms. The same patina of hypocrisy that facilitates the domination of the Deumes of this world over their foreign subjects also covers their conjugal relationships.

Ariane's intrinsic loathing of masculine power and dominance, both sexual and political, calls into question from the very beginning Solal's perception of her as a passive worshipper of masculine power. Thus the manifest mythological opposition between the descendant of Aaron and the descendant of Europa immediately becomes doubtful. Philippe Zard has demonstrated that for Cohen, Europe as a general concept is consistently represented by a woman—Adrienne, Aude, Ariane—the woman Europa, in short, whom Solal desires as much as he despises her. Ariane, however, abhors precisely what the mythological Europa secretly desired—the phallic order and the phallus. Solal himself openly suggests this equation between Ariane and Europa. Following an evening at the circus, where Ariane is moved by the power of the tigers, Solal imputes a generalized pagan disposition to her: "Excited, unsettled by the tiger, yes, like the good woman Europa by the bull! Not stupid, Jupiter, he knew women! The long-locked virgin Europa surely most certainly said to the bull, eyes chastely lowered, 'you are a strong one, my darling.'"† The irony here is double: first Ariane may obviously get a frisson from this or that act but is not fundamentally beholden to masculine ethos and aesthetics; secondly, this is a reprise of an identical scene in Cohen's first novel *Solal* where the protagonist Solal single-handedly rescues a circus trainer from a tiger's claws, impressing Aude, and thus definitively winning her heart in the most pagan fashion imaginable.[6]

But in her transparent interiority, Ariane is anything but a *tauroparthenos* ("virgin dedicated to the bull").[7] Cohen's specific charge against the pagan Eu-

*la drôle d'épilepsie du monsieur qui s'occupe des territoires sous mandat (*BdS,* 177)

†"Excitée, troublée par le tigre, oui, comme la bonne femme Europe par le taureau! Pas bête, Jupiter, il connaissait les femmes! La vierge Europe aux longues tresses a sûrement dû dire au taureau, les yeux chastement baissés: 'vous êtes un fort, vous, mon chou.'" (*BdS,* 779; cited in Zard, *Fiction de l'Occident,* 263)

ropa is not that she was abducted and raped by Zeus—for that could happen to even the most chaste daughter of Zion—but rather that, being in love with the bull's beauty, and above all his horns, she secretly desires her own abduction and rape. Roberto Calasso sums up this pagan psychological topos with poetic precision:

> All of a sudden [Europa and her friends] find themselves surrounded by a herd of bulls. And one of those bulls is dazzling white, his small horns flashing like jewels. There's nothing in the least threatening about him. So much so that, though shy at first, Europa now brings her flowers to his white muzzle. The bull whines with pleasure, like a puppy, slumps down on the grass, and offers his little horns to the garlands. The princess makes so bold [a move] as to climb, like an Amazon, on his back.[8]

This description captures the pagan metaphor of the bull as a sign of strength and beauty, of the powers of cunning and domination, which constitute the ultimate currency in the state of pure nature in Cohen's worldview. Philippe Zard, however, suggests a less metaphorical and more disturbing reading of the myth:

> For Solal, there is no doubt that beauty is the decorous expression of force and that the playful game with the animal leaves the suggestion of temptation by bestiality. "Jupiter . . . knew women!": before being raped by the god, Europa might have desired the beast, like Pasiphaë—Aria[d]ne's mother—[who] was attracted by the bull of Poseidon. What could have passed as the trickery of a god corresponds in fact to a secret wish of the young girl: *the ladykiller's guile fulfills the unavowed desires of the victim.*[9]

Cohen repeats this litany against the pagan in all his fiction and essays—except that Solal, his protagonist, despite his assertion of the contrary, is also a pagan bull. Zeus and Theseus follow essentially the same pattern of seduction: they covet, abduct, rape, and abandon, leading their victims to shame, despair, and ultimately suicide. And this is precisely the narrative sequence of Solal, protagonist of "La Geste des Juifs" (Cohen's early title for *Belle du Seigneur*). Cohen's first novel, *Solal,* offers a particularly protean version of this narrative. Solal covets the French consul's wife (Adrienne); he abducts her in the middle of the night (she consents); after a period of sexual frenzy, they part ways; Solal makes her jealous by seducing her niece (Aude); she despairs and commits suicide, which has no effect on Solal whatsoever. Except for Aude, all of Solal's lovers commit suicide, just as most abducted maidens in Greek mythology are eventually forsaken to their own chagrin and lonely deaths on rocky islands. Furthermore, that Cohen absolutely insists on the explicit identification with the animalistic and predatory male is evident in Solal's Russian head-to-toe fur outfit, which gives him the appearance of a bear, and a particularly frightful one when he is seen galloping on horseback.

But Ariane does not belong to this category of passive maidens of pagan antiquity, these Europas, flower-collecting virgins who bathe innocently in a pond while secretly desiring wild bulls who spy upon them. "[At] heart," she says in her second important stream of consciousness, "until now I was just a kind of virgin raped from time to time by the iram [an anagram for *mari,* husband]."* Ariane belongs, at least in the level of desire and fantasy, to the category of skilled huntresses of inviolable virginity: Diana, Aura, Nikaia: "me oh me me me," she affirms to her sister Eliane in a stream of consciousness, "a fierce independent virgin my costume the day of the costume ball you know as Diana the huntress I kept it Eliane my Dear."† Diana is the militant virgin: she does not yield to a singular bull who will have her virginity as a prize for his cunning and force; she abhors the phallic order and thus remains alone in the forest, committed to the slaughtering of beasts. Her greatest nightmare is being penetrated by one of them. Calasso spins it in a neutral manner: "All [Diana] wanted was virginity and strength, nothing else"—namely, all she wanted was to avoid males (to keep her virginity intact) and never be their subject.[10] All she wanted then was to avoid the nightmare that haunts Ariane: "an animal above an animal below," subject to the beast's "canine haha" as he falls into his "epilepsy." Ariane's surest Diana-like instinct is the one she displays first with Solal by hurling a glass at him, drawing first blood. Her initial reaction to the intrusive Zeus, disguised as an errant Hassidic Jew wearing the tie of the diplomatic commander, is a confident and bloody NO!

When viewed through the prism of this mythological syncretism, the conflict between Solal and Ariane is patently absurd. On the one hand, a descendent of the first Hebrew priest, Aaron, Solal possesses and displays many of the characteristics of Zeus ("Poor Solal man or beast?"),‡ all the while berating Ariane for her supposed pagan adoration of phallic bestiality. But the accused pagan woman in fact identifies with inviolable forest-dwelling virgins who would rather be killed by beasts than copulate with them, would rather dwell alone in the forest than live under the sign of the phallus in the city. And in his turn the supposed priest of the Law is closer in conduct and temperament to Zeus

*[A]u fond jusqu'à présent j'ai été une sorte de vierge violée de temps en temps par l'iram. (*BdS,* 612)

†moi oh moi moi moi indépendante vierge farouche mon costume le du bal masqué tu sais en Diane chasseresse je l'ai gardé Éliane chérie (*BdS,* 179)

‡pauvre Solal homme ou bête (*BdS,* 903)

than to Aaron. This is a singular mismatch. Yet when these absurd juxtapositions are viewed as components of a single dissonant persona, Solal-Ariane, surprising parallels come to the fore.

For example, while contemplating herself in the mirror from her steamy bath, absorbed in her shape, peering beneath the hue of her narcissistic image, the now-married woman cannot—still!—acknowledge her own conception in and by coitus, cannot accept that her parents were capable of *ça* and that her own origin is soiled by the bestial and chthonic "above below." Notwithstanding imperatives and disbelieving exclamations, Ariane reiterates what she most desires to elide: "no more thinking about Papa Mama doing that oh that hurts that disgusts me how is it possible that Papa and yet it is certain because of Eliane and me in the night Papa on top of Mama it's terrible parents should never."*

But she then ponders the relationship between "that" *[ça]* and her own love for her exotic Russian girlfriend: "Varvara maybe that is why I loved her so much."† The causal link *(pour ça)* puzzles at first. But Varvara's silky embraces contradict the repellent aspects of her parents' sexuality, namely, the penetration of the pious mother by the goatish, bestial father. Varvara dispels all traces of the animal that Ariane so abhors. Is it an accident that her name contains two V's, as if to reiterate its non-phallic nature, just as Chauchat in *The Magic Mountain* embodies in her very name a feline wildness absent in proper German women? For Ariane, Varvara can never be transitive with any male-female experience. Never could the names Ariane and Varvara be substituted for Papa and Mama in the next fragment: "Papa whom I respect so much dreadful Papa on top of Mama and handling her like an animal Papa also pushing the dog's cries haha haha how is this possible."‡ And then comes the satire of the supposedly elected Protestants of Geneva, promised to eternal bliss in heaven, violating their angelic wives and then shamelessly advertising the result, as if the infants were the fruit of an ethereal meditation: "obviously all people since there are always births Monsieur and Madame Turlupin have the joy of announcing the birth announcing the birth [repetition in original] of their little Turlupette what nerve to acknowledge it publicly in this way and everyone finds natural suitable this birth announcement yes everyone partakes in these

*ne plus jamais penser à Papa Maman faisant ça oh ça fait trop mal ça me dégoûte comment est-ce possible que Papa et pourtant c'est sûr puisque Éliane puisque moi dans la nuit Papa sur Maman c'est épouvantable les parents ne devraient jamais (*BdS,* 186)

†Varvara c'est peut-être pour ça que je l'ai tant aimée (*BdS,* 186)

‡Papa que je respecte tant Papa affreux sur Maman la maniant aussi comme une bête Papa poussant aussi des cris de chien haha haha comment est-ce possible. (*BdS,* 177–78)

horrors and nine months later they are not ashamed to announce it all of them even respectable people dressed during the day and all these ministers who give speeches."*

Solal shares Ariane's phallus phobias in identical terms. Traces of this dread abound everywhere in the novel, but they flare up at the very end when the two lovers are living in their isolated oceanfront Mediterranean villa named "La Belle de Mai." Love loses the support lent to it by the entire social web of recognition: political power, cocktail parties, dinners, clubs, without which the ennui of carnal desire in a (hostile) vacuum slowly, but very cruelly, appears. Unmediated by the high-octane mix of the Social, carnal desire must now be teased out by the invention of senseless cruelties, scenes of jealousy and reconciliation, capped by passionate love-making. Thus a painful scenario precedes every instance of passion, without which there remains only the boredom of eating and looking at the vast Mediterranean. Pain keeps interest alive. These situations bring about Cohen's most explicitly Proustian moments, as jealousy piques Solal's imagination, just as it did for Swann with Odette or Marcel with Albertine. Solal obsesses over the careful gathering of details concerning past affairs, possible infidelities, torment and delight mingle as he imagines these past deeds. But soon enough Ariane commits a grave mistake by confessing to an extramarital love affair with a German orchestra conductor during Solal's courtship. Worse, she admits to having copulated with the conductor the very same day that Solal seduced her at the Ritz, where she pretended to be an innocent virgin, spiritually playing religious chorals by Bach on the piano before the rarified copulation and then assuring Solal that she would stay awake for the rest of the night to savor the singular and miraculous experience. And this after a day during which she copulated with her lover, lied to her husband, and was seduced by yet a second lover. Ariane thus becomes for Solal the ultimate hypocritical female who, despite all outer appearance of propriety, secretly adores the bull: "Oh, the face of a child and a saint, but of a saint who was getting bonked! No, no, enough."† Paradoxically, Ariane becomes for Solal the paragon of what she herself most explicitly abhors. Even more interestingly, the clearly zoological terms used by Ariane in her first stream of consciousness

*évidemment tous les gens puisqu'il y a tout le temps des naissances monsieur et madame Turlupin ont la joie de vous part de la naissance faire part de la naissance de leur petite Turlupette quel toupet d'avouer ainsi publiquement et tout le monde trouve naturel convenable cet avis de naissance oui tous font ces horreurs et neuf mois après ils n'ont pas honte de l'annoncer tous même des gens respectables le jour habillés et aussi ces ministres qui font des discours. (*BdS,* 178)

†Oh, ce visage d'enfant et de sainte, mais d'une sainte qui recevait des chocs! Non, non, assez. (*BdS,* 961)

to describe copulation are here taken up by Solal. The same discourse, slightly altered by voice and circumstances, circulates from character to character across all Cohen's novels and essays (from Louise Cohen to Saltiel to Mangeclous to Ariane to Solal). Solal imagines Ariane copulating with Serge (whom Solal keeps misnaming Dietrich): "And now the baby of the orchestra loosened his incisors and passed his hairy tongue, his ox's tongue on the nipple more pointed than a German helmet! And while the bull licked, she smiled, the choral-playing pianist! Oh, the hairy hand that now lifted the skirt!"* These words fully reiterate the disgust that Ariane herself felt toward copulation in her first stream of consciousness, although she articulates it more convincingly and more lucidly, free as she is from Solal's infantile resentment.

Serge becomes the focal point of these scenes of jealousy and violence and is the pretext for a spiral of violence. Solal focuses his ire on the black moustache of Ariane's lover, using it as a condensation of male body hair, the most disturbing feature of the masculine body, which most likens it, as in the passage quoted just above, to the body of a bull *(taureau)*. Serge passes his hairy tongue *(langue poilue)* over Ariane's breasts while his hairy hand *(main poilue)* lifts her skirt. But beyond his body hair lies that black moustache, a trait that contrasts with the conductor's white hair, a pure sign of the orchestra conductor's imperious virility: "Oh, the white hair, oh this black moustache that she loved! . . . But then why had she authorized the hairy hand?"† And again: "Oh, the black moustache on the golden breast! Oh, she lovy-doving under the mouth of the moustached baby with the white mane that suckled."‡ Serge obviously serves a synergetic function: he is German and his phallus is compared to the spiked *Pickelhaube* helmet worn by German troops in World War I *(plus pointu qu'un casque allemand!)*, which is just another permutation on Cohen's perennial loathing of the horned, forest-dwelling Teutonic man who covers his longing for the pagan (romantic naturalism, for example) with a thin patina of Christian piety, symbolized by the (spiritual) white hair that crowns the black moustache. Ariane sees Serge for the first time when he conducts Beethoven's Pastoral Symphony. In short, Solal sees the German conductor as a composite of all he abhors: a bull, a warrior whose phallus points

*Et maintenant le bébé d'orchestre desserrait ses incisives et passait sa langue poilue, sa langue de bœuf sur le mamelon plus pointu qu'un casque allemand! Et pendant que le taureau léchait, elle souriait, la pianoteuse de chorals! Oh, la main poilue qui soulevait la jupe maintenant! (*BdS,* 955)

†Oh, ces cheveux blancs, oh cette moustache noire qu'elle aimait! . . . Mais alors pourquoi avait-elle autorisé la main poilue? (*BdS,* 954)

‡Oh, la moustache noire sur le sein doré! Oh, elle tourterellante sous la bouche du bébé moustachu à crinière blanche qui tétait (*BdS,* 955)

up from the center of his black moustache to the pointed end of his savage German helmet; Zeus, masquerading as a Christian, who seduces a married woman. The German is, in sum, not unlike Solal.

But this is not our first encounter with the moustache. We recall yet again that Cohen contemptuously qualifies his father as the "male and tamer with the strong moustache." This black moustache stands for the animal-male regime of the father. And this same moustache now defiles Ariane, just as it defiled that other "elected" woman, the mother. We have again come full circle: from the autobiography to the stream of consciousness, the same motif resurfaces. What appears at first as an absolute contrast, the adultery of a Swiss aristocrat with a German symphonic conductor, reenacts in exact detail, through the metonymy of the moustache, the most private and humiliating of domestic scenes that took place in the Coens' modest apartment in Marseille. Difference and otherness are merely narrative lures here. The moustache always refers to the tyranny of the father and the incessant repetition of the trauma that it causes. Solal desires to be with Ariane, just as he would have liked to be with his mother, outside of the regime of nature, outside the grip of masculine power. But at every turn, his fantasy is defiled by the hairy male(s).

This is no interpretive leap that hinges on a fanciful interpretation of the moustache metonymy, for Cohen himself offers this precise analysis in the crystal lucidity of Solal's own crucial stream of consciousness. As the lovers slide into boredom and thus into mutual cruelty as a panacea against this boredom, and just before their erotic life is recharged by the omnipresence of the German conductor and his black moustache, Solal's stream of consciousness leaves no doubt as to the true nature of his overt longing, regret, desire:

> no longer need to act as the bastard of expensive maliciousness to please her to relieve her from boredom yes as early as tomorrow son and mother forever and enough of this mucous business and get out of here man the dreadful the bestial *the father with whom she deceived me deceived her son* I'll ask her if she loves me more if she loves her son or the man who slammed she will tell me yes . . . what do I care I'll live as a madman until my dying day if I can finally love her in truth oh my love I'll be able to love you with a love that does not perish.*

*"plus besoin de faire le salaud de cher méchant pour lui plaire pour la désennuyer oui dès demain fils et mère à jamais et assez d'entreprises muqueuses et hors d'ici l'homme le bestial l'affreux *le père avec qui elle m'a trompé a trompé son fils* je lui demanderai si elle m'aime davantage si elle aime davantage son fils que l'homme qui a claqué elle me dira que oui . . . que m'importe de vivre en fou jusqu'à ma mort si je peux enfin l'aimer dans la vérité ô mon amour je vais pouvoir t'aimer de l'amour qui ne périt point" (*BdS,* 916–17; emphasis added)

The dread of repetition hovers over this paragraph. Solal is interchangeable with his father, Ariane with his mother, and the dread resides in repeating their bestial acts that the little Albert so resented. This is perhaps the most convincing and explicit thematic hybridization of *Le Livre de ma mère* and *Belle du Seigneur.* Looking at Ariane, Solal sees his mother. Thinking of himself, he sees his father. Acknowledging the cruelty of their relationship, he recalls his father's wrath, his mother's submission, his own resentment—and his enduring fantasy of being at last—be it a few moments before death—liberated from the regime of the black moustache. The paradigmatic shifts of man, beast, father and of Ariane and the mother are clear. Solal is then at once the moustached tyrant, the betrayed son, and the future androgynous, feminine, sororial companion, and Ariane is the harlot who pretends to adore the moustache, the mother and that lover, sister, mother with whom no sticky (mucus) bodily fluids need be exchanged. Solal and Ariane mimic that which they abhor. And to cap it all, this montage can only be more generally understood in terms of the overreaching moral experiment that is at play here: were Ariane capable of loving Solal in the guise of an old Hassidic Jew, the pair would have been liberated from "the mucous business," liberated from the necessity of playing stupid roles not of their making and (real) desire, and capable, finally, of "lov[ing] in truth . . . able to love . . . with a love that does not perish." (Needless to add that, as we saw in the previous chapter, the inverse of this moral experiment is also true: were Solal able to love a woman, were Solal capable of seeing beyond bestiality and power, were he not seduced himself by Solal the powerful seducer, were he able in short to love Rachel rather than Ariane—he would altogether have avoided "the mucous business" and the comic but humiliating necessity of playing "a bastard of expensive maliciousness" (*BS,* 916). But that is not an option for a narcissistic masochist who secretly delights in his own dismemberment, itself inscribed in the grand history of a martyred people on the eve of yet another holocaust.)

But, going further in the game of substitutions in this stream of consciousness, Cohen also imports the dwarf Rachel from the Berlin underground into this synthetic montage: "my little slightly crooked cardboard [Purim] crown to make a crazy king but kind *[sympathique].*"* Solal yearns for a crooked baton, a crazy baton, yearns for the kingdom without a phallus, a "sympathetic" phallus in sum. He is an infant king; Ariane, a mother queen, the two living in *douceur* and complicity, a paradise free from the moustached king(s): "a son

*ma couronne de carton un peu penchée de côté pour faire roi toqué mais gentil (*BdS,* 916)

does not have to lie [with a woman] a son has only to cherish."* Now circling back to Ariane's first stream of consciousness, we also see that Solal and Ariane not only share the same phallic phobias but also an identical vision of paradise.

Ariane's interlocutor in paradise is a postmenopausal woman, irrevocably operating outside the orbit of the moustache. To be available, the old woman must be isolated at the edge between life and death, at the edge of the ocean of death. This is how Ariane imagines their conversation:

> it's funny I almost never think about my brother a grandmother that's what I need a wrinkled little pippin very good in the solitary house on the top of the dune I'll go see her so that she consoles me with café-au-lait the wind howling outside but we'll be happy inside in the warmth what's going on Ariane I don't know grandmother I am unhappy I need something need what my darling a real girlfriend that's it a friend to whom I would tell all that I would admire for whom I would kill myself and not be raped by a stranger yes my poor little one I understand I understand you but perhaps you will find it this great friendship.†

To the grandmother, Ariane will tell the truth: males are beasts who kill and rape, and desire exists only for "une amie" such as Varvara. To the grandmother Ariane will recount the pain of submitting to a fumbling fool of a husband. Only with the grandmother could Ariane ever cease pretending, stop acting out the comedy of desire.[11]

This fantasy of paradise also occurs, and in identical terms, in *Le Livre de ma mère.* The only escape from the phallic order—which Cohen deftly characterizes as "this continual duo between humans, this disheartening refrain of the baboon. 'I am bigger than thou. I know I am smaller than you. I am bigger than thou. I know I am smaller than you. I am bigger than thou. I know I am smaller than you.' And so on, always, everywhere, Baboons, all of them!"‡—lies in retreat with the isolated grandmother, where the macabre syntax and semantics of domination and submission, of the *thou* and the *you*

*un fils n'a pas à coucher un fils n'a qu'à chérir (*BdS,* 915)

†drôle je ne pense presque jamais à mon frère une grand-mère voilà ce qu'il me faudrait une petite reinette ridée très bonne dans la maison solitaire en haut de la dune j'irais la voir pour qu'elle me console avec du café au lait le vent dehors hurlant mais on serait bien au chaud qu'est-ce que tu as Ariane je sais pas grand-mère je suis malheureuse j'ai besoin de quelque chose de quoi ma chérie d'une vraie amie voilà une amie à qui je raconterais tout que j'admirerais pour qui je me tuerais et pas être violée par un étranger oui ma pauvre petite je comprends je te comprends mais tu la rencontreras peut-être cette grande amitié (*BdS,* 186)

‡"ce duo continuel parmi les humains, cet écœurant refrain babouin. 'Je suis plus que toi. Je sais que je suis moins que vous. Je suis plus que toi. Je sais que je suis moins que vous. Je suis plus que toi. Je sais que je suis moins que vous.' Et ainsi de suite, toujours, partout. Babouins, tous!" (*BdS,* 366)

(tu/vous), dueling about the *more* or *less,* no longer dominate. Cohen's version of paradise mirrors Ariane's to such an extent that it merits a second full quotation:

> Wide awake, I dream and speak to myself of what it would be like if she were still alive. I would live with her, *in a little way [petitement]*, in solitude. A *little* house, beside the sea, far from men. The two of us, she and I, a *little* house a bit crooked, and no one else. A very quiet *little* life without talent. I would make myself a new soul, a *little* old lady's soul like hers so that she should not be bothered by me and so should be completely happy. . . . Two old sisters, she and I . . . two real *little* old ladies. . . . And this is how I imagine paradise.*[12]

There is the same visceral loathing of baboonery; the same desire to step out of the shadow of the father and be with the mother alone, like two old sisters, two postmenopausal women, self-sufficient unto themselves. No longer subject to the wheel of phallic necessity of domination and submission, the two women will be like parasites of each other, but parasites in a symbiotic relationship.[13]

Yet the wheel of necessity is relentless. Isolation at the edge of the ocean with an unconditionally loving grandmother is not an option. Two alternatives exist: immediate suicide (as on the first page of the novel) or life in the shadow of the male (either by imitation, spite, or inversion). The novel resolves this tension by its use of many voices, discourses, and fluid identities, a literary shadowboxing match, where Solal-Ariane assumes both gender roles, and, as life slowly fades out, shuttle between the two identities in the most theatrical fashion. The first suicide having been botched, and lacking courage for another attempt, Ariane finally turns her attention to Solal, her elected ferryman to accompany her down the Styx into Hades. She begins with a description of a sexual-gender ideal that foreshadows Solal's true identity. Ariane is again very lucid and prescient: beneath Solal the super male, the Zeuslike Don Juan, hidden in turn beneath Solal the old rabbi, she perceives the feminine son who occupies a place somewhere between Serge and Varvara.

Ariane's erotic ideal resembles "a beautiful naked woman who would at the same time be a man isn't that good . . . yes who would be at the same time a man."† She goes further when describing her sexual fantasy about a powerful

*Toute éveillé, je rêve et je me raconte comment ce serait si elle était en vie. Je vivrais avec elle, *petitement,* dans la solitude. Une *petite* maison, au bord de la mer, loin des hommes. Nous deux, elle et moi, une *petite* maison un peu tordue, et personne d'autre. Une *petite* vie très tranquille et sans talent. Je me ferais une âme nouvelle, une âme de *petite* vieille comme elle pour qu'elle ne soit pas gênée par moi et qu'elle soit tout à fait heureuse. . . . Deux vieilles sœurs, elle et moi. . . . deux vraies *petites* vieilles. . . . Et c'est ainsi que j'imagine le paradis. (*LM,* 751–52; emphasis added)

†une belle femme nue qui serait en même temps un homme pas bien ça . . . oui qui serait en même temps un homme (*BdS,* 175)

hermit who will handle her just the way she wishes to be handled: "I would like so very much there I am flat and my hermit folds me into halves and then quarters like a piece of cloth and stuffs me into his sack *he is a man but without hair* and when one gets close to the source of the shades he opens his sack and unfolds me it's so good"* The male/hermit overwhelms Ariane in his power to manhandle her, yet he is hairless, smooth but powerful, aggressive but not cannibalistic. The ideal sexual being thus is both female and male, possesses a phallus, may be aggressive at times but is never hairy. If a phallus there must be, then let this phallus project itself out from the smooth curves and soft skin of a feminine body. In a later stream of consciousness, Ariane's ideal of a perfect erotic being transpires with even more detail: "it's crazy how I feminize myself I would rather enjoy being a man for a certain thing but to keep all the rest female the hips the breasts that would be in sum the perfect being."† Such is Ariane's erotic ideal: the man-woman, the she-man whom she will soon enough recognize in Solal the oriental dandy.

The Two Belles

Ariane once again waits for Solal in her bath, where she delves into her second important stream of consciousness, another entire chapter (chapter 70), another twenty pages, 700 lines of unpunctuated free-flowing text. After weeks of waiting, he is to return from Berlin and the lovers are to be reunited. Even though the train arrives at seven, Solal is not expected at Ariane's for another two hours, because he must prepare himself with extreme care: "that brings him here at nine o'clock all that because monsieur wishes to please bathe for an hour and perhaps a meticulous shave," which leads Ariane to reveal the meaning of Solal's preciosity, "it's your feminine side my dear feminine also are your glances in the mirror you look at yourself a bit too often a weakness my dear and also comedianlike with his dressing gowns too lovely too long oh my friend this is thus how we are we others your slaves."‡

*j'aimerais tellement voilà je suis plate et mon ermite me plie en deux puis en quatre comme une étoffe m'enferme dans sa besace *c'est un homme mais sans poils* et quand on arrive près de la source des ombrages il ouvre sa besace et il me déplie c'est tellement bon (*BdS,* 185; emphasis added)

†c'est fou ce que je me féminise j'aimerais assez être un homme pour une certaine chose mais garder tout le reste féminin les hanches les seins ça serait en somme l'être parfait (*BdS,* 618)

‡qui s'amène ici à neuf heures tout ça parce que monsieur veut plaire bain d'une heure peut-être rasage minutieux c'est d'ailleurs votre côté féminin mon cher féminins aussi vos coups d'œil dans la glace vous vous regardez un peu trop une faiblesse ça mon ami et puis comédien avec ses robes de chambre trop belles trop longues oui mon ami c'est ainsi que nous sommes nous autres vos esclaves. (*BdS,* 604)

When seen in his transparent interiority or even just in his domestic setting, this overbearing male is feminine at heart. When Solal gazes in the mirror, he reflects Ariane's own vain and narcissistic glance—and vice versa. That shared narcissistic gaze constitutes the site of their particular truth, revealed by Solal from the very beginning of the novel, where the man who is "beautiful enough to [make you] vomit" intersects with "the most beautiful woman in the world."[14]

But Ariane's last statement: "[T]his is thus how we are we others your slaves" drives the equation between the two to its limit. To wit: this is how we women are; we are your slaves, whom you, Solal des Solal, resemble. Slave and master concurrently, man in the mirror of the eyes of other men; woman in the mirror of your bedroom. Solal simultaneously plays the role of the Beauty and of the Beast, of the Belle and of the Seigneur, or of the Belle subjugated to her Seigneur, of the Seigneur torturing his Belle, that is—himself. That baboon game of domination and submission, of the *you* and *thou* and the *more* and *less* is played out within the self, within the Belle and the Seigneur. This matrix proposition could have applied to each episode so far discussed; simply substitute the notion of Hassidic Jew for that of woman and you have a convincing reading of the theme of the Jew as marginal stranger. The statement "You are like us, despite our subjugation to you" could have been addressed to Solal by the Valorous in the underground of the Château Saint-Germain, or to Solal by the dwarf Rachel and her uncles in the Berlin underground. To recognize the dynamic identity between disparate categories is to grasp Solal's epic dissonance, which is repeated in different novelistic montages throughout *Belle du Seigneur.*

But nowhere is the identity between Solal and Ariane as categorically asserted as in the observations that the old maid Mariette makes on the subject of the two in her chapter-long streams of consciousness.[15] This allows Cohen to focalize on Solal-Ariane from the point of view of a maid—awkward and colloquial, but all too observant. Describing the daily routines of the two "priests of love," the mirror imaging of the two convincingly comes to the fore. In a way, here, Mariette describes the best period of their charmed exile in the south of France, their utopian wager against the principle of the real: to exist as two lovers, two women, one fully feminine, the other phallic but hairless, in the utopia of romance from which all traces of the beast are rigorously excluded. And thus Mariette's stream of consciousness offers a minute and highly comic description of Solal and Ariane's life in the secluded villa. Mariette's narrative strongly suggests the gender symmetry between Solal and Ariane, the two precious women—except that they are nevertheless condemned to play their traditional gender roles, and thus the potential feminine-feminine utopia turns into yet another nightmare.

The crucial text for us is chapter 90 (pp. 801–16), where Mariette focuses on the lovers' orchestration of a ritualized ideal existence of unending erotic romance in the Mediterranean villa. Solal and Ariane see each other only when they are impeccable—ready for love-making, a promenade, or a meal. Ideal lovers, they must never betray the slightest hint of bodily functions—burping, coughing, flatulence, urination, or defecation—and, when indisposed or ill, they simply avoid each other altogether. Their separate bathrooms and toilets are arranged in such a way that there is never the hint of their real usage. The sound of a toilet flushing is pure horror, because it might also flush away the allure of the nondefecating erotic body, always seductive or seducing, embodied, to be sure, but never outside the bounds of ideal representation, which excludes the urinary and intestinal tracts. The words "soiled underwear," for example, are never to be mentioned by the maid, even though, she insists, neither Ariane nor Solal actually ever soil their underwear: "monsieur's dirty underwear is never dirty either."* Mariette repeatedly emphasizes, by means of these revealing parallels, the symmetry between the two.

To be seen, each must be at once "ready and visible" *(prêt et visible),* which means that by definition they rarely see each other in full. Circuitous ways must therefore be concocted to communicate while being partially hidden or separated. This is the stuff of a farce. Bells are installed so that an elaborate code of rings communicates their degree of readiness and visibility. Two rings signify that Ariane should come and talk to Solal from beyond the closed door; three rings signify that Ariane is asking Solal whether she can freely circulate in the house without his coming out of his room, and so on. "[I]t's the house of electrical phantoms I was telling myself."† When the electricity is cut off, the maid serves as intermediary between the two impeccable beauties. Notice in the following passage the symmetry between Ariane and Solal: "go ask monsieur if I can move around because you understand she does not want to be seen without being dolled up enough, *and the same goes for him.*"‡ Through the keyhole, Mariette observes even more farcical scenes: Ariane enters Solal's room walking backward and talks to him facing the other way, because neither

*"il est jamais sale non plus le linge sale de monsieur" (*BdS,* 815)

†"[C]'est la maison des fantômes électriques je me disais" (*BdS,* 811)

‡"allez demander à monsieur si je peux circuler, parce que vous comprenez elle veut pas être vue pas assez pomponnée, *et lui même chose"* (*BdS,* 812; emphasis added)

is "ready and visible"; or she enters his room and talks to him with her eyes covered by a scarf, because the Beau Seigneur de la Belle is neither ready nor visible.[16]

Mariette's lucidity is exemplary. She recognizes this purely theatrical staging for what it is, namely, the narcissism of two females, bound in a rigid priestly ritual, whose ideal, physical perfection in its optimal mise-en-scène, renders their existence morbid and entombs them in the house of the dead: "there they go acting as bishops of love in their tomb."* Mariette focuses here on the essential, the protean formula of the whole novel: *the self-fashioning of death with the other who is at heart the same.* And no one articulates this identity, the farcical theater of "electrical phantoms" and the morbidity of it all as well as the old maid Mariette does, the naïve buffoon who, like Mangeclous elsewhere, tells the truth in her proletarian patois.

Dressed in their robes, prisoners of romantic rites and rigid routines that force the magical onto the banal, they are "bishops" of love, officiants at a romantic sacrifice. Their carefully choreographed encounters read like those of two women: "He would enter, and it would be a wonder to contemplate each other, demi-gods in their robes of priestly love, poetic and cleaned."† And then the comedy of dressing, watching, adjusting; the whole coquettish montage that occupies much of Ariane's time, just as it does that of her counterpart: part Varvara, part Serge: "a beautiful naked woman who would at the same time be a man isn't that good?"

In the novel, the Solal-Ariane hybrid identity is suggested by Solal from the first scene, which is subsequently reiterated in so many ways (mimicking, mirrors, fantasies). But to posit this hybrid identity of the two in the one in a more explicit or categorical manner would simply disable the narrative both for the novelist and for the critic. To succeed, narratives require that identities between disparate parts be suppressed, antagonisms exaggerated, and a plot woven around supposed differences. The same identity in two would collapse the structural cohesion of a narrative. On the face of it, Ariane must come off as a Bovaryesque or Kareninaesque dupe of phallic mystification, and Solal must appear as a phallic Zeus struggling with a Jewish shadow. Cohen's effectiveness as a novelist springs from his narrative juxtapositions of probing streams of consciousness and a strong plot, resulting in a comic interplay between the inner lucidity of the characters and their sense of obligation to act

*"ça s'en vont faire les évêques de l'amour dans leur sarcophage" (*BdS,* 816)

†Il entrait, et c'était la merveille de se contempler, demi-dieux en leurs robes d'amoureuse prêtrise, poétiques et nettoyés. (*BdS,* 710)

out plots not of their making, not of their desire, but ultimately fatal in these particular historical circumstances. If Solal-Ariane is truly a single identity montage, which is my thesis here, then they must be split apart and pitted against each other in the same way that dissonant voices may clash in psychotic discourse but nonetheless belong to a single empirical subject.

Apotheosis and Jouissance

We now turn to the second half of Ariane's first stream of consciousness, which moves outward from the modes of interior confession and recollection to a narrative of possibility, a turn toward Solal, who incarnates the possible, constitutes the other who is at first tortured then worshiped. From the very first stream of consciousness, the trajectory of this movement, its narratives and metaphors, constitute a mise-en-abyme of the whole novel, not just in the prediction of the unfolding of events but also for their interpretation. Ariane's stream of consciousness already anticipates a reading of *Belle du Seigneur.*

The novel begins and ends in blood. Ariane draws first blood by throwing a glass at Solal's face, thus finally drawing the blood that the dwarf Rachel craves but does not dare spill. Solal walks away from their first one-on-one encounter wearing his cherished new flesh wound like expensive jewelry, a crown of thorns bestowed by the "elected" one as a first gesture in a blood-soaked epic. The wound constitutes their first exchange of goods—his Purim Carnival against her Easter Passion. Afterward, they are even, his intrusion into her bedroom redeemed by the wound over his peeping eye. It also occasions their first moment of complicity, as the undersecretary-general conceals how he earned his fleshy jewel and Ariane withholds how and why she bestowed it. Blood is their first bond; it will also be their last.

Ariane's outburst of violence against Solal parallels her phallic phobias, and the glass hurled at the intrusive male becomes the spear with which Diana would have pierced any intruder. Finally, she can inflict the wounds that she secretly desires to deliver to her imprisoning satyr of a husband. Yet she remains intrigued all the same, as if Solal's blood is merely a foretaste of fleshy thrills to come. What a mise-en-scène this strange fellow has concocted! The felonious audacity of intruding through the window late at night, the carnivalesque histrionics of customs, accents, and gestures, the philosophical contempt heaped on a stranger in her bedroom. With this one extraordinary act, Solal's singularity as a conceptual montage easily overtakes Varvara in the hierarchy of desire: "oh so beautiful to have wanted to be loved as a hideous old

man."* And when she thinks of Solal's anti-feminine tirade at the Ritz, Ariane concludes, "it's not Varvara who would have said that."† However sweet, silky, soft, and unthreatening, Varvara lacked this imaginative capacity for the dramatization of being. Ariane understands Solal as a poet of existence and his theatrical maleness as a secondary feature—another mask among many. Once she has overcome her primary repulsion from the hairy bull (and from the Jew), there transpires a far deeper desire for ecstasy in pain. Solal is a "nasty man who is good and the others are good men who are nasty."‡ No matter how contemptuous Solal seems, his venom, compared to Adrien's saccharine affection, is the poison that heals.

Solal's magnetism resides in the cruelty that his smile betrays: "he can be nasty that is what is chic about him damn *[zut]* at the Ritz he said a bunch of things against too bad me *his cruel smile devastates me with happiness.*"§ The "cruel smile" refers to Ariane's masochistic joy and Solal's sadism, but, more abstractly and self-referentially, it also alludes to the very painful joy of the writing of the novel—always an aesthetic yet masochistic enterprise where the polyphonic, dissonant, satirical, and thus fundamentally cruel redescriptions, meet their perfect expression in language. After all, Albert Cohen himself defines the novelist as someone in possession of a good heart and a mean eye.[17] By definition, the great novel offers both writer and reader this "cruel smile that devastates," because it chronicles in minute details the desire and even orgiastic joy of dying after one's fashion, of being one's own executioner in the most delectable manner.

The sensual aggression comes to the fore in the second half of the stream of consciousness, only to build—through surprising pivots—into a Christian Passion play ending with a sacred orgasmic crescendo worthy of Molly Bloom's repeated orgasmic "Yes's." At first Ariane sees Solal only as an imposter of the worst kind: a court Jew, a libidinal male, and an impolite intruder to boot. She viscerally despises this phallic intrusion into her privacy. The depressed housewife finally pours out all her wrath as she fantasizes about cruelly torturing and humiliating the ultimate other against whom she defines herself: Germanic, she is not a Jew; lesbian, she does not desire the male; Genevan Protestant, she loathes Solal's baroque and very oriental theatricality. But she

*oh si beau d'avoir voulu être aimé en vieil affreux (*BdS,* 610)

†c'est pas Varvara qui aurait dit ça (*BdS,* 610)

‡un méchant qui est bon les autres c'est des bons qui sont méchants (*BdS,* 610)

§il peut être méchant c'est ça qui est chic zut au Ritz il a dit un tas de choses contre tant pis moi *son sourire cruel me dévaste de bonheur* (*BdS,* 613; emphasis added)

can always put this seemingly ultimate other on the wheel of torture and thereby remain close to him while torturing him: "the chic thing would be to whip him and that he should yell out of of pain yell my dear yell yes that he should yell and that he should beg me to stop it all in tears with such comic grimaces I beg you madame I beg forgiveness on my knees and me I shall laugh oh there there on his knees and without his monocle he begs me with his hands joined with a contemptible expression of horror."*

This is more than generic sadomasochism. Solal may indeed be an audacious undersecretary-general of the League of Nations, revered by Ariane's husband as his superior, but Ariane sees him first and foremost as a Jew, and as a lowly oriental one at that, and with this visceral contempt, the otherwise tender woman quivers with delectation as she tortures her victim:

> oh the tears flowing from his eyes the to and fro [*dzin et dzan*] on the tears no pity the tears furrowed the cheeks of *Yaourt ben Solal ben Zouli Tapis* but the brave young woman whipped him without respite and on the kike's wretched face the red lines were turning white and really stood out and he begged to the point of cleaving the soul but the beautiful young woman unperturbed whipped on without respite and *dzin* and *dzan* that will teach you my good man to have such a conk was telling him the admirable young woman with a caustic irony oh how much he bore he is at the end of his wits he can no longer go on†

Ariane taunts her victim with a name that in itself tells a complete story: "Yaourt ben Solal ben Zouli Tapis"—which stands in obvious opposition to her aristocratic name: "Ariane Cassandre Corisande d'Auble." *Yaourt,* for the French invective "youpin/youtre," which we have encountered in the street hawker trauma. *Ben,* a Hebrew word, meaning "son of"; then Solal, both a proper name and a surname. She mocks his unusual name of Solal des Solal, whose redundancy she correctly interprets as Jew of Jews—a tautology trying disparately and theatrically to create a difference. Finally, *ben Zouli* evokes the

*le chic serait de le cravacher et qu'il hurle de douleur hurle mon cher hurle oui qu'il hurle et qu'il me supplie de m'arrêter tout en larmes avec des grimaces tellement comiques je vous en supplie madame je vous demande pardon à genoux et moi je rirai oh là là à genoux et sans monocle il me supplie les mains jointes avec une expression abjecte de terreur (*BdS,* 181)

†oh les larmes coulent de ses yeux dzin et dzan sur les larmes pas de pitié les larmes sillonnaient les joues de *Yaourt ben Solal ben Zouli Tapis* mais la courageuse jeune femme le cravachait sans répit et sur l'ignoble visage de Yaourt les raies rouges devenaient blanches bien en relief et il suppliait à fendre l'âme mais la belle jeune femme impavide cravachait sans trêve et dzin et dzan ça vous apprendra mon bonhomme à avoir un tel pif lui disait l'admirable jeune femme avec une ironie mordante oh ce qu'il en a reçu il est à bout de forces il ne peut même plus (*BdS,* 181; emphasis added)

Orient, and *Tapis* refers to the lowly class of oriental rug peddlers, Solal's progenitors in Ariane's mind. The name *Yaourt ben Solal ben Zouli Tapis* might be translated into English as "Kike son of a Sephardic [son of an] oriental rug merchant." No name could be further from the mythological Ariane Cassandre Corisande of the noble lineage of Auble. Her name is not a tautological name; it is a string of predicates and noble genitives. Solal the feminized oriental *metèque* repels Ariane to her core: "oh really that a woman could truly be attracted by this type of seedy shadowy man with *eyes like a Turkish dancer* it's unbelievable I wouldn't want to meet him at the corner of a bazaar."*

The good whipping accomplished, Ariane releases the Jew to his native and rightful place, saying: "off you go to the synagogue go have your wounds dressed by large noses on small legs."† Solal's rightful place is certainly not in the Palace of the League of Nations. Ariane thinks: "Your place is not here with me, Europa, but with the disfigured subhumans in your recalcitrant synagogue full of grotesque Rachels and Jérémies and Mangeclous who will tend your wounds." Thus the fictional stream of consciousness of the beloved repeats the autobiographical street hawker's invectives on Cohen's tenth birthday and with the exact plot of the Berlin underground where Solal is wounded by the "blond beasts" and healed by the deformed Rachel. Ariane's language bears an uncanny resemblance to that of the street hawker: "'You there, you are a Yid, aren't you? . . . you're not quite French, are you? . . . a little thoroughbred kike . . . you can slip by on, we've seen enough of you, you don't belong here, this is not your country, you have no business being here, go . . . get the hell out of here go to Jerusalem and see if I'm there."‡ Everything is a question of places and displacement, of love and repulsion. "off you go to the synagogue," "off you go to Jerusalem," "just go away": therein lies Solal's catastrophic odyssey—climb up and down the secret staircase of the Château Saint-Germain, crouch in the Berlin underground, hide behind the wall of the Palace of the League of Nations spying on your kin. Never can Solal just belong *(en être)* naturally and at ease, either as a spectator of a street hawker or even (or especially) as a participant in a sadistic fantasy. That normalcy in its

*oh vraiment qu'une femme puisse être attirée par ce genre d'homme louche ténébreux avec *ses yeux de danseuse turque* c'est incroyable j'aimerais pas le rencontrer au coin d'un souk. (*BdS,* 187; emphasis added)

†allez hop à la synagogue allez faire panser vos blessures par des gros nez sur des petites pattes (*BdS,* 182)

‡"Toi, tu es un Youpin, hein?'" . . . "tu es encore un Français à la manque, hein? . . . un petit Youtre pur sang. . . . tu peux filer, on t'a assez vu, tu es pas chez toi ici, c'est pas ton pays ici, tu as rien à faire chez nous, allez . . . va un peu voir à Jérusalem si j'y suis." (*Ô vous,* 1052)

most banal or most bizarre forms remains ontologically foreign to him. His *en être* is a permanent utopia (no place); his name, permanently an index both to his tautological overdetermination as a Jew and his permanent displacement—Solal des Solal wandering misty Europe, repelled by his own people, repelling others. His lot is to be a Hebrew, a *passeur* from identity to identity, costume to costume, slipping in through a window, kicked out through a door, and always disturbing the peace.[18]

But Solal is also that perverse erotic subject who takes a great deal of masochistic joy in being tortured at the hands of the blonde beast, especially when Ariane spits in his face the identical invectives that derailed his life at the age of ten and turned him into a suicidal subject that fateful evening at the Marseille public lavatories. No doubt Solal identifies at some perverse level with Ariane's description of him and of where he ultimately belongs—which is why he disguises himself as an old Jew in the first place. In that sense, in this torture scene, Ariane is simply a montage of all the anti-Semitic hatred that defines Solal's identity as the hated Jew whom he both abhors and cherishes, which he suffers from and performs. Ariane and Solal are alloyed into a single montage, of which the deepest points of contact are to be found in the seemingly meaningless recesses of this stream of consciousness chatter. Ariane in this case is just the active agent in an *autophagic organism;* she is the half that consumes the other half of the same entity. She is the internalized street hawker reincarnated in the image of Viviane, his childhood imaginary playmate.

More specifically, Ariane's sadistic fantasy resonates with two recurrent motifs in Cohen's most elemental montage: Ariane bleeds Solal, just as Rachel was tempted to bleed him but did not because Solal viewed her as an unworthy torturer. Deep down, Ariane, the "elected one," wants to bite and castrate Solal as much as the despised Rachel does: "I'd love to smoke a cigar . . . I'd like to have a chocolate candy when I eat one I would look at him before putting it in my mouth putting it in my mouth I turn it on all sides and . . . then snap I bite again bite again the presents that [Adrien] gives me."* Solal is the gift brought by Adrien, which Ariane would now like to crack in her mouth. The oral castration even surfaces in the whipping phantasm , for as she tortures Solal with a whip *dzin et dzan* in the face, forcing him to kneel and beg for mercy, she fantasizes about taking a break between strokes to contemplate her work: "I'll chain him up tightly so that he can't hurt me so I can whip him at

*j'aimerais fumer un cigare . . . j'aimerais un bonbon au chocolat quand j'en mange un je le regarde avant de le mettre dans la bouche le mettre dans la bouche je le tourne de tous les côtés et . . . puis crac je remords remords les cadeaux [his penis] qu'[Adrien] m'apporte (*BdS,* 175–76)

my leisure and eating a chocolate truffle after each snap of the whip one truffle for me"*

Likewise, she laces her *dzin* and *dzan* whipping with the street hawker's invectives, which act as the verbal correlative to the whip's lashing, and appear just as perversely satisfying to both torturer and victim. These practices, of course, continue Solal's secret delectation in anti-Semitic discourse and acts. Ariane simply serves as a vehicle for Solal's own fantasies in the most novelistically efficient manner: Let the adversary perform the vivisection.

The Aryan aristocrat torments the oriental Jew. Absolute difference, spiteful phobia is inscribed in blood. This torture phantasm marks the moment of absolute polarity and conflict between the two (who are but one). Ariane lashes the flesh of Solal, searching above all for that humiliation in his eyes. Contemptuous of her victim, despising every detail of his existence, she recoils in horror at the thought of any contact with him, except for the highly intimate exchange between torturer and victim. But as much as she resists the mere thought of Solal, this resistance, evident in the torture fantasy, only inserts him even deeper into her mind. And while she soon pivots in the stream of consciousness from apparent repulsion to desire, the sadomasochistic modality of the relationship is stamped once and for all. The torture-passion trope remains constant; only the roles of torturer and victim oscillate: Solal becomes the dominant Savior (Seigneur) and Ariane his subjugated disciple on all the sadomasochistic levels, hence its death-bound dimensions.

In truth, even before the turn, despite conscious hostility to Solal, Ariane spends her days and nights waiting for this rabbinical clown to deliver her salvation (what a scenario!). She recognizes his singularity, his suicidal insanity, as a fitting complement to her own. She slowly realizes what Solal understood at once at the Brazilian reception. Slowly the two halves converge. Although conflicted, she knows that the madman will return, and that she will then cede to him; and she awaits Solal, naked in her bathtub with the window wide open, her gaze fixed upon the open space just beyond, her expectations heightened.

To effectuate such a shift from repulsion to desire, from torturing "Yaourt ben Solal ben Zouli Tapis" to venerating the intimate yet sacred "Sol," a bridge phantasm must operate on both sides. This would provide a perfect *fantasme embrayeur,* capable of articulating contradiction, of overcoming obstacles, of rendering the real magical. The figure of Jesus Christ acts as that *fantasme embrayeur.* Jesus allows Ariane to almost seamlessly transform the oriental Jew

*Je le ferai bien enchaîner pour qu'il ne me fasse pas mal pour le cravacher à mon aise en mangeant des truffes au chocolat après chaque coup de cravache une truffe pour moi (*BdS,* 181)

into a figure of Genevan reverence, while allowing Solal to assume this role without negating his identity as an oriental Jew. After all, Jesus was himself a Mediterranean Jew, as Solal reminds himself obsessively when celebrating Easter in the first novel.[19] Both Solal and Ariane play at the edge of their identity horizons, the exchange is symmetrical and the complicity mutual.

Ariane transforms Solal himself into Christ in the last page of her stream of consciousness, as in a perfect metaphorical and sensual dénouement, overcoming all contradiction, entering the zone of post-reality utopia (this is the ontotheological dimension here), and ending in the phantasm of sexual penetration and orgasm. The sequence in these last two pages is quick and worthy of close attention, for it all ultimately culminates in the aesthetic suicide motif that drives the whole novel. Ariane thinks of her suicidal state of mind "the black ideas about my life come more often when I brush my teeth."* She then freely admits to having performed a ritual that consists of waiting in her bathtub for another of Solal's "break-ins," which the phantasm of torturing Solal served to obfuscate. Only then does the crucial Christ phantasm appear; she awaits her Savior, who is now just barely perceptible over the horizon beyond the open window: "there he is I see him over there in the white robe he goes quickly on the blindingly powdery road one would say that he does not place his bare feet on the ground there he is closer me very pure all naked but not flat it's not the moment that's it he pushed the barrier he is holy he is royal it's the lord hermit me on my knees a very grave disciple."†

The roles are reversed. Solal advances in the stream of consciousness from one who is chained and whipped to one who walks on water and floats, semi-immaterial, toward his submissive disciple, who no longer cruelly dominates but readies herself on her knees. The sexual dimension is underlined by the semantic slippage of the word "hermit." Four pages beforehand, "hermit" refers to the infantile imaginary sexual partner, who powerfully folds and unfolds Ariane, all while *not* being a hairy beast. And now, it is another "hermit," the "lord hermit" who comes to fold and unfold his "grave disciple." Solal will henceforth occupy this tragicomic space between Savior and sex toy, upon which is hinged the whole aestheticization of their hetero-master/slave-but-not-hairy-beast performance of a relationship—the object, as we saw above, of Mariette's scorn.

*les idées noires sur ma vie viennent beaucoup plus quand je brosse mes dents (*BdS,* 188)

†le voilà je le vois là-bas dans sa robe blanche il va vite sur la route poudreuse aveuglante on dirait qu'il ne pose pas ses pieds nus par terre le voilà plus près moi très pure toute nue mais pas plate c'est pas le moment ça y est il a poussé la barrière il est saint il est royal c'est le seigneur ermite moi à genoux très grave disciple (*BdS,* 188)

For the fantasy to complete itself, the Seigneur must disdainfully discipline his Belle. Ariane finally submits, not out of necessity, as she was compelled to do with her husband, Adrien Deume, or out of boredom, as with the German conductor, Serge. Rather, she follows a willful strategy of being, in this case the mode best suited to accompany her down the Styx toward her self-fashioned death. Her Savior is in fact Chiron; he acts as the perfect ferryman for a one-way voyage. This Savior Chiron is as dominating as Zeus, as smooth as Europa, as cruel as human fate. That this vicious aspect of the Seigneur should differ from the Gospel's image of Jesus is beside the point, because all of Cohen's mythological allegories are marked by syncretism, the significance of which remains internal to Cohen's particular montage.

Notice that Ariane not only desires to submit but emphasizes the disdainful scorn that the Seigneur must perforce exhibit toward her: "he *scorns* me a bit otherwise it does not work I am *nothing* next to him just a kind glance and only once a sort of smile and afterward he doesn't *condescend* anymore it's moving this kindness and this smile only once from the *disdain* and then I am madly his *servant.*"* For this Belle du Seigneur relationship to work, dominance must be established, although mediated through the Savior narrative, thus thinly disguising the sadomasochistic mode, which becomes obvious before their first kiss and later dominates the decline and dénouement of their passion in death.

In a later stream of consciousness, Ariane's phantasms become even more sexually submissive: "I am chained and he overcome with a male fury I can't escape him he makes me submit to the worst indecencies I don't see any disadvantage to the male fits of rage *it's right up my alley [ça fait tout à fait mon affaire].*"† A literal reading may suggest that Ariane has pivoted 180 degrees. Why would a Diana, allergic to the hairy male, hater of penetration, desire this humiliation in the hands of "male fury"? But this question misses the point, as the last clause clearly intimates: "it's right up my alley." That is, it corresponds perfectly to my core desires of erotic and morbid self-dramatization. That Solal takes her from time to time, that she lives a parenthetical "love affair," does not change Ariane's self-understanding as that virgin who is raped

*il me *dédaigne* un peu sinon ça marche pas je ne suis *rien* à côté de lui juste un regard de bonté une seule fois une sorte de sourire et après il ne *daigne* plus c'est émouvant cette bonté et ce sourire une seule fois du *dédaigneux* et alors je suis follement sa *servante* (*BdS,* 189; emphasis added)

†je suis enchaînée et lui il est pris d'une mâle fureur je ne peux pas lui échapper il me fait subir les derniers outrages je ne vois aucun inconvénient aux mâles fureurs *ça fait tout à fait mon affaire* (*BdS,* 622; emphasis added)

from time to time. But this violation now becomes more theatrical, aristocratic in appearance, feminine in essence, and, through its linkage to the ultimate sacrificial narrative, much more acceptable. Ariane now submits to a male but a Savior, to a male but a feminine dandy God, to a "hermit" who is both religious and phallic. Thus intimacy occurs with this simulacrum of a male, which with any other real, non-dramatized male (e.g., Adrien, Serge) would have been all but impossible. Of course, reversing all the terms here, the same could have been said of Solal: he gets his female, but one who at heart abhors phallic baboonery—an acceptable female, even if both "women" (Ariane and Solal) must play along in the hetero-phallic comedy of romance. Cruelty mediates the horror of the same loving the same, and no narrative could be as evocative as this Solal-as-Christ one with all its macabre subtexts: the Trial (banishment from the League of Nations), the Via Dolorosa (the various torture scenes), the Stabat Mater (Ariane on her knees at Solal's feet), and the Crucifixion (the suicides).

This is why in the first stream of consciousness, the notion of intimacy and disdain is so explicitly linked; "disdain and then I am madly his servant" followed directly by a concessive clause: "nevertheless there is a mysterious intimacy since in the end he accepts that but at this very moment without looking at me he speaks of God with this all eluding gaze he teaches me the path toward the truth and life me I listen on my knees very pure he is no longer speaking now."* So Solal, as Jesus, is at once intimate and distant, carnal and ethereal in a way that no male ever was—not a Hebrew prophet and certainly not a Greek god. Solal incarnates wisdom from beyond, while accepting that Ariane should prostrate herself in front of him—both as a supplicant disciple and as a woman to be taken. This penetration becomes explicitly sacramental. Far from the repulsive "above below" *(dessus dessous)* and the canine "haha haha" of the other hairy males, this copulation represents the gravitas of a mass of multiple consumptions tinged with the comedy of banality, a distinctive characteristic of Cohen's style:

> he remains upright before me because he knows what will come I am very moved I bow down I genuflect great respect now I rise I shall go and fetch the ewer of perfumed water scented oil would be more sacramental but it makes the hands sticky it would be stupid to wash my hands with soap dur-

*pourtant il y a une intimité mystérieuse puisque à la fin il accepte que mais en ce moment sans me regarder il parle de Dieu avec ce regard ailleurs il m'enseigne le chemin de la vérité et la vie moi j'écoute à genoux très pure il ne parle plus maintenant. (*BdS,* 189)

> ing the rite that would destroy the charm so scented water instead okay there I've returned naked with the ewer I very religious he always royal he ignores me necessary that he should ignore me then on my knees I gently pour the water on his bare feet dusty from the road very gently I let down my hair it's very long in the rite with my long hair I wipe his sacred feet I do it for a long time a long time oh it's nice he lets me do it because he deserves everything [*tout lui est dû*] I love it more more now I kiss his feet he lets me do it he does not punish me for my audacity lips pressed to the sacred feet a long time a long time now I lift my head and it's his marvelous smile his smile that accepts that I oh I tremble as I approach I am going since he allows that yes I oh it feels good more more me oh me more oh my lord more more of you more lord inside me.*[20]

This passage is riddled with inverted religious imagery. Ariane would like to anoint Solal with perfumed oil, but she does not because the sacred oil would make her hands sticky (the novelist cannot resist laughing at Ariane's combination of gravitas and idiocy, her enduring tragicomic signature). Instead, she washes his feet with perfumed water, which places her in a pious position, prostrate at the Savior's feet. A humble servant yet fervent in her devotional duties, subjugated yet initiating copulation with the man-god—such is the sacred orgiastic rite, the erotic self-fashioning that allows Ariane as Diana, and now as Mary Magdalene, to allow the descendent of Aaron to penetrate her body, not in humiliating violation but in orgiastic joy with this demi-god, man-woman, Savior, and ferryman, all at once: "oh my lord more more of you more lord inside me." This is Ariane echoing Molly Bloom's orgasmic "Yes," the assertion of both love and death, of the one phantasm-montage that reconciles Solal with the idea of being a male like his father, a female like his mother, and phobic to both, while performing both roles admirably through a sacralized reiteration—erotic, messianic, and morbid. Ariane's first stream of consciousness is an interpretive cornerstone of the whole novel, the well-

*il reste debout devant moi parce qu'il sait ce qui va venir je suis très émue je m'incline je fais une révérence grand respect maintenant je me lève je vais chercher l'aiguière d'eau parfumée l'huile parfumée serait plus sacramentelle mais ça poisse les mains ça serait bête d'aller se savonner pendant le rite ça couperait le charme donc eau parfumée d'accord voilà je suis revenue nue avec l'aiguière moi très religieuse lui toujours royal il m'ignore faut qu'il m'ignore alors moi à genoux je verse doucement l'eau sur ses pieds nus poudreux de la route tout doucement je dénoue mes cheveux ils sont très longs dans le rite avec mes long cheveux j'essuie les pieds sacrés je le fais longtemps longtemps oh c'est bon il me laisse faire parce que tout lui est dû j'adore ça encore encore maintenant je baise les pieds il me laisse faire il ne me châtie pas de mon audace lèvres collées sur les pieds sacrés longtemps longtemps maintenant je lève la tête et c'est son sourire merveilleux son sourire qui accepte que je oh je tremble en approchant je vais puisqu'il permet que oui je oh c'est bon encore encore me oh me encore ô mon seigneur encore encore de vous encore seigneur en moi. (*BdS,* 189)

camouflaged mise-en-abyme that understands and states it all, from deep psychology of sexual identity to aesthetic self-fashioning of a most dramatic and morbid type.[21]

The rest of the novel is little more than the consummation of this narrative. Their love affair is akin to a walk down a gallery of late medieval and early Renaissance art dominated by sacred devotion, thorns, nails, blood, scorn, and the orgasmic beauty of evil (crucifixion) culminating in (self-)execution—not unlike the macabre promenade Solal takes with Rachel in the Berlin underground, except that here the couple do pause from time to time to consume each other. For Solal, there is never the shadow of a doubt that he will soon die, that he will soon turn his snubbed-nose companion *(compagnon trappu),* the revolver that has accompanied him since the opening pages, on himself.

In a later stream of consciousness, Solal imagines his death like this: "I am the one who nails myself to this door of a cathedral in the mountains I am the one who pierces my side with a nail of the underground one of the long nails that she gave me as souvenir."* "I am the one who" emphasizes Solal's deliberate agency in his dramatic suicide-crucifixion; the woman who gave him the nails is, of course, the dwarf Rachel, a metonymy for modern Jewish disfigurement, which implies suffering, repulsion, and eternal crucifixions. The nails represent Solal's studded bad conscience, related to the fact that he does not love his mother, did not love Rachel at all except as an abstraction; the permanent guilt about his searing ambivalence—sharp nails with which he crucifies himself. But in mid-thought, Solal shifts back to his desired interlocutor, not Rachel, but Ariane: "yes my love I love you more and inside myself I cry it out to you while you gently sew"†—to which I would add: "While you weave gently the story of my death which you gently foretold to them for me in your first flowing chatter, meaningless and true as my soon to be death is meaningless but also real."

Solal and Ariane do commit suicide in the end, and it is not a heroic one. Their suicide results from a sordid spiral of self-destruction at the Ritz after nights of drug-induced debauchery. A banal suicide by veronal sleeping pills at the Ritz is the final cruel joke on these two (really one) who so ardently wanted a death of their own heroic self-fashioning, anointed with perfumed water and hot, scented oil. Instead, they die miserably and anonymously—

*c'est moi qui me cloue à cette porte d'une cathédrale dans la montagne moi qui perce mon flanc avec un clou de la cave un des longs clous qu'elle m'a donnés en souvenir. (*BdS,* 906)

†"oui mon amour je t'aime toujours plus et en moi-même je te le crie pendant que tu couds gentiment." (*BdS,* 906)

more like Madame Bovary than like Jesus Christ. Or, more correctly, more like a Madame Bovary, yes, but with the conscious self-understanding of a failed Joseph endowed with a lyrical and prophetic and messianic temperament, as the shift from an indicative narrative to a delirious phantasm in the last paragraph of *Belle du Seigneur* makes all too obvious.

However cagey Cohen remained till the end of this life about the political, messianic, and specific historical dimensions of *Belle du Seigneur*, the last paragraph of the novel could not be more eloquent and categorical. Cohen clearly directs us toward the real submerged Josephic and messianic plots, as if he were afraid that the real plot was buried too deep in the romance. We are in Geneva, late 1936, at the Ritz Hotel. Ariane has already taken the lethal dose of sleeping pills that will put her to rest, and Solal, who also intends to commit suicide shortly after her, carries Ariane in his arms . . . down into the Berlin cellar where Rachel is awaiting him. Here is David Coward's translation of this crucial last paragraph:

> Suddenly his legs buckled and coldness came upon him, and he set her down on the bed and lay by her side and kissed her virginal face, softened now by just the shadow of a smile and as beautiful as it has been on that first of their nights, kissed her hand, which was still warm but heavy now, held her hand in his, kept her hand in his until he reached the cellar where a dwarf was weeping, weeping openly for her comely king who was dying transfixed with nails to the wart-studded door, her doomed king who was weeping too, weeping for forsaking his children on earth, his children whom he had not saved, what would they do without him, and suddenly the dwarf enjoined him in ringing tones, ordered him to offer up the last prayer in accordance with the ritual, for the hour had come.*

The whole Solal-Ariane-Rachel montage is spelled out here in detail: Solal carries Ariane's body to Rachel's Berlin cellar. That is, he deposes in the Jewish cellar, the corpse of his narcissistic female double and then proceeds to his own death with the proper form of intoning the *She'ma Israel* prayer *(Hear, Israel, the Lord is our God, the Lord is One.)* just before his death, exactly as many

*Chancelant soudain, et un froid lui venant, il la remit sur le lit, et il s'étendait auprès d'elle, baisa le visage virginal, à peine souriant, beau comme au premier soir, baisa la main encore tiède mais lourde, la garda dans sa main, la garda avec lui jusque dans la cave où une naine pleurait, ne se cachait pas de pleurer son beau roi en agonie contre la porte aux verrues, son roi condamné qui pleurait aussi d'abandonner ses enfants de la terre, ses enfants qu'il n'avait pas sauvés, et que feraient-ils sans lui, et soudain la naine lui demanda d'une voix vibrante, lui ordonna de dire le dernier appel, ainsi qu'il était prescrit, car c'était l'heure. (*BdS,* 999)

Jews did in the gas chambers. But in this last hallucinatory phantasm, his death is not passive, not induced by an overdose of sleeping pills, as the preceding paragraphs imply. He is the "comely king who was dying transfixed with nails to the wart-studded door"; he is the king who has forsaken his children—children that this Joseph was supposed to save. The Savior is crucified like Jesus, but not for the purpose of expiating the sins of humanity. This Savior is crucified because of a political failure at the crucial historical juncture of 1936 to save those who were to perish soon afterward. And so Solal weeps, and his death is sanctified by the weeping dwarf: his Jewish double, his mother.[22]

Epilogue: Ézéchiel, *or Abject Origins, Suicidal Destiny*

So nothing is as sweet as a man's own country,
his own parents, even though he's settled down
in some luxurious house, off in a foreign land
and far from those who bore him.
No more. Come,
let me tell you about the voyage fraught with hardship
Zeus inflicted on me, homeward bound from Troy . . .

Homer, The Odyssey *9.38–43*

No book on Cohen should begin nor conclude without a reflection on his paradoxical status in our contemporary literary consciousness. The question of why, particularly in academia, Cohen is *known* but not *read,* and when read, then most often misread, has motivated virtually all aspects of this book. Dissonance has been the musical analogy used to describe the discomfort that the reader experiences while reading Cohen, for he strikes certain familiar notes but rarely returns to the expected and comforting keys. He therefore leaves the reader suspended in a foreign space, estranged as in a nightmare.

What I propose by way of conclusion is an explicit reflection on the reasons for Cohen's marginality. But I would like this conclusion to be as concrete as possible, lest the Sirens of abstraction dilute Cohen's searing dissonance and lure us away again from the harshness of his disruptive texts into the soft anesthesia of historicism and theory where allegories and analogies drowned in the ether of "contextual relativism" allow the reader to smartly resist and repress the unthinkable. Cohen offers us this very experience of total dissonance and even repulsion in his 1932 play *Ézéchiel*—his most controversial piece, the subject of much painful and repeated public reprobation. In the economy of a one-act, two-man play, Cohen distills his ambivalence and darkest nightmares in crisp expression. But most critically, the brevity and theatrical nature of the piece make it impossible for the audience to circumvent the meaning of these nightmares. No wonder, then, that *Ézéchiel* resulted in an open confrontation between an unusually aggressive Cohen and spectators of the play in 1933, some of whom defensively attacked the author by sarcastically identifying him as none other than the new German chancellor Adolf Hitler, using "the pseudonym of Albert Cohen." These spectators could no longer afford to tiptoe around the burning coals Cohen flung at them. They had to engage the spectacle, respond to Cohen, or withdraw in silence, ashamed or satisfied, depending on their perspective. A critical reading of this play in terms of the dynamics of Cohen's œuvre as a whole, and with the circumstances of its performance in Paris in the early 1930s in mind, would be a lacerating experience—a reading of a Jew's pathological self-hatred, hysterical rage, and bitter resentment. Yet we shall never understand the problem of Cohen's literary reception without fleshing out *Ézéchiel,* this taboo play about an abject father, whose ghost haunted Cohen throughout his life.

Ézéchiel is not a minor product of circumstances. First published in the *Palestine-Nouvelle revue juive* (1930), it won the *Comoedia* one-act competition and was first performed at the théâtre de l'Odéon on April 1, 1931. In May and June 1933, the Comédie-Française included a second version of *Ézéchiel* in a program of five one-act plays. But between the first performance at the Odéon in 1931 and the performances at the Comédie-Française in the spring of 1933, the atmosphere in Paris had soured, and many Jews and anti-Semites alike reacted virulently. The stinging rebukes *Ézéchiel* received remained with Cohen his entire life. Seventeen years later, when he was writing the final version of *Le Livre de ma mère* (1950–53), he also rewrote its complement, *Ézéchiel* (which could easily be retitled "The Book of My Father"), and this third version of the play was published by Gallimard in 1956. That same year, Cohen gave the Comédie des Champs-Élysées permission to stage the play, and again, to Cohen's dismay and ongoing frustration, the same open reprobation ensued. Again the play was subject to a de facto boycott by the Jewish establishment. From then on, Cohen no longer authorized any public performance of the play. Since his death in 1982, the play has been performed sporadically, no doubt as a kind of oddity. More significantly, besides the biographical and bibliographical treatments, the existing criticism on Albert Cohen is all but silent on the subject of *Ézéchiel,* with not a single article or book chapter devoted to it. This play is too unsettling, too abject to be allegorized and intertextualized with the usual fare of Stendhal and Tolstoy! Here the intertextual dismays: *The Merchant of Venice, The Protocols of the Elders of Zion,* Édouard Drumont's *La France juive* (1886). And yet Cohen, who reworked this play at least three times between 1927 and 1956, considered it a major work, a significant statement of who he was (not) and what he was (not).

So let us plunge into this theatrical, father-centered nightmare, from which we shall emerge capable of accounting for Cohen's relative marginality in canonical French and Jewish literature.

The action of the play unfolds on the island of Cephalonia, in the house of Ézéchiel, a rich banker who is the leader of the local Jewish community and the father of Solal, Britain's chancellor of the Exchequer (minister of finance). The stage set is claustrophobic. Ézéchiel's house is one of those psychotic, paranoid spaces of closure in Cohen's writing, of which the basement of the Château Saint-Germain in *Solal* (see Chapter 3) and Rachel's Berlin cellar in *Belle du Seigneur* (see Chapter 5) are telling examples. Cohen's prefatory notes on the décor are categorical about its pathological nature:

> Very low ceiling. White walls. A door in the foreground and to the left. In the background, to the left and in a separate section, the front door round at the top. The double doors are covered with metal fittings and enormous bolts. Gigantic lock and deadbolt. Above the door, a large inscription in Hebrew letters. To the right and pretty high, a small window round at the top. In the front plane and to the right, a table, a cathedra [a thronelike chair], and a stool. These pieces of furniture are massive. On the table an old Bible, a big chandelier with seven candles, an ink pot in which rests a goose quill, a glass ewer, a round loaf of bread, a knife, the portrait of Ézéchiel's son.*

But the spectator's eye would immediately be riveted on the center rear of the stage, where

> an old safe *[coffre-fort]*, gigantic, monstrous, looms like a fortress. It is covered with large bolts, which are like the warts of a monster. Heavy chains riveted to the walls and to the ceiling keep the safe captive. These chains, the safe's enormous tentacles, two of which cross the room lengthwise and heightwise, are the main decorative elements of this sad house. Three steps lead to the safe, which is like an immense spider, whose chains would be its feet. The safe and all the pieces of furniture are black.†

*Plafond très bas. Murs blancs. Une porte au premier plan et à gauche. Au fond, à gauche et en pan coupé, la porte d'entrée, dont la partie supérieure est arrondie. Les deux battants de la porte sont bardés de ferrures et d'énormes boulons. Serrure et verrou gigantesques. Au-dessus de la porte, une grande inscription en caractères hébraïques. À droite, et assez haut, une petite fenêtre dont la partie supérieure est arrondie. Au premier plan et à droite, une table, une cathèdre et un tabouret. Ces meubles sont massifs. Sur la table, une vieille Bible, un grand chandelier à sept branches, un encrier dans lequel est trempée une plume d'oie, un broc en verre, un pain rond, un poignard, le portrait du fils d'Ézéchiel. (*Ézéchiel,* 781)

†un vieux coffre-fort, gigantesque, monstrueux, dominateur comme une forteresse. Il est bardé de gros boulons qui sont comme les verrues du monstre. De lourdes chaînes rivées aux murs et au plafond le maintiennent captif. Ces chaînes, énormes tentacules du coffre, et dont deux traversent la pièce dans sa longueur et dans sa hauteur, sont le principal élément décoratif de cette triste demeure. Trois marches conduisent au coffre qui est comme une immense araignée dont les chaînes seraient les pattes. Le coffre et tous les meubles sont noirs. (*Ézéchiel,* 781)

This safe, where Ézéchiel keeps all of his capital, represents the totality of Ézéchiel's being *in reductio:* it is most obviously the typical representation of a paranoid miser's home, somewhat like Shylock's home, although very different from the home of Molière's miser, Harpagon, in that the *cassette,* or safe, is not ashamedly hidden in the garden but dominates the interior of the house. In other words, the safe here is not a matter for shame and taboo but, on the contrary, set on a pedestal as a ritual fetish; the sacred altar of the house, the holy of holies. Furthermore, tentaclelike ropes secure and choke the safe in all directions, making the safe the prisoner of the suffocating room and, by analogy, Ézéchiel a prisoner of his own safe, prisoner of his money psychosis. He is thus much more than a mere miser in the classical Plautian tradition who just happens to belong to the Jewish nation. Rather, the suffocating room, the safe, and above all the ropes, represent, according to Cohen, the essence of the Jewish condition—that of being the proud prisoners of an insane project: on the one hand, the negation of nature, which is the rule of force over the ethical, the total negation of paganism, in short; and, on the other hand, the need to accumulate wealth as a response and an antidote to a history of persecution. Thus from the "natural," pagan point of view, the Jew is twice deformed. This is why Cohen's emphatic décor descriptions are laden with such overdetermined symbolism. No doubt can be entertained as to the meaning of the stage décor. This play is not going to be an exercise in subtlety.

To prepare his evening prayer, Ézéchiel opens the locked doors of the safe, as a Jew would open the holy of holies in the synagogue, and prays facing it as if it contained the Torah scrolls, instead of placing himself closest to the east-facing wall as required by Jewish custom. Ézéchiel translates the pathological fetishism of money into flagrant idolatry and his relationship to God into a form of oriental bazaar quid pro quo: "O powerful [father] of Jacob, I present to You the two million gold drachmas with which it pleased You to bless my commercial and financial ventures. Bestow long life and fecundity upon these two million so that they may praise You and pay tribute to Your power, O Landlord of the world."* To pray is to bargain for earthly things. Worse, to pray is to allow money the honor and agency of praising God. Money is not an abstract means of exchange, a guarantor of survival for a persecuted minority—no, it acquires a voice of its own. And thus Ézéchiel opens the safe, dons the prayer shawl, and begins to sway in prayer. Stage, décor, gestures, and

*Ô puissant de Jacob, je Te présente les deux millions de drachmes-or dont il T'a plu de bénir mes entreprises commerciales et financières. Accorde longue vie et fécondité à ces deux millions afin qu'ils Te louent et qu'ils rendent hommage à Ta puissance, ô Propriétaire du monde. (*Ézéchiel,* 783)

opening monologue reveal the truth about this deranged miser even before a single dialogue ensues. We see all of this before and during the prefatory monologue. The subsequent dialogues and dramatic developments seem superfluous; the meaning of the silent but all too eloquent stage montage overdetermines the meaning of what follows.

The two main characters make their entrances separately, and each is assigned an expository monologue. Ézéchiel is dressed in his best attire for his son's arrival: black velvet frock coat lined with gray fur, black boots, a fur hat, and a silver chain, at the end of which hangs the enormous key to his safe. His initial interior monologue is like a collage of Jewish miser jokes. "Seven candles," he begins, "thirty cents a piece, that adds up to exactly two drachmas and ten cents. Two drachmas and ten cents, at a reasonable interest rate of five percent, after a ten-year period, yield exactly interest of sixty-three cents. A candelabra with three branches would have done just as well. These candelabras with seven branches are wasteful and are consequently the ruin of the chosen people."* Ézéchiel then laments aloud (echoing Molière's Harpagon shouting in panic, "Où est ma cassette?") "Who stole my thirty-seven matches? Zacharie! . . . Zacharie, where are my thirty-seven matches? Where are my thirty-seven matches? . . . Zacharie! Zacharie!"† And when he finds them, he splits them lengthwise for the sake of economy. Later we learn that cooling by way of ventilation for Ézéchiel means hard work: he sways and rotates himself in front of the fan, lest the fan actually be used and thus possibly damaged. After two minutes of the play, the spectators know that Ézéchiel is miserly, paranoid, hypocritical, and, above all, sacrilegious to the core.

Jérémie, a poor, uncouth, itinerant Eastern European Jew, with a short red beard, dressed in tattered Levite garb, an old suitcase in one hand, and a broken handcuff around one wrist, then enters, accompanied by a small dog named Titus. He is, in sum, the very character that Solal pretends to be in the macabre Purim play in the opening scene of *Belle du Seigneur* where Solal tries to seduce Ariane. The square suitcase, held together by ropes and complicated knots, covered in stickers reading: "*Emigrant. To be Disinfected. To be turned*

*Sept chandelles, à trente centimes l'une, cela fait exactement deux drachmes et dix centimes. Deux drachmes et dix centimes, au taux raisonnable de cinq pour cent, produisent exactement, au bout d'une période de dix années, un intérêt de soixante-trois centimes. Un chandelier à trois branches eût tout aussi bien fait l'affaire. Ces chandeliers à sept branches sont dispendieux et sont en conséquence la ruine du peuple élu. (*Ézéchiel,* 783)

†Qui m'a volé mes trente-sept allumettes? Zacharie! . . . Zacharie, où sont mes trente-sept allumettes? Où sont mes trente-sept allumettes? . . . Zacharie! Zacharie! (*Ézéchiel,* 784)

*back. Undesirable. Fourth class."** And handwritten in big letters: "*International Bank. Marriages. Open at Night.*"† Alongside the eloquent chained safe, this roped suitcase completes the stage décor: they represent two versions of essentially the same exilic Judaism in its full bipolarity. Opulent or destitute, self-confident or paranoid, in command or marginal, Ézéchiel and Jérémie are essentially the same character in different guises. From a secular European point of view, the immaculate velvet frock coat of the one is symbolically identical to the tattered Levite dress of the other. And whether they carry a suitcase around desolate train stations or are imprisoned in a prosperous house for the sake of a safe, both are symbolically chained to insanity, a perpetual insecurity, a symbolic pariah state; both "international bankers" are insane and repulsive, although Jérémie, Solal's surrogate, possesses a lucidity that Ézéchiel's utter narcissism, paranoia, and fetishism preclude. "No, Master Ézéchiel, [Judaism] is not a religion, it's a catastrophe."‡ "But it is a beautiful catastrophe,"§ Jérémie adds in a burlesque scene in *Mangeclous.*[1]

The plot is simple. Ézéchiel is awaiting the arrival of his illustrious son from England. But Solal has died aboard ship the day before. Daunted by the prospect of announcing such terrible news to the patriarch of their community, the Cephalonian Jews entrust this mission to Jérémie, who charges them five drachmas to execute the dreadful task. Upon meeting Jérémie in his living room, the rich Sephardic banker has nothing but contempt for his poor Eastern European coreligionist. Yet Jérémie is himself incapable of abruptly announcing Solal's death. And so ensues a comic scene that is all about delaying the inevitable, during which Cohen draws on his usual bag of tricks. Jérémie introduces himself as a banker, attempts to talk Ézéchiel first into buying an option to build a bridge in Turkey, and then into investing in a scheme to run tubes through every house in Argentina so as to provide a continuous distribution of café-au-lait to each and every home at any hour of the day. Finally, as a last resort, he pulls out a fake ruby ring and haggles with Ézéchiel about its quality and price. Time flies, the boat that has unloaded Solal's body now leaves the harbor, as indicated by a blowing of its fog horns, and Jérémie finally carries out his charge and informs the old patriarch that his son is dead. Ézéchiel is at first apparently shattered by Solal's death, but he quickly recovers. He then asks Jérémie whether his daughter is fertile and decides to marry

**Émigrant. À désinfecter. À refouler. Indésirable. Quatrième classe.* (*Ézéchiel,* 780; emphasis in original)
†*Banque internationale. Mariages. Ouvert la nuit.* (*Ézéchiel,* 780; emphasis in original)
‡*Non, seigneur Ézéchiel, ce n'est pas une religion, c'est une catastrophe. (*Ézéchiel,* 788)
§C'est ine *[sic]* catastrophe mais belle (*Mangeclous,* 548)

her himself the next day so that he can sire another son. He decides to name the future son David and wishes him not only to be more politically and financially important than the British chancellor of the Exchequer but also the Messiah in person. As the play ends, Ézéchiel orders his Greek notary to contact members of the extended Solal clan in Brussels, Zurich, and New York to place limit orders for shares in the Union minière du Haut Katanga, Nestlé, and Dupont. "Without commission, of course."*

We are now positioned to account for the driving force behind this theatrical performance in terms of the repetitive montages that Cohen broods over. The saga of Solal begins on Cephalonia in *Solal* with the bar mitzvah of metaphysical estrangement, Solal's revolt against his father and flight from the island to urban Europe, and ends in *Ézéchiel* with his return to the island and to his father. We have come full circle, or just about, since it is only a cadaver that actually returns home. Solal dies en route.

The most obvious aspect of this play is an absence. This is Cohen's only fiction or essay where the fictional Solal or the autobiographical "I" is absent. The wandering son, now British chancellor of the Exchequer, does not live to see father, hearth, community again.[2] He will not be the prodigal son. Only his corpse arrives. Yet we are told nothing about the surprising death of this vigorous young man on board a modern ocean liner. However, we are by now quite familiar with Solal's perennial urge to commit suicide; and we can conclude that Samson Solal, just like Solal in *Belle du Seigneur,* kills himself. Suicide, rather than the eternal wandering of Abraham, the glorious return of the prodigal son, or the cunning return of Odysseus, is the true Cohenian destiny. *Ézéchiel* is an odyssey with no return; or, alternatively, the story of return as a suicide.

For Solal, the nothingness of death is preferable to facing the father. No reconciliation is possible between this vile father and his suave son. This is another variation on the complete exhaustion of the Joseph narrative. Solal will not be the "augment," the hidden leavening that will exist apart from the tribe, estranged from the father, and yet who will guarantee their survival by his skill, intelligence, and cunning. Unlike Joseph, who is ultimately reconciled with Jacob, his brothers, and their kin, all while remaining apart from them, Solal opts for death.

Solal cannot inhabit the paternal space, cannot identify with it under *any* circumstances. The staging and gestures, in their grotesque overdetermination, make that clear. Having analyzed Cohen's nightmares—the underground of

*Sans courtage, bien entendu (*Ézéchiel,* 803)

Château Saint-Germain, Berlin, the Rosenfelds (Chapters 3 and 5)—we read these scenes as symbols of Solal's searing ambivalence about Jews, that is, about himself: he repeatedly identifies with Jews in the abstract and rejects them in the concrete. The subterranean spaces are reserved for those others who are the same as, but essentially different from, Solal, whether they be the paternal Rabbi Gamaliel hidden in Château Saint-Germain or the dwarf Rachel burrowing about in Berlin, infected with multiple deliria of grandeur. These images of an insane subterranean vermin constitute the most negative pole in Cohen's dialectics, in his desire to "show the glory of Israel to those who see only Jews." These moments of visceral denigration make the serious transmission of Cohen's literary works extremely difficult.

Proud and narcissistic, the father seeks to mirror himself in the splendor of his son's worldly success. This is why Ézéchiel does not go to the harbor to greet his son: he does not want their encounter to be diluted by the crowd. He looks forward to an intimate scene of return as the crowning experience of his life. The contemptuous son, however, refuses to raise such a mirror to his father's face. Instead, Jérémie, Cohen's favorite grotesque surrogate, first tortures the father. This surrogate then carries out his commission and delivers the son, or in his absence, the son's death certificate. Solal's message through the surrogate is the following: "A certified death; my death, which redeems my impossible presence before you in your house."

There is, however, something very surprising in Cohen's decision to employ Jérémie as a surrogate for the dead Solal. This scenario is weak in comparison with Cohen's more spectacular and very effective scenarios where he disguises Solal as Jérémie. Although colorful and moving, Jérémie cannot but be a stiff character, a clown of sorts, hemmed in by his real limitations. But Solal-*cum*-Jérémie bristles with comic potential, and especially on the comic stage. It is Cohen's favorite Purim play, his most striking self-dramatization. Think of the first scene of *Belle du Seigneur,* where Solal-*cum*-Jérémie conducts the famous moral experiment on Ariane. Think of all the times Solal disguises himself as a Jérémie just to be mocked in the streets (the Christological phantasm of being a mocked king), including the crucial Berlin episode, where the undersecretary-general of the League of Nations disguises himself as a Jérémie and almost actually satisfies his suicidal wish to be martyred by the Nazis. And think of all the episodes where Solal pulls his Eastern European Hassidic costume out of a suitcase (in which he also keeps his favorite anti-Semitic tracts) in the privacy of his hotel room and gazes at himself in the mirror, gesticulating like a pious Jew. One often has the impression that whenever Solal looks into a mirror, he sees a dissonant double image of himself as both virile master of the world (Joseph) and itinerant Jewish clown (Jérémie). So the absence of Cohen's signature baroque Purim play in *Ézéchiel* raises the question: Why does the presence of the father exclude his son's favorite mise-en-scène?

The answer is rather obvious. When a mask is worn, it can be removed. When, on the other hand, a character dies, he cannot be revived (at least in realistic fiction). In other words, the cadaver and its surrogate render impossible the father-son encounter. It will not happen, come what may. Had Solal only disguised himself (as he does with the Valorous, Jérémie, Ariane, and countless other strangers), the mask would have acted as a catalyst for further dramatic development. The mask always comes off and the real encounter takes place—which is precisely what cannot take place with this father. Solal does meet the Valorous in the Joseph/Purim play in which he performs the role of a "monstre à tete de gaze" and then recognizes and reconciles with them; and with Ariane, once the Jérémie mask comes off, the real encounter takes place. To mask oneself, as Solal does, is to play a *Fort! Da!* game of now I have it, now I don't. Death, life; rejection, recognition; cruelty, generosity. Again, this is Cohen's signature topos, so rich in dramatic and existential possibilities. But in Cohen's scheme this British minister, Samson Solal, prefers death to a reunion and therefore a surrogate is sent, a burlesque caricature, to represent Solal, as a final and macabre poisoned gift to an impossible father for an impossible encounter. *Ézéchiel* is short-circuited from the beginning; the play has no dramatic potential except that of admitting the cruel truth, and making a spectacle of it at the Comédie-Française to boot.

As noted, both *Ézéchiel* and *Le Livre de ma mère* were rewritten concurrently in the early 1950s. In both cases, the portrayal of Cohen's parents is fraught with wishes for their death. While the death wish with respect to the mother is veiled by moments of sincere tenderness and remorse, the aggression toward the father is almost unmediated. Cohen puts his mother on a death train; and in *Ézéchiel,* his own corpse is disembarked: death instead of return and reconciliation. Unable to kill his father, even symbolically, he takes his revenge by killing himself. The mourning process that is so rich in literary potential does not take place in the play *Ézéchiel.* The deep ambivalence so evident in the case of the mother is simply absent here.[3] Instead of the affective and poetic charge, whose deepest source is found in the ambivalence about the people we mourn, Cohen employs *Ézéchiel* as the repository of the vilest stereotypes concerning the Jews, as well as the apologist for these character deformations: "My money, yes. Our money, our old ally which is there *(he points* *toward the safe)* in this fortress, in our fortress. Our money that has permitted us to remain a strong people, that has permitted us to resist, to wait, to be patient, that has permitted us to endure despite our persecutors, that has permitted us to have contempt for their contempt!"* In the end, however, this combination of stereotype and platitude is sterile, which explains why *Le Livre de ma mère* is the best-loved of Cohen's writings and *Ézéchiel* the most neglected. Yet despite all these differences, the core dynamic remains the same. Writing about his father or his mother brings on another scenario of self-execution, whether through entombing oneself in writing about death, as in the case of the mother, or through absence by suicide and surrogacy, as in the case of the father.

In this brief analysis of *Ézéchiel,* we have revisited many of the arguments of the present book. For those familiar with Cohen's recurrent montage, *Ézéchiel* offers an incomparable advantage over all his other texts. Because of its brevity and theatrical nature, the signal is exceptionally clear. Absent the usual background noise, the essential elements of the Cohenian montage come through all the more explicitly. Here the Alexandrian alibis of comforting intertextuality, analogy, and allegory are missing entirely. Here there is no escape to Stendhalian narratives; no bored Madame Bovary, no passionate Anna Karenina, no Proustian bisexuality and jealousy; no Joycian self-consciousness to hold us up, to buffer the assault of Solal's nightmares. Here, in this one-act play, there is no hiding in the inner folds of a richly polyphonic novel, where many wrinkles and devices may satisfy our desire to elude acknowledging what is at stake. No, here the spectator who has just stepped into the Comedie-Française to see five short plays must witness Cohen's most masochistic vision: abject origins, suicidal destiny, the son absenting himself from the presence of a father impossible to love.

The spectator must have had the feeling of being trapped: theater has the ability to force a confrontation with a real, concrete representation, which you must view with others, in a given place and at a given time, all your escape routes blocked. You are in front of the massive safe and the tattered suitcase, both props held fast by snakelike chains and ropes: the Medusa's head of Judaism that reduces Solal to yet another mise-en-scène of his own death. In the darkness of the theater, you must experience Ézéchiel and Jérémie as real beings; your nervous system intermingles with theirs; your imagination with

*Mon argent, oui. Notre argent, notre vieil allié qui est là *(il montre le coffre-fort)* dans cette forteresse, dans notre forteresse. Notre argent qui nous a permis de rester un peuple fort, qui nous a permis de résister, d'attendre, de patienter, qui nous a permis de durer malgré nos persécuteurs, qui nous a permis de mépriser leur mépris! (*Ézéchiel,* 799)

their deliria. You, like Cohen, become the sadistic spectator, to your delight or horror, or both. Cohen forces you to experience *Ézéchiel* exactly as he experiences Judaism in his darkest moments, with this searing admixture of visceral repulsion and historical pride. This is, of course, the inner theater of Cohen the poet and not that of Cohen the diplomat, the tireless public militant of Jewish causes. But staging this private nightmare in the agora of French cultural life—the Comédie-Française—was a *political* act, its impact surpassing by far that of any printed text, and it therefore took on a different communicative status and earned for itself a public reception commensurate with its political audacity.

Here is perhaps the most disturbing passage in the play. Jérémie has just extolled his scheme to conduct hot café-au-lait to every home in Argentina, and Ézéchiel's objection is that the milk will curdle in the tubes:

> JÉRÉMIE: We'll charge more for it! Curdled milk, it's very good for your health. Would you like to underwrite the business? There are millions to be made!
>
> ÉZÉCHIEL, *he puts his prayer shawl back on:* Go make them elsewhere. Leave me in peace, it's the hour of prayer *(He begins to recite a prayer in Hebrew.)* Baruch ata Adonai Elohénou melech . . .
>
> JÉRÉMIE, *taking candles out of his Levite coat:* Four candles that I bought from an Eskimo tribe!
>
> ÉZÉCHIEL, *after sniffing them, returns the candles:* Melech aolam asher bachar banou . . .
>
> JÉRÉMIE: Pure whale tallow!
>
> ÉZÉCHIEL: Buying never interests me. One always pays too much. Bachar Banou micol aamim . . .
>
> JÉRÉMIE, *enthusiastically handing over a ring:* A gold ring!
>
> ÉZÉCHIEL, *after sniffing the ring, gives it back to Jérémie:* This ring is copper. Micol aamim venatan lanou eth torato torath . . .*

*JÉRÉMIE: Nous le vendrons plus cher! Le lait caillé, c'est très bon pour la santé. Voulez-vous commanditer l'affaire? Il y a des millions à gagner!

ÉZÉCHIEL , *Il remet son châle de prière:* Va les gagner ailleurs. Laisse-moi en paix, c'est l'heure de la prière. *(Il commence à réciter une prière en hébreu)* Baruch ata Adonaï Elohénou melech . . .

JÉRÉMIE, *sortant des chandelles de sa lévite:* Quatre chandelles que j'ai achetées à une tribu d'Esquimaux!

ÉZÉCHIEL , *après les avoir flairées, rend les chandelles:* Melech aolam asher bachar banou . . .

JÉRÉMIE: Pur suif de baleine!

ÉZÉCHIEL : L'achat ne m'intéresse jamais. On achète toujours trop cher. Bachar banou micol aamim . . .

JÉRÉMIE, *tendant avec enthousiasme une bague:* Une bague en or!

ÉZÉCHIEL , *après avoir flairé la bague, la restitue à Jérémie:* Cette bague est en cuivre. Micol aamim venatan lanou eth torato torath . . . (*Ézéchiel,* 790)

Imagine the reactions such a scene must have provoked! The "Dossier de presse," included in the Pléiade edition of Cohen's *Œuvres,* and other documents from the time allow us to partially reconstruct the reactions to *Ézéchiel.*[4] For the sake of argument, I divide the audience into three very roughly delineated groups: republicans, anti-Semites, and *Israélites.*

Let us also stipulate a starting point: irrespective of his deep ambivalence about Judaism, Cohen, at least on a conscious level, surely saw this play as an open challenge to anti-Semitic discourse, ranging from *The Merchant of Venice* to *The Protocols of the Elders of Zion* and Drumont's *La France juive.* In order to subvert that discourse by exhausting its rhetoric (the logic of self-derision), Cohen then turns the libel into a litany against anti-Semitism.[5] This argument constitutes the most plausible "defense" of the play. (I assume here that *Ézéchiel* is not read and understood, as we have done above, as a function of the whole Solal-Cohen saga.)

Sympathetic democratically minded republican audiences, eager to bestow recognition on ghetto Jews, were consequently inclined to swallow *Ézéchiel* as an exotic, indigestible lump, untouched by the enzymes of thought. The most typical sympathetic reactions betray this acceptance without reflection: "*Ézéchiel* is a profound and savory study of the Jewish soul" (*Oeuvres,* 1321); "[in] this work . . . the Jewish soul is reflected, is totally synthesized" (1321); "a brilliant study of the Jewish soul" (1324). What do these platitudes mean? How can one assert that the "Jewish soul" is distilled in a forty-minute tragic farce involving a repulsive and blasphemous orthodox miser haggling with a delirious vagabond? Would anyone ever label a sordid dialogue about money and debt between Madame Bovary and her village merchant, Monsieur Lheureux, as a "savory study of the French soul"? If not, then a good question would be: What "French" plays correlate with *Ézéchiel,* that is, reflect "the French soul, . . . a total synthesis of it?" Sometimes, simple logic can go a long way in simplifying questions that seem impenetrable on the surface.

But the most bewildering instance of the sympathetic critics' will not to know concerns the recurrent allusions to the "mysticism" of the play. I count seven such allusions in the Pléiade's "Dossier de presse." If anything, Ézéchiel himself is rudely opposed to mysticism of any kind. He represents himself as a strict legalist. As for Jérémie, he never makes any mystical illusions. He subscribes to the school of Hillel, which is more liberal in its interpretation of the Law, but betrays no hint of mysticism properly speaking. At best, if we put aside the fact that Ézéchiel is altogether blasphemous, the difference between Ézéchiel and Jérémie can be seen as a conflict between Sephardic legalistic elit-

ism and Ashkenazi populist orthodoxy. But nowhere are allusions to the "connection between God and creation, the existence of good and evil, and the path to spiritual perfection" or, on the more pragmatic level, to the "practice of deep meditation for the purpose of linking the soul with the Deity"—features common to all monotheistic mysticisms—to be found in Cohen's play.[6]

"What shocks me in the first place is the continual passage from the profane to the sacred," Cohen's lifelong friend and admirer Vladimir Rabi wrote, in what is perhaps the most penetrating review of *Ézéchiel.*[7] In other words, these juxtapositions of the sacred and the repulsive, which the sympathetic audience mistook as "mystical," stand out as the most transgressive and grotesque aspects of the play: substituting a safe for the holy of holies (the golden calf for the Torah) and interspersing Hebrew liturgy with vile haggling. Would the same critics have recognized Christian mysticism in an Harpagon praying and bowing in front of a safe in lieu of a cross for the safety of his golden louis, while mixing Latin liturgy with particularly crass haggling?

It is necessary to examine the chain of displacements that allowed these reviewers to disregard Jérémie's insightful assertion that "[Judaism] is not a religion but a catastrophe"—which would be the most obvious beginning of an interpretation—and assert instead that aesthetic "mysticism" constitutes the positive affirmation of the play. How and why does the grotesque become the sublime and mystical, and to what end? Answering these questions will go a long way in accounting for Cohen's permanent marginality.

It is unlikely that any Gentile republican in the audience had actually had any real contact with traditional Jews such as Ézéchiel and Jérémie. These picturesque Jews were eccentric even for the assimilated French *Israélite.*[8] Mysticism therefore becomes a solvent for irreducible differences: their ghettoized style of speech, exuberant body gestures, and ancient Hebrew are all markers of differences that cannot be assimilated by the republican ethos except as exotic curiosities. This displacement allows repression or forgetting of the actual questions the play poses. Instead of recognizing the "catastrophe of being a Jew," these spectators recognize an affirmation of the mystical "soul of Judaism." Acknowledging mystical exoticism, however, never represents a genuine recognition of historical realities in their full human dimension. It is rather the symptom of the will not to think, not to recognize. Better yet, in affirming that this play represents the soul of Judaism, when in fact it represents the catastrophe of Judaism, the critics unwittingly suggest that the soul of Judaism is catastrophic. Ironically, they end up reading the play correctly despite themselves.

For the typical French republican, the *Israélite* was the model (former) Jew. The credo of the *Israélite* was "Be a Jew on the inside, and a human being on the outside"—which is another version of the Josephic-Marrano paradigm writ large and legitimized by the Napoleonic offering of full citizenship to the Jewish community in exchange for its assimilation into French republican culture. (The Valorous, who are anything but *Israélite,* love Napoleon and talk incessantly and patriotically about France as a land of liberation and civilization.) The most important thing for an *Israélite* was to be invisible, to remain always indistinguishable from all other citizens while in public. Proust provides the most lucid description and analysis of the *Israélite.* This assimilation was *not* experienced by the Jewish community in France as an imposed and humiliating constraint. Alain Finkielkraut's analysis of the state of mind of French Jewry during the period spanning from the revolutionary and Napoleonic periods through the Dreyfus Affair and up to Vichy is pertinent in understanding what happened in the Comedie-Française when *Ézéchiel* was performed: "[N]ever before has a nation granted full citizenship to the entire Jewish community, it was therefore not narrow interest *[calcul],* but gratitude that dictated the behavior of the descendents of Moses. To conform to the French people, they left behind all that could, in their laws, risk marking them as foreigners. . . . Far from feeling guilty, the Jews of that period experienced the sweet certitude of obeying the most elementary justice and morality: they acquitted their debt [to the Republic] by de-Judaizing themselves."[9] No conversion to Christianity was necessary; only a conversion to secular republicanism. The only condition for becoming a part of the French nation (*en être,* in Cohenian parlance) was to make one's Jewishness visible only to one's family and intimate circle. Kosher at home, T'aref at work, in sum. In general, the Jewish population embraced this legal emancipation with messianic fervor—they saw the French Revolution and Napoleon as the modern equivalents of the biblical exodus from Egypt, a new Passover.[10] The *Israélite* in other words was a pseudo-Marrano with a clear conscience.

And no one is more fit to tell us this story than Albert Cohen. We have seen in Chapter 1 how the little Albert passionately constructed a religious altar to the French Republic and was in love with an imaginary playmate named Viviane. His romance with the French Republic came to an abrupt and violent end on his tenth birthday when the street hawker drove him from his *Israélite* paradise into the inferno of the "catastrophe called Judaism." In the novel *Solal,* M. de Maussane tells his son-in-law, a Jewish Greek immigrant, what will secure his success in France: "If such is your desire, there is but one

possible attitude. No ambiguity. French and only French and everything that this implies. . . . I repeat . . . love your parents, but from afar, in God's name, from afar! Don't be upset, my friend, and let me tell you something just between the two of us: my great-grandmother, indeed yes, from Alsace. You see then that I have no prejudice. Besides, my best friends. But not so pure."*

Throughout his life Albert Cohen attempted to straddle both positions—that of the Jew and that of the *Israélite.* Although publicly a Zionist and Jewish activist, he always remained a zealot of the *Israélite* dream to the point of recognizing the French language and culture as his true motherland.[11] Thus, he inverts the *Israélite* scheme: publicly, he is a Jewish nationalist, but in private, he remains an unconditional lover of France and would have preferred to become a member of the Académie française than to occupy any public position in Israel.[12] But all apparent inversions or conversions are simply just forms of an even more insistent repetition of the original scenario.

In a word, for the sympathetic republican spectator—and, by extension, for the *Israélite* sitting right beside him—traditional Judaism per se was aberrant, except, perhaps, as a form of fossilized exoticism. Ézéchiel and Jérémie must therefore be displaced into the excessive and "mystical" expression of the Jewish "soul" (as opposed to the sober and rational mind of the *Israélite*) so that they do not provoke repulsion even in liberal and assimilated minds as they do with the more vulgar militants of the Action française. This same dynamic would have been true of the less offensive *Fiddler on the Roof,* but Cohen considerably raises the stakes by offering a sacrilegious Shylock as the apologist for the Jewish community. Could there be a better illustration than the personage of Ézéchiel for those on the Right, Left, and Center of the political spectrum who, overtly or covertly, associated Judaism with a cosmopolitan, conspiratorial form of capitalism? The liberals had to smile and charitably displace this montage into a soft universal "mysticism" of Judaism. The *Israélites* (including Léon Blum, who was in the audience), on the other hand, were horrified by *Ézéchiel,* and their emphatic rejection of it would soon become a mantra in Jewish circles in Paris: "Under the pseudonym of Albert Cohen, Mr. Adolph Hitler had the shrewdness of presenting at the Comédie-Française a one-act play entitled *Ézéchiel.*"[13]

*"Si c'est là votre désir, il n'y a qu'une attitude possible. Pas d'ambiguïté. Français, uniquement français et tout ce que cela comporte. . . . Je le répète . . . aimez vos parents, mais de loin, au nom du ciel, de loin! Ne vous fâchez pas, mon ami, et laissez-moi vous dire une chose en toute confiance: mon arrière-grand-mère, oui parfaitement, d'Alsace. Vous voyez donc que je n'y mets aucun préjugé. Mes meilleurs amis, d'ailleurs. Mais pas si purs" (*Solal,* 275)

The anti-Semites, alerted by the fact that the national theater that Molière had built was going to be desecrated by a Cohen representing a Jewish subject, resorted to whistling and hissing to show their displeasure during the performance. You can imagine the clash that this sparked between the *Israélites,* who defended Cohen's right to present his play, despite their dislike of the content and tone; the enlightened republicans, who twisted uncomfortably in their seats, opening their liberal hearts to the "mysteries" and the "essences" of the Jewish "soul"; and the anti-Semites, who hated the very idea of the play but must have secretly rejoiced in its content and tone, if only for the final affirmation: "Now [that my son Solal is dead], I have only my money to love. My money, yes. Our money, our old ally, which is there (*he points toward the safe*) in this fortress, in our fortress. Our money has permitted us to remain a strong people, has permitted us to resist, to wait, to be patient, has permitted us to endure despite our persecutors, has permitted us to have contempt for their contempt."* No wonder Jacques Marteaux begins his review in the *Journal des débats*: "There was, yesterday afternoon at the Comédie-Française, what in the Middle Ages one called 'a big commotion *[hutin],*' a little revolution with hubub and brouhaha. *Ézéchiel* by Mr. Albert Cohen was what caused it."[14]

One can easily imagine the standard arguments offered for and against the play. But writing from the perspective of the year 2004, with easy access to Cohen's entire œuvre in the two handy volumes of the Pléiade edition, these arguments seem beside the point. None of the standard arguments about appropriateness of content and about the specificity of historical timing, none of the generic arguments about what Philip Roth calls Jewish self-censorship based on the fear of "what the goyim will think,"[15] address the specificity of the Cohenian nightmare, that of Cohen's need to have Solal commit suicide rather than face his father, that of his further aggression in sending Jérémie as a buffoon surrogate for Solal. In the perspective of the whole œuvre, *Ézéchiel* is simply one in a series of macabre Purim plays about the "catastrophe of being a Jew." Solal's absence must have perplexed many a spectator at the Comédie-Française, especially given the fact that many in the audience, as is evident from the reviews, had read the novel *Solal.* The sadistic spectator desired to witness the cruel reunion between the orthodox Sephardic patriarch

*Maintenant, je n'ai plus que mon argent à aimer. Mon argent, oui. Notre argent, notre vieil allié qui est là *(il montre le coffre-fort)* dans cette forteresse, dans notre forteresse. Notre argent qui nous a permis de rester un peuple fort, qui nous a permis de résister, d'attendre, de patienter, qui nous a permis de durer malgré nos persécuteurs, qui nous a permis de mépriser leur mépris! (*Ézéchiel,* 799)

and his high-flying son, a privileged topos of Jewish literature since the Enlightenment. This is the very scene that Cohen offers the readers in *Solal:* after being spurned by Solal for weeks, Rabbi Gamaliel interrupts a diplomatic reception, and Solal, under pressure from his surrogate father, that is, his father-in-law, the liberal republican senator M. de Maussane, crosses himself in front of his father. In *Ézéchiel,* Cohen goes further. As the *Israélite* comes back to the Jew—he dies of his own will. An encounter with the father is no longer even imaginable.[16] Solal's classic double bind leads him to suicide, as one of those gloomy Austro-German *Luftmenschen* described by Theodor Lessing and Sander Gilman in their respective books on Jewish self-hatred, and not as the charismatic, sun-loving Sephardic Messiah, the virile, biblical poet who sings the glory of Israel.[17] But Cohen is both *Luftmensch* and *Solalic* (sun king) at once, or he represents both personae at once. Such is the pain that underwrites these books, and such is the pain that readers and spectators do all they can to avoid acknowledging when confronted with his work.

It is interesting to note that Cohen was so taken aback by the reception of his play, that, as his friend and biographer Gérard Valbert writes, he was to brood over the *Ézéchiel* fiasco many years after the actual events.[18] There is, it seems, a permanent disconnect between Cohen's narrative drives and his readers. Cohen tells and retells the story of this "catastrophe of being a Jew," torn between abject origins and a suicidal destiny. But the novels are so baroque in their combination of style and rhetoric, in their interlacing of voices and perspectives that the repetitive montage, the raw material that he continuously regurgitates, may be overlooked, eclipsed, or even repressed by his readers.

A close examination of the enthusiastic and copious reception of *Belle du Seigneur* in 1968–70 only proves this point to a surprising degree. This reception is exemplary in terms of what is said and, more important, what is left unsaid. There are many excellent commentaries on the language, the eroticism, the social satire of bureaucracy in international organizations; there are also some vague allusions to "the Jewish gaze on the world," and, to account for Cohen's morbidity, the inevitable reference to the metaphysical theme of the "Vanity of Vanities," as if this phrase incarnated the quintessence of the Jewish spirit, which is completely wrong. But with the exception of a single sentence by Jean Blot, no mention is made of the crucial chapter about the Berlin underground and the dwarf Rachel, which is the linchpin of the plot. Many critics assert that it is a novel so vast and so complex, a modern *A Thousand and One Nights,* that it is about everything—and therefore really about nothing in particular. The submerged Josephic political plot, the obscure Estheric drama figuring Ariane as an androgynous projection of Solal—in other words, the essentials!—are completely ignored.[19] What I suggested in the Prologue bears restatement: whereas Cohen's comedy and romance are universal, his tragedy is specifically Jewish in character. And most readers labor so as not to recognize this tragedy, not to recognize what is really at stake in this monumental novel, namely, the Shoah.

But the analogous oversight is not possible in *Ézéchiel,* due to the very nature of theater, the brevity of the play, and its monological, almost didactic tone. And if Cohen remained stunned by the reception of *Ézéchiel,* it is because he was always engrossed by his own need to write these macabre montages, and too little appreciated the impact of such a montage once presented on stage in a theater. Perhaps Cohen did not even care, being both naïve and narcissistic—driven by his need to tell his story in his way, come what may with the republicans, *Israélites,* and anti-Semites. But in doing so on stage he forced the public to reveal itself, to be both fascinated and phobic in reaction to his words, his private theater of nightmares. And thus all that is not said, or said obliquely between the lines, about his prose, comes to the fore here. Cohen forced the issue and was wounded. And this is why the study of *Ézéchiel* and its reception is invaluable for understanding Cohen's paradoxical status in our culture.

Ézéchiel therefore brings into the open the reasons for Cohen's marginality within the institutions invested with the transmission of culture, be they French, Israeli, or American, Jew or Gentile. Who would invest in promoting such a disruptive vision, in which every link to a symbolic identity is undermined? The answer is that Cohen is largely the property of enthusiastic readers worldwide. His masochistic and dissonant montages would preclude the possibility of an appropriation by any normative discourse within academia, including the discourses of demand for redress and the discourses of resentment. To fully account for this, one would have to carry out a full cultural psychoanalysis of France, the United States, and Israel. I conclude nevertheless with a few suggestive reflections on the dynamics of this resistance to Cohen's work.

The French angle is the most perplexing, but also the most obvious. From the early 1920s, key cultural figures such as Jacques Rivière, director of the *Nouvelle revue française* at the time, had recognized Cohen's literary potential and were extremely generous in terms of publishing venues and long-term financial support. As noted in the preface, Cohen's work is formally canonized in its entirety in the prestigious Bibliothèque de la Pléiade collection, and attractive French paperback editions are readily available. This means that Cohen is read, even widely read, relative to other authors of his generation. Yet he remains, if not taboo, then at the margins of French official culture: he is rarely to be found in the national examination syllabi *(concours, textes au programme),* and is virtually untaught in graduate programs.[20]

That Cohen is read by individuals but ignored by institutions should not surprise us. There are simply no grounds for his appropriation by or assimilation into the French collective conscious. Nothing in Cohen is amicable to a "republican" pedagogy or to the French historical memory. As late as the 1980s, one could have gone through a complete curriculum of French *belles lettres*—as I did—either in French or American universities, without once directly addressing the issue of Judaism in France. Pascal's complex relationship to Judaism is glossed over quickly, when not altogether elided, and Voltaire's *Dictionnaire philosophique,* a true manual of systematic modern anti-Judaism, is again carefully edited, if not in the text, then in assigned readings and topics of discussion. Proust might have given us the opportunity for just such a discussion, but even with *À la recherche du temps perdu,* the Jewish dimension, so crucial to understanding the novel, remains largely in the background, subsidiary to the Dreyfus Affair. In a literary culture largely based on careful selection, the Jew has been excerpted out. Either there is no such thing as a Jewish problem, since the *Israélite* is a well-adjusted citizen—end of discussion; or, more accurately, from a French point of view—even an enlightened, liberal vantage point—the Jew and the French are simply incompatible, unless the Jew erases himself completely, changing his name (like André Maurois), incarnating another destiny. Rather than present a multitude of arguments and proofs for this assertion—I submit the following extended passage by none other than André Gide:

> It is absurd, it is even dangerous to attempt to deny the positive aspects of Jewish literature; but it is important to acknowledge that there is today in France a Jewish literature that is not French literature, that has its own virtues, its own meaning, and its own tendencies. What a wonderful job could be done and how helpful it could be to both the Jews and the French if someone would write a history of Jewish literature—a history that would not have to go back far in time, moreover, and within which I can see no disadvantage to fusing the history of Jewish literature from other countries, *for it is always one and the same thing.* This would clarify our ideas somewhat and would perhaps check certain hatreds that result from false classifications.

> There is still much to be said on the subject. One would have to explain why, how and as a result of what economic and social factors the Jews have been silent up to the present. Why Jewish literature goes back hardly more than twenty years, fifty at most. Why during these last fifty years its development has followed a triumphant progress. Have they suddenly become more intelligent? No, before that they did not have the right to speak; perhaps, they did not even have the desire to, for it is worth noting that amidst all those [Jews] who now speak, there is not one who does so through an imperious need to speak—I mean whose eventual aim is the word in itself and the work, and not *the effect* of that word, its material and moral results. They speak louder than we because they do not have our reasons to speak often in an undertone, to respect certain things.[21]

This quotation should stand without comment, except to note the abyss separating Jews and Frenchmen, and to note how unrequited the love was that Jews felt for postrevolutionary France. This quotation expels all the Cohens as Cohens from the "true" French literature, in the same manner that the street hawker expelled the little Albert from the fraternity of citizens.[22]

No wonder the Gides of the world had to displace the aggressive and uncouth *Ézéchiel* into exotic mysticism—and charitably left the foreign play at that. In perhaps an unconscious urge to legitimate Cohen's work, French academic critics now tend to position him within the sphere of French *lettres,* and, for the most part, their arguments are reasonable. In doing so, the critics followed in the footsteps of Albert Cohen himself, who in a slew of mostly regrettable interviews following the publication and celebrity of *Belle du Seigneur,* succumbed to the narcissistic fantasy of cultivating his literary legend by asserting that he was not a writer, but rather a "Don Juan," and tacitly assented to trivial readings of his fiction that ignore the tragic main plot.[23] No doubt, Cohen is inspired by Stendhal, obsessed by Proust, fascinated by Don Juan, and so on. However, if my reading of Cohen is correct, the essential plot lies elsewhere—and this elsewhere is what blocks his institutional transmission.

This "elsewhere," which *Ézéchiel* gives us in protean form, is the following: Cohen's narratives of dissonance and self-mutilation, combining the affirmation of Judaism in the abstract and its negation in the concrete, combining the desire to be French at all cost with the lucidity of knowing that no Jew could ever become fully French, combining the will to belong *(en être),* with suicidal resignation (which is the result of the realization that such a desire to belong will never be fully reciprocated)—this narrative that conjugates to no end and without allegories the "catastrophe of being a Jew" in the specific circumstances of the interwar period in France is just too inimical to French institutional ideology. Once they are closely studied, Cohen's narratives could never become institutional tools in the transmission of French culture, such as *textes au programme* in various centralized state examinations.[24]

But could this masochistic excavation of the "catastrophe of being a (French) Jew" become even today a part of the self-representation of French institutions without, for example, the alibis of a talmudic ethical thought recast in the language of phenomenology with the purpose of a further deepening of the liberal Republic? (Emmanuel Lévinas).[25] I doubt it. This irredeemable lament about the "catastrophe of being a Jew" and the correlated suicidal quest would have no place in a polity predicated on the disappearance of just such irreducible differences, even though few Jews today subscribe to the *Israélite* delusion. Unable to tame the texts, the institutions remain de facto phobic to Cohen, who insistently confronts them with their irredeemable failure to nullify centuries of anti-Semitism through political revolutions and their related "enlightened cultures."

The resistance to Cohen in Israel is even more total. His works have been translated into Hebrew, yet they have been largely ignored there, with the modest exception of *Le Livre de ma mère*.[26] Although considered by many to be the preeminent Sephardic author of the twentieth century, he is not part of the literary conversation in Israel.[27] A. B. Yehoshua, for example, one of Israel's most preeminent novelists, and a Sephardi, never mentions Cohen, even though Yehoshua's magnum opus *Mr. Mani* is itself the morbid story of successive insanities and deferred suicides over five generations.[28] What would the Sephardim do with Cohen, who combines the cultural and existential psychosis of a converted Austrian Jew with a clownish Mediterranean exuberance, the whole montage unanchored in faith, family, and community—and, above all, lacking political hope of any kind? Who in Israel would invest in the transmission of Cohen's bleak version of the Jewish catastrophe? Who in Israel, where the staging of the *Merchant of Venice* was taboo until very recently, would even think of putting *Ézéchiel* on stage? The answer is obvious. Notwithstanding his distinguished Zionist cultural and diplomatic career, Cohen is simply not readable in Israel—at least at present.

To read Albert Cohen for what is properly his, to surmount the profound resistance to him, we must first overcome the historical stage in which Jewish writers and intellectuals live their Judaism as a permanent catastrophe—a catastrophe that is rarely openly admitted and is experienced chiefly as a set of symptoms—and start constructing a reflective relationship, self-conscious and perhaps altogether ironical, with this masochism-as-identity, with this montage that Daniel Sibony correctly characterizes as "the sado-masochistic relationship of everything-for-the-other," which is inherently self-destructive and ultimately suicidal.[29] Philip Roth's recent American Trilogy is well along on this road, while regrettably—in my opinion—the Levinasian and Derridian turn toward ethics and "nonlogocentric justice" only exacerbates the moral masochism inherent in catastrophic Judaism, in which the Jew shoulders every ill and all the guilt of the world—the perfect Cohenian Christlike suicidal montage, all over again.[30]

Within the American academy a more positive tectonic shift has already begun with the illuminating contributions of, among others, Arthur Hertzberg, Jeffery Mehlman, and Alice Kaplan, which are all, to a certain degree, exercises in self-conscious balancing of the attraction to and repulsion of Jews from French culture. Their work is free of willful French republican forgetfulness and in tune with Jewish concerns that are at least more lucid about the *Israélite* double bind—all while remaining sympathetic or even in love with France, as was the ten-year-old Albert Cohen—allowing for more reflective readings of authors such as Voltaire, Maurice Blanchot, and Céline.[31] Overcoming the abjectness of the other is certainly easier than overcoming the abjectness of the same—but is it not time that we also create a space for reading Albert Cohen?

Perhaps the United States of America, free of the feudal and fundamentally anti-Semitic heritages of France and Europe, and their corrective republics, revolutions, and counterrevolutions, and equally free of an exclusive investment in a nationalist solution for the Jewish people, will host this historical transformation of Jews into actors in postcatastrophic Judaism, and thus also become receptive to a frank reading of Albert Cohen. One has to get past the catastrophe to take full measure of the catastrophe's colossal scope, including its brilliant literary epiphanies. This book is intended as a contribution to this budding conversation.

Notes

Prologue: The Cohen Paradox

Epigraph: Cohen, *BdS,* 850: "Ici, dans cette chambre, il a le droit de faire ce qu'il veut, de parler hébreu, de se réciter du Ronsard, de crier qu'il est un monstre à deux têtes, un monstre à deux cœurs, qu'il est tout de la nation juive, tout de la nation française. Ici, tout seul, il pourra porter la sublime soie de synagogue sur les épaules et même, si ça lui chante, se coller une cocarde tricolore sur le front. Ici, terré et solitaire, il ne verra pas les regards méfiants de ceux qu'il aime et qui ne l'aiment pas." French citations refer to the 1994 Bibliothèque de la Pléiade edition of *Belle du Seigneur;* the translations of *Belle du Seigneur* are based, with some modifications, on David Coward's rendering of the novel, except for the stream-of-consciousness translations in Chapter 6, which are my own. All other translations of Cohen are my own.

1. See Bibliography for details of French and English editions of Cohen's writings. The English translation of *Belle du Seigneur* is not currently in print.

2. Marks, *Marrano as Metaphor,* 62.

3. Cohen expresses this notion of the "catastrophe of being Jewish" in many different ways; e.g.: "Why was he Jewish? Why this unhappiness *[malheur]*?" (*Solal,* 123); "No, Sir Ézéchiel, Judaism is not a religion, it's a catastrophe" (*Ézéchiel,* 788); "Enough, enough, finish with this Jewish leprosy"; "And above all the crime of being born a Jew" (*Mangeclous,* 551, 583); and, in particular: "She will not know the misfortune that awaits me, as it awaits all the Jews, these specialists in catastrophes. It is our house special *[specialité maison],* misfortune. You know, in fancy restaurants, there's the house pie. With us, it is the house misfortune, speciality of the house, [sold] wholesale, semi-wholesale, and retail" ("Chant de mort," *France libre* 1 [June 15, 1943]: 105).

4. See Citati, *Kafka.*

5. I am thinking for example about the way René Girard uses the concept of the nineteenth-century "romantic reader" in his discussion of *Don Quixote* and the resistance of readers to acknowledging external mediation, who thus see in the novel "little more than the contrast between Don Quixote the *idealist* and the *realist* Sancho" (Girard, *Deceit, Desire, and the Novel,* 4).

6. Tonnet-Lacrois, *Littérature française et francophone de 1945 à l'an 2000,* 175–76: "Le grand thème du roman de Cohen, c'est la passion amoureuse, qui est

à la fois glorifiée et démystifiée parce que soumise elle aussi à la dégradation. En même temps l'œuvre peint avec beaucoup de verbe satirique les milieux de la diplomatie internationale à Genève dans l'Europe antisémite des années 30, tout en suggérant, par le jeu de la derision, le néant et l'illusion des sentiments et des idéologies. Mais le roman est dominé par la figure fulgurante de Solal, le séducteur passionné quoique lucide. Le récit emporte par le soufflé puissant et baroque, est souvent lyrique, épique, tragique, mais également comique, burlesque même."

7. In 1919, upon his Swiss naturalization, the vowel "h" was added to Coen.

8. *Colloque de Cérisy: Albert Cohen dans son siècle* (forthcoming).

9. On the two endings of *Solal,* see Cohen, *Œuvres,* 155–56.

10. The 1995 English translation wisely retained the French title *Belle du Seigneur,* which does not translate easily.

11. See Cohen, *Écrits d'Angleterre,* 49–84; Valbert, *Albert Cohen, Le Seigneur,* 369–70.

12. See Bibliography for details of Bella Cohen's books about Albert Cohen.

13. Bernard Pivot interviewed Albert Cohen for *Apostrophes* in his Geneva apartment in December 1977 (Seuil Vision, I.N.A., 1977).

14. See esp. *Radioscopie de Jacques Chancel* (transcripts of a series of radio interviews with Cohen in 1980), passim.

15. See the chronology in the Pléiade edition of *BdS,* lxxi–cvii.

16. Cohen on Proust: "Proust cette perversité de tremper une madeleine dans du tilleul ces deux goûts douceâtres le goût épouvantable de la madeleine mêlé au goût pire du tilleul féminité perverse qui me le donne autant que ses hystériques flatteries à la Noailles en réalité il ne l'admirait pas ne pouvait pas l'admirer il la flattait pour des motifs sociaux non pas le lui dire ça la peinerait elle aime la petite phrase de Vinteuil les clochers de Martinville la Vivonne les aubépines de Méséglise et autre exquiseries." *BdS,* 878.

17. This tendency to split Cohen, making him metaphysical or burlesque, can be seen in the work of Carole Auroy, who emphasizes the metaphysical and romantic Cohen, and Judith Kauffman, who emphasizes the burlesque Cohen. See Auroy, *Albert Cohen,* and Kauffmann, *Grotesque et marginalité.* On this contrast, see also Weingrad, "Juifs imaginaires."

18. *BdS,* 152–53.

19. See Bella Cohen's remarks on the subject of Cohen versus Solal in her prefatory essay "Albert Cohen" in *BdS,* lv, lvi.

20. See Braud, *Tentation du suicide dans les écrits autobiographiques,* passim.

21. Milkovitch-Rioux, "Tristan et Iseut: Fortune et avatars du mythe dans *Belle du Seigneur.*"

22. See Lessing, *Haine de soi,* esp. the section entitled "Six vies humaines," 63–167; Gilman, *Jewish Self-Hatred,* esp. chap. 4, "The drive for assimilation"; Loewenstein, *Psychanalyse de l'antisémistisme,* chap. 3, "Psychopathologie collective."

23. For a similar formulation of the relationship of Cohen's work to the Shoah, see Kauffmann, *Grotesque et marginalité,* 159–73.

24. On criticism as delectable self-mutilation, and Judaism and masochism, see Mann, *Masocriticism,* esp. chap 2.

25. "Consonance is the quality inherent in an interval or chord which . . . seems complete and stable in itself. . . . The opposite of consonance is dissonance (or discord): the quality or tension inherent in an interval or chord which . . . involves a clash between adjacent notes of the scale and create the expectation of resolution on to consonance by conjunct motion." *Oxford Companion to Music,* 297–98.

26. See the classic discussion of this predicament in Lessing, *Haine de soi;* Loewenstein, *Psychanalyse de l'antisémistisme;* and Gilman, *Jewish Self-Hatred.*

27. Cohen is acutely aware of this incongruity, see *Les Valeureux,* 864.

28. For an example of this kind of reading, see Morganroth-Schneider, "Literary Struggle with Ambivalence."

29. See Blot, *Albert Cohen;* Valbert, *Albert Cohen: Le Seigneur.*

30. I am well aware that, due to its pejorative etymology ("little pigs"), my usage of the term *marrano* and its derivatives may elicit discomfort in some readers. I do not believe, however, that the term should be replaced by *crypto-Jew* because the latter term is to my ear and sensibility too sterile and simply does not possess the rich resonance of marranism. As with my analysis of Cohen, I tend to adhere to the vocabulary in which a speaking subject describes and/or understands himself (e.g., the Social, baboonery), rather than revise it to reflect current vocabulary. Being at heart a Montaignian nominalist, I know that in some abstract sense signs are arbitrary and at the same time words are laden with rich historical sedimentation, which is not arbitrary. This cannot be easily changed by fiat. I am skeptical of any semantic constructivism. Changes in vocabulary do not, to my mind, transform in any meaningful way the reality of what is being represented. They just impoverish its representation.

One: The Double Bar Mitzvah

Epigraphs: Sibony, *Perversions,* 95: "L'enjeu est d'être identique à son nom, de l'incarner"; id., *Psychanalyse et Judaisme,* 91: "[Le] Père . . . a cette manie de forcer le fils au sacrifice."

1. See the Epilogue for a more extensive discussion of the terms *Israélite* and *Juif;* and see also Blot, *Albert Cohen,* 29–30.

2. See detailed discussion of this "election" in Chapter 2.

3. Cohen is verging here on the Augustinian and Pascalian type of argument, which has its ultimate origin in a conception of matter as fallen, or as stained forever by original sin. This strand of thought exists in some marginal Jewish thought, but is never dominant. On the other hand, it is true that exilic Judaism, which was concerned with, survival, transmission of the Law, and the pragmatic patriarchal management of the community, tended to become more puritanical. See, e.g., the discussion of marriage and sexuality in the Sephardic book of bibli-

cal commentaries *MeAm Lo'ez, Genesis I* [People of Strange Language (The Torah Anthology)], in Hebrew, 124–29. For a discussion of the duality of nature and anti-nature in Cohen, see Schaffner, *Le Goût de l'absolu,* 39–46.

4. *Pirke Avot* [The Ethics of the Fathers], 3.9, in *Daily Prayers,* trans. Philips, 469. And see also *Living Talmud,* trans. Goldin, 127–28.

5. Sibony, *Trois Monothéismes,* esp. appendix, "Lecture des Dix Commandements."

6. *BdS,* 899–900.

7. I am borrowing the notion of God's actions as "blessing or scattering" from Harold Bloom's commentary on Genesis in *Book of J,* trans. Rosenberg, ed. Bloom, 192.

8. Cohen, *Paroles juives,* 47.

9. Schaffner, "Paroles juives," in *Albert Cohen: Colloque du centenaire,* 69–86.

10. For a general description of the concept of romance, see Rougement, *L'Amour et l'Occident.*

11. Cohen substitutes the name of the Popular Front prime mininster Léon Blum (1936–38) for that of Alfred Dreyfus, the army officer falsely accused of treason.

12. This pogrom corresponds to a real (or the threats of an) anti-Semitic pogrom in Corfu that took place in 1891, which precipitated the decline of the Jewish community there and resulted in the emigration of the Coen family in 1895. See Valbert, *Albert Cohen: Le Seigneur,* 29, and Blot, *Albert Cohen,* 17–23.

13. For a differing viewpoint on the mother and on the image of Jewish women in Cohen, see Bensoussan, "Aude, Adrienne, Rébecca, Rachel," 54–59.

14. Sibony, *Psychanalyse et Judaisme,* 139.

15. See, e.g., Glenn Frankel "For Jews in France, a 'kind of Intifada': Escalation in Hate Crimes Leads to Soul-Searching, New Vigilance," *Washington Post,* July 16, 2003, A1, and, more extensively, Taguieff, *Nouvelle Judéophobie,* passim.

16. Celan was similarly inclined to see himself as having a homeland in a particular language, German in his case. See Felstiner, *Paul Celan,* 94.

17. Here's how Romain Gary, *Les Clowns lyriques,* 33–34, explains the ideal that France represented politically to a Polish Jew at the beginning of the twentieth century. "When [La Marne, nom de guerre] was a child and his Polish classmates treated him as a kike *[youpin]* and gave him a good thrashing, he did not begrudge them, because they were not French. They were poor little barbarians. . . . At that time, they taught in the Russian and Polish ghettos about France, the Revolution, the rights of man, liberty, equality, fraternity to teach the children to breathe, and it so happens that La Marne was particularly sensitive to this breathing exercise."

18. These pages are a perfect illustration of the situation of persons of Jewish origin in France from the time of Napoleon to 1945. See Finkielkraut, *Juif imaginaire,* 79–80.

19. See Prager, *Presenting the Past,* esp. chap. 4, "Trauma and the Memory of Wars."

20. See Michon-Bertout, "Cohen et l'antisémitisme," 55–74.
21. See Miernowska, *Dialogue des discours dans les romans d'Albert Cohen,* 129.
22. Valbert, *Albert Cohen: Le Seigneur,* 393.

Two: Identity Montage

Epigraphs: Mann, *Joseph the Provider,* 109. Trigano, *Philosophie de la Loi,* 230: "Joseph . . . —est l'expérience et la problématique d'Israël pour s'assembler, pour former un peuple, constuire sa multiplicité et lui donner un sens."

1. Cohen repeatedly uses the term *le Social* to refer to the sense of familiarity, comfort, and belonging in the world of European Gentiles, and I am using "the Social" here in the same sense.

2. For a recent example of this tendency of favoring European over Hebrew origins, see Schaffner, ed., *Albert Cohen: Colloque du centenaire,* where the first section of the book, "Itinéraires intertextuels," includes papers on Virgil, Homer, Tristan and Isolde, Proust, and Albert Camus, but no reference to the biblical intertext.

3. See *Radioscopie de Jacques Chancel,* passim.

4. Judith Kauffmann has certainly understood the concrete historical dimensions of Cohen's fiction. See Kauffmann, *Grotesque et marginalité,* 159–73.

5. This point is strongly made by Blot, *Albert Cohen,* 15; and Marks, *Marrano as Metaphor,* 62.

6. Trigano, "Mystère d'Esther et de Joseph," 11.

7. All my citations from Genesis are based on Alter, *Genesis: Translation and Commentary.* All other biblical citations are based on the New Oxford Annotated Bible.

8. I am referring here to the "documentary hypothesis" with respect to the composition of the Hebrew Bible, according to which the biblical text consists of four distinct layers: Jahwist (J); Elohist (E); Deuteronomist (D); and Priestly (P).

9. Trigano, "Mystère d'Esther et de Joseph," 13.

10. Survival is paramount, even at the price of transgression, including incest. Even very modern texts are marked by this "obsession," as is evidenced, e.g., by A. B. Yehoshua's *Mr. Mani,* in which transgression and survival play a pivotal role in a modernist retelling of Genesis.

11. Whedbee, *The Bible and the Comic Vision.*

12. See Auroy, *Albert Cohen,* 63–75.

13. *Solal,* 306.

14. Solal's repeated provocations are in stark contrast to Joseph's prudential attitudes: "[Potiphar] is not greater in this house than I, and he has held back nothing from me except you, as you are his wife, and how could I do this great evil and give offense to God?" (Gen. 39: 9).

15. The father substitution here (Maussane for the "old man with the beard") is just one more in a long chain of family romance type of substitutions, of which

Adrienne de Valdone, Solal's first lover, is the first, because she substitutes for Rachel, who is as repulsive to Solal as his father, Gamaliel, that "old man with the beard."

16. Kauffmann, *Grotesque et marginalité,* passim.
17. On the *Fort! Da!* game, see Freud, *Beyond the Pleasure Principle,* 14.
18. *Book of J,* trans. Rosenberg, ed. Bloom, 237.
19. Mangeclous, 570.
20. *Book of J,* trans. Rosenberg, ed. Bloom, 235.
21. Trigano, *Philosophie de la Loi,* 230.
22. Trigano, "Mystère d'Esther et de Joseph," 17.
23. Mann, *Joseph the Provider,* 358.
24. Ibid., 379.
25. See Aciman, "Le Juif intérieur."
26. McGaha, *Coat of Many Cultures,* xv.
27. Whedbee, *The Bible and the Comic Vision.*
28. See discussion in the Epilogue.
29. Mann, *Joseph the Provider,* 109. See also Sibony, *Don de soi ou partage de soi,* 264, where he offers the following definition of the Hebrew person: "The Hebrew book symbolizes an identity broken like the famous Tables of the law, but alive, out of place, de-centered, in movement vis-à-vis itself and the others, thanks to this brokenness which resonates with the ontological brokenness between *being* and that-which-is. It's less about inclusions than *passing* through inclusions. This is what the word *passeur* [Hebrew] means."
30. See McGaha, *Coat of Many Cultures.*
31. Doniach, *Purim,* 36.
32. Judith Kauffmann sees in the Purim festival a major chronotope in Cohen's fiction. See Kauffmann, *Grotesque et marginalité,* 144–55.
33. Quoted in Díaz-Mas, *Sephardim,* trans. Zucker, 139–40.
34. Quoted in Gopnik, "Purim Story," 130.
35. I am referring to Giles Deleuze's concept of *habitus,* in Deleuze, *Différence et répétition.*
36. Armand Abécassis, *Pensée juive,* 3: 323.
37. See Yovel, *Spinoza,* chap. 4, "Marranos in Mask and a World Without Transcendence: Rojas and *La Celestina.*"
38. Roth, *History of the Marranos,* 188.
39. Yovel, *Spinoza,* xl, cited in Marks, *Marrano as Metaphor,* 134.
40. Aciman, "Le Juif intérieur"; Marks, *Marrano as Metaphor.*
41. Jama, *L'Histoire juive de Montaigne,* 23–24.
42. See Hertzberg, *French Enlightenment and the Jews,* 268–313.
43. See Blot, *Albert Cohen,* 183–97, and Valbert, *Albert Cohen: Le Seigneur,* 325–30.
44. The principal reason for this failure was the opposition of the Quai d'Orsay (the French Foreign Ministry), motivated by British fear that such an army would eventually be detrimental to British interests in Palestine. See Valbert, *Albert Cohen: Le Seigneur,* 330.

45. Mann, *Joseph the Provider,* 404.
46. See *Mangeclous,* 855–64, for a final recap of the story of the Valorous. On their language, see Elbaz, *Albert Cohen.*
47. *Solal,* 93.
48. Weingrad, "Juifs imaginaires," 12.
49. *Mangeclous,* 569.
50. Whedbee, *The Bible and the Comic Vision,* 118–19 (Gen. 45: 3).
51. Brooks, *Reading for the Plot,* 234.
52. Ibid., 171.
53. Whedbee, *The Bible and the Comic Vision,* 122.

Three: The Jewish Saint-Germain

Epigraph: Trigano, *Philosophie de la Loi,* 232.

1. See on eyes and castration, Freud, "The Uncanny," in *The Standard Edition of the Complete Psychological Works of Sigmund Freud,* ed. Strachey et al., 17: 219–52.
2. For a more extensive discussion of this point, see J. I. Abecassis, "Camus' Pulp Fiction," 633.
3. See Zard, *Fiction de l'Occident,* 167, on "la tentation marcionite de l'Occident." And see also Lowenstein, *Psychanalyse de l'antisemitisme.*
4. Brazilai, *On the Structure of Judaism,* esp. 143–65.
5. Sibony, *Trois Monothéismes,* esp. "Religion et point de vue de l'être," 292–97.
6. Bakhtin, *Dialogic Imagination,* esp. the third essay, "Forms of Time and the Chronotope in the Novel."
7. Steiner, *No Passion Spent,* esp. the essay "Through a Looking Glass Darkly," 328–47.
8. See Benhaïm, "Synagogue perdue." And see also Von Simson, *Gothic Cathedral,* 121 n.
9. See Lowenstein, *Psychanalyse de l'antisémitisme,* esp. the reference to Arnold Toynbee, for whom Jews are "fossils of the Syrian civilization" (115).
10. Sibony, *Trois Monothéismes,* 328: "L'origine de la haine, c'est la haine de l'origine."
11. Zard, *Fiction de l'Occident,* 172.
12. On the chronotope of the cave/cellar in Cohen, I consulted Léwy-Bertaut, *Albert Cohen,* 307–11, 340–43; Schaffner, "Château gothique de Solal"; Zard, *Fiction de l'Occident,* 164–74; and Kauffmann, *Grotesque et marginalité,* 38–53.
13. "[L]a pratique de la religion ne se borne pas aux cérémonies accomplies par la communauté à des moments prescrits. Au contraire, tout acte de la vie courante, comme le fait de manger ou de travailler, tend à être sanctifié par Dieu ou encore le devoir religieux tend à pénétrer même dans les actes qui, chez les Chrétiens, restent profanes." Lowenstein, *Psychanalyse de l'antisémitisme,* 179.

14. The association between blood rituals and Jewish origin is so strong that even in otherwise "liberal" authors such as Thomas Mann the imputation is clear. In *The Magic Mountain,* Naphta's origin as the son of a *shohet* (ritual Kosher butcher) is described in gory detail as being soaked in fresh blood.

15. See Lowenstein, *Psychanalyse de l'antisémitisme,* on the blood of Christ dripping on the Jews, 243–46.

16. Steiner, *No Passion Spent,* 334.

17. Sibony, *Psychanalyse et Judaisme, 260:* "Si la grace remplace la loi, la jouissance remplace l'interprétation."

18. Solal has already characterized his mother as a worm: "Rachel Solal, une épaise creature larvaire qui se mouvait avec difficulté, et dont les yeux faux luisaient de peur ou de désir" (*Solal,* 97). According to Cohen in his interview with Bernard Pivot, the title of his first poem was "Dans l'antre de la négation" (In the den of negation).

19. This analysis of the name Solal des Solal is consonant with an important insight by Alain Schaffner in *Albert Cohen: Colloque du centenaire,* 75: "All of Albert Cohen's work seems to be a product of the will to vindicate the name of Cohen, which signifies priest in Hebrew."

20. See the original ending of the novel *Solal,* reproduced in full in Cohen, *Œuvres,* 1255–56.

21. On the relationship between Judaism and Christianity, see Sibony, *Trois Monothéismes,* 318–34.

Four: Kaddish and Shivah

Kadish: Jewish prayer of sanctification for the departed; Shivah: ritual "sitting" on the ground for seven days after burial of a dead Jew.

Epigraph: The Pakistani Urdu poet Faiz Ahmed Faiz to Alun Lewis, Burma, ca. 1943; see *The True Subject: Selected Poems of Faiz Ahmed Faiz,* trans. Naomi Lazard (Princeton, N.J.: Princeton University Press, 1988), v.

1. See Cohen, *Œuvres,* 1258–67, "Dossier de presse."

2. Marcel Pagnol quoted in Valbert, *Albert Cohen: Le Seigneur,* 380: "La grande réussite et la grande audace d'Albert Cohen, c'est d'avoir écrit un chef-d'œuvre sur le plus commun des lieux communs."

3. Georges Altmann quoted in ibid., 379: "André Gide, ce Lucifer petit-bourgeois, proclamait un jour qu'on ne peut faire de bonne littérature avec de bons sentiments. Bien des œuvres du passé et du présent démentent cette boutade. *Le livre de ma mère* est de celles-là."

4. *Book of My Mother,* trans. Bella Cohen, 11. English translations here are my own.

5. Although the texts studied here differ completely from those studied by Leo Strauss in *Persecution and the Art of Writing,* I am certain that my analysis of concealment in Cohen owes a considerable debt to Strauss's approach.

6. Duprey, *Albert Cohen,* esp. chap. 2, "Les Figures parentales," 35–40.

7. On the femininity of the boy Albert Cohen, see Winter, *Errants de la Chair,* 68–77.

8. The critical literature on this issue is prolific. I find Barzel, *On the Structure of Judaism,* 152–65 ("Man's unique place—here and now") particularly persuasive and richly documented. Unfortunately, it is in Hebrew.

9. See Brooks, *Reading for the Plot,* chap. 8, "Narrative Transaction and Transference."

10. *Mangeclous,* 570.

11. A particularly good example here is *BdS,* chap. 94.

12. Shivah is the name for the seven-day mourning period that follows the burial of a close family member. "The expression 'sitting shivah' alludes to the custom of mourners' remaining at home during the first seven days of mourning, sitting unshod on a low stool." Birnbaum, *Book of Jewish Concepts,* 578.

13. On mourning, see Freud, "Mourning and Melancholy," 152–70, and Klein, "Mourning and Its Relation to Manic-Depressive States," in *Selected Melanie Klein,* ed. Mitchell, 146–74 and Sánchez-Pardo, *Cultures of the Death Drive,* chap. 2, "Kleinian Metapsychology," 55–71.

14. See Adam, *Promises, Promises,* "Coming to Grief," 257–66.

15. Cohen's text here takes on the rhythm of the mourning incantation, achieved by its usage of repetition of the same phrases and syntactical structures, akin to the mourner's tearful monologue. For example: "Jamais plus . . . Jamais plus" (*LM,* 720); "Amour de ma mère . . . Amour de ma mère" (*LM,* 740–41); and "Autour de ma mère . . . Autour de ma mère (ibid.).

16. On the regression fantasy, see Klein, "Mourning and Its Relation to Manic-Depressive States," in *Selected Melanie Klein,* ed. Mitchell, 148.

17. Kristeva, *Génie féminin,* vol. 2: *Melanie Klein,* 104.

18. For discussion of Christlike scenarios in Cohen, see Auroy, *Albert Cohen,* 63–74.

Five: Purim in Berlin

For an earlier version of this paper, see J. I. Abecassis. "Les clous d'Albert Cohen." Fragments of this article are translated and reprinted here with permission.

Epigraph: *BdS,* 501. Said by Rachel.

1. I am using the 1995 English translation by David Coward of *Belle du Seigneur.* However, I have considerably modified all these translations.

2. Blot, *Albert Cohen,* 162–69, develops this point.

3. Here, I cannot but think of Prosper Mérimée's fantastic tale "Lokis," in which a countess is raped by a bear and bears a son who is half human, half animal.

4. *New Oxford Annotated Bible.*

5. See Schaffner, "Paroles juives," in *Albert Cohen: Colloque du centenaire,* 76.

6. Bakhtin, *Rabelais and His World,* 10.

7. See, by way of analogy, Sibony, *Don de soi ou partage de soi,* esp. chap. 1, "Un Éthique de coupable," for the idea that the relationship between the "I" and "Thou" only makes sense if mediated by a third, superior "being" (i.e., God).

8. On Solal's mother, see *Solal,* 123. Cohen reproaches himself for not being able to rescue his parents in "Chant de mort," *France libre* 6, no. 33 (July 15, 1943): 198.

9. Reality deflates the Rabelaisian verbal plethora of the narrative here, ending its seriocomic verve. See Elbaz, *Albert Cohen,* 93.

10. E.g., Goitien-Galperin, *Visage de mon peuple,* 101–3.

11. *BdS,* 857.

12. On the one-way election, see Fix-Combe, "Sous le soleil de Solal."

13. See discussion of a similar point in Chapter 4: "Comme quoi on peut être presque antisémite même avec sa mère" ("Chant de mort," *France libre* 1 [June 15, 1943]: 103).

14. It is revealing that David Coward, the English translator of *Belle du Seigneur,* is clearly resisting the force of the French syntax, and here therefore the meaning of the whole stream of consciousness. "Je veux tout aimer de mon peuple" does not translate into "I will treasure my people and everything about my people." There is no hint of the future tense in the French verbal construction; only strong insistence on the act of conscious volition "Je veux," which contrasts with the absence of such conscious volition, such hard work on oneself, when it comes to the sentences in the same stream of consciousness describing his love for Ariane.

Six: Ariane-Solal

Epigraph: Winter, *Errants de la chair,* 71: "Ariane, c'est tout autant Albert Cohen que Solal." I met the psychoanalyst Jean-Pierre Winter at the "Albert Cohen dans son siècle" colloquium at Cerisy-la-Salle in September 2003 and learned that he had come to the same conclusion as I had concerning the fluidity and transitivity of Ariane's and Solal's identities.

1. For a formal discussion of this intimate "notebook" *(cahier)*, see Stolz, *Polyphonie dans "Belle du Seigneur" d'Albert Cohen,* 180–83.

2. See Léwy-Bertaut, "L'Androgyne," 124–44, and Politis, "Bisexualité chez les personages d'Albert Cohen," 145–54.

3. I am aware that in psychoanalytical literature the term "phallus" is not synonymous with the penis but has a more complex symbolic function. But for my purposes here, I use "phallus" to refer to the anatomical penis (it makes sense in terms of what Ariane says in her stream of consciousness), and I use "phallic order" to refer to the more symbolic patriarchy based on strict power, which Cohen abhors throughout his writings. See Cohen's description of the world of baboons in *BdS,* 366, as a perfect illustration of what I mean in the Cohenian context by

"phallic order." See *Dictionnaire de la psychanalyse,* 599–609, s.v. *phallus.* In the same vein, I make a distinction between the terms "fantasy" and "phantasm." "Fantasy" connotes a conscious wish fulfillment thought, whereas "phantasm" refers to unconscious or subconscious desire of scenarios that are most readily available to the reader in the seemingly random montages of themes of which the streams of consciousness are constructed.

4. See Stoltz, *Polyphonie dans "Belle du Seigneur" d'Albert Cohen,* 27–38. For a more general discussion, see Boone, *Libidinal Currents,* 142–71.

5. Cohn, *Transparent Minds,* 225.

6. See *Solal,* 186.

7. Calasso, *Marriage of Cadmus and Harmony,* 7.

8. Ibid., 4.

9. Zard, *Fiction de l'Occident,* 263–64; emphasis added.

10. Calasso, *Marriage of Cadmus and Harmony,* 27.

11. There is another variation of this phantasm in which Ariane takes refuge with her grandfather, with whom she essentially repeats the same scenario of refuge from the world at the edge of natural boundaries (here, it is in a mountainous forest). See *BdS,* 181.

12. See full discussion in Chapter 4.

13. "Ma mère était mon gui" ("My mother was my mistletoe"), *Livre de ma mère,* 743.

14. He looks at himself in Ariane's bedroom mirror thinking that he is "sickeningly beautiful" (*beau à vomir* [*BdS,* 9]); Ariane, in turn, gazes upon herself and thinks that she is "the most beautiful woman in the world" (*la plus belle femme du monde* [*BdS,* 34]); see previous discussion of this scene in Chapter 5.

15. See Duprey, "Mariette."

16. Exactly the same scene is related by Cohen's daughter Myriam about their cohabitation in Paris during the 1930s. Myriam Champigny Cohen, *Livre de mon père,* 86–87.

17. Cited in Blot, *Albert Cohen,* 000.

18. See Sibony, *Don de soi ou partage de soi,* 264.

19. See *Solal,* 164.

20. The orgasmic end of Ariane's stream of consciousness recalls the end of Molly Bloom's stream of consciousness in James Joyce's *Ulysses,* 643–44: " . . . a girl where I was a Flower of the mountain yes when I put the rose in my hair like the Andalusian girls used or shall I wear a red yes and how he kissed me under the Moorish wall and I thought well as well him as another and then I asked him with my eyes to ask again yes and then he asked me would I yes to say yes my mountain flower and first I put my arms around him yes and drew him down to me so he could feel my breasts all perfume yes and his heart was going like mad and yes I said yes I will Yes."

21. For a discussion of the Passion in *BdS,* see Schaffner, *Goût de l'absolu,* 158–66.

22. For a different interpretation of the last paragraph of *Belle du Seigneur*, see Kauffmann, *Grotesque et marginalité*, 196–67.

Epilogue: Ézéchiel, *or, Abject Origins, Suicidal Destiny*

A earlier version of this chapter was presented at the Colloque de Cérisy, "Albert Cohen dans son siècle," September 3–8, 2003; see *Colloque de Cérisy: Albert Cohen dans son siècle* (forthcoming).

Epigraph: Homer, *The Odyssey*, trans. Fagles, 212.

1. *Mangeclous*, 548.
2. Solal does return once to Cephalonia in the novel *Solal*, but remains in the hotel, never visiting his father.
3. See Freud, "Mourning and Melancholy," in *Collected Papers*, ed. Jones, 4: 152–70.
4. I would like to thank Mme Daisy Politis for providing me with all the available documents at the Atelier Albert Cohen, Paris.
5. On the specific nature of Jewish humor, see Rabinovitch, *Sourire d'Isaac*, passim; Ted Cohen, *Jokes*, passim; and Kauffmann, *Grotesque et marginalité*, 174–88.
6. Birnbaum, *Book of Jewish Concepts*, 533.
7. Cohen, *Œuvres*, 1337.
8. It is true that by the 1930s, many Eastern European Jews had immigrated to Paris and could be seen, but they had not yet made any inroads into French society, and they were, in fact, the first to be sent to the death camps under the Franco-German Vichy regime.
9. Finkielkraut, *Juif imaginaire*, 79–80.
10. Ibid., 80.
11. See discussion of this point in Chapter 1.
12. Albert Cohen was offered an ambassadorship to the state of Israel but declined. He never visited Israel, where a forest was planted in his honor close to Jerusalem.
13. Valbert, *Albert Cohen: Le Seigneur*, 277.
14. Cohen, *Œuvres*, 1326.
15. See Roth, *Reading Myself and Others*, 205–11.
16. We recall that in *Mangeclous*, Solal hides his father in a secluded villa.
17. On the specific nature of Jewish self-hatred, see Lessing, *Haine de soi;* Gilman, *Jewish Self-Hatred.*
18. Valbert, *Albert Cohen: Le Seigneur*, 271.
19. See *BdS*, 1003–27, "Dossier de presse." I have also consulted the archives of the Atelier Albert Cohen.
20. Politis, "Presence d'Albert Cohen dans le secondaire," 131–34.
21. André Gide, *Journal*, 175–76, cited in Marks, *Marano as Metaphor*, 59–60;

translation modified, emphasis added. For a more general discussion of Judaism in French literature, see Weingrad, "Juifs imaginaries," passim.

22. Cohen is a self-consciously anti-Gide novelist: see *Solal,* 175, and *BdS,* 334, where he pokes fun at the refined French novel and its elegant prose.

23. Valbert, *Albert Cohen: Le Seigneur,* 78.

24. Marks, *Marrano as Metaphor,* 62, insists on the uncompromisingly Jewish character of Cohen's writings: "Albert Cohen (1895–1981) is one of the major French writers of the twentieth century who is Jewish by birth and whose narrators are never not conscious of their own Jewishness and the Jewishness, or relation to Jewishness, of most of the important characters in their fictional world."

25. Lilla, *Reckless Mind,* passim.

26. I thank Cohen's translator Nitsa Ben Ari for discussing Cohen's place in Israel with me. I also thank Professor Judith Kauffmann of Bar Ilan University for her insights on the subject of Cohen in Israel.

27. See Bensoussan, "L'Image du Sepharade dans l'œuvre d'Albert Cohen."

28. See Horn, *Facing the Fires.*

29. Sibony, *Don de soi ou partage de soi?* 65: "le rapport sado-maso du tout-pour-l'autre."

30. See Lilla, *Reckless Mind,* chapter on Derrida; Delacampagne, *Le Philosophe et le Tyran.*

31. See Hertzberg, *French Enlightenment and the Jews;* Mehlman, *Legacies of Anti-Semitism in France;* Kaplan, *French Lessons.*

Bibliography

Cahiers Albert Cohen (Études, Critiques, Événements), published by the Atelier Albert Cohen and edited by Philippe Zard, is an indispensable tool in Cohen research, and includes conference proceedings, articles, book reviews, and notes about new editions and reprintings of Cohen's works and on professional meetings. The periodic bulletins of the Atelier Albert Cohen include complete bibliographical references to all relevant recent publications. Other documentation, including Cohen's early writings that are out of print, original documents, and complete collections of reviews and scholarly articles about Cohen, can be consulted at the Atelier Albert Cohen, 115, avenue Henri-Martin 75116 Paris. Mme Daisy Politis, secretary of the Atelier and editorial secretary of the *Cahiers Albert Cohen,* can be contacted at atelieralbertcohen@net-up.com.

Albert Cohen's Works in the Bibliothèque de la Pléiade

Belle du Seigneur. Edited by Christel Peyrefitte and Bella Cohen. Paris: Gallimard 1994 [1968]. 1,034 pp. This invaluable edition contains a comprehensive introduction by Peyrefitte and an introductory essay by Bella Cohen, a complete annotated chronology, notes and variants, and selected reviews.

Œuvres. Edited by Christel Peyrefitte and Bella Cohen. Paris: Gallimard 1993. 1,436 pp. This volume includes the complete texts of *Paroles juives, Solal, Mangeclous, Le Livre de ma mère, Ézéchiel, Les Valeureux, Ô vous, frères humains, Carnets 1978,* and *Churchill d'Angleterre.* This edition also includes notes and variants and selected reviews.

Paperback French Editions of Albert Cohen's Writings

Solal. Paris: Gallimard, 1930.

Mangeclous. Paris: Gallimard, 1938.

Le Livre de ma mère. Paris: Gallimard, 1954.

Belle du Seigneur. Paris Gallimard, 1968. 845 pp.

Les Valeureux. Paris: Gallimard, 1969.

Ô vous, frères humains. Paris: Gallimard, 1972.

Carnets 1978. Paris: Gallimard, 1979.

Radioscopie de Jacques Chancel. Monaco: Éditions du Rocher (Radio France / France Inter), 1999. Transcripts of a series of radio interviews with Albert Cohen on March 31 and April 4, 1980.

Écrits d'Angleterre. Paris: Les Belles Lettres, 2002. Wartime writings and writings related to the legal status of refugees in the post–World War II period.

Albert Cohen's "Chant de mort," the first draft of *Le Livre de ma mère,* appeared in *France libre* 6, no. 32 (June 15, 1943): 99–105; 6, no. 33 (July 15, 1943): 189–99; 7, no. 40 (February 15, 1944): 280–87; and 8, no. 43 (May 15, 1944): 47–54. Cohen's "Le Jour de mes dix ans," the first draft of *Ô vous, frères humains,* appeared in *France libre* 10, no. 57 (July 16, 1945): 193–200, and 10, no. 58 (August 15, 1945): 287–94, and *Esprit,* 114 (September 1945): 460–79.

English Translations of Books by Albert Cohen

Belle du Seigneur. Translated by David Coward. New York: Viking, 1995. Out of print.

Book of My Mother. Translated by Bella Cohen. With a Foreword by David Coward. UNESCO Collection of Representative Works. London: Peter Owen, 1997.

Solal. Translated by Wilfrid Benson. New York: Dutton, 1933. Out of print.

Biographical Studies of Albert Cohen

Blot, Jean. *Albert Cohen.* Paris: Balland (Biographies) 1995 [1986]. Complete biography.

———. *Albert Cohen, ou, Solal dans le siècle.* Présence du Judaisme. Paris: Albin Michel, 1995.

Cohen, Bella. *Autour d'Albert Cohen.* Paris: Gallimard, 1990. Useful documentation.

———. Albert Cohen, *Mythe et réalité.* Paris: Gallimard, 1991. Controversy as to the identity of Ariane, protagonist of *Belle du Seigneur.*

Cohen-Champigny, Myriam. *Le Livre de mon père, suivi de, Les Lettres de ma mère.* Arles: Actes Sud, 1996. Revealing reminiscences by Cohen's only daughter, with his letters to his first wife, Elizabeth Brocher.

Valbert, Gérard. *Albert Cohen: Le Seigneur.* Paris: Grasset, 1990. Complete biography.

———. *Albert Cohen, ou, Le Pouvoir de vie.* Lausanne: L'Âge de homme, 1990 [1981].

———. *La Compagnie des écrivains.* Lausanne: L'Âge de homme, 2003. Ten years of friendship and conversations with Albert Cohen recalled by an astute observer.

Albert Cohen Criticism

Abecassis, Jack I. "Les Clous d'Albert Cohen." *Cahiers Albert Cohen,* no. 12 (September 2002).

———. "La Synagogue à la Comédie-Française." In *Colloque de Cerisy: Albert Cohen dans son siècle.* Forthcoming.

Auroy, Carole. *Albert Cohen: Une Quête solaire.* Paris: Presses de l'Université de Paris-Sorbonne, 1996.

Benhaïm, André. "'Mon plus beau livre' (Albert Cohen)." *Revue des sciences humaines,* nos. 266–67 (April–September 2002): 413–25.

———. "La Synagogue perdu: Proust et Cohen." In *Colloque de Cerisy, Albert Cohen dans son siècle.* Forthcoming.

Bensoussan, Albert. "L'Image du Sepharade dans l'œuvre d'Albert Cohen." *Les Temps modernes,* May 1979.

———. "Aude, Adrienne, Rébecca, Rachel: L'Image de la femme dans l'œuvre d'Albert Cohen." *Les Nouveaux Cahiers* 91 (Winter 1987–88).

Duprey, Véronique. "Mariette: Entre le sérieux et (ou) le comique d'une enterprise langagière." *Cahiers Albert Cohen (Jouissances et réjouissance),* no. 6 (1996): 59–76.

———. *Albert Cohen: Au nom du père et de la mère.* Paris: Sedes, 1999.

Elbaz, Robert. *Albert Cohen, ou, La Pléthore du discours narratif.* Paris: Publisud, 2000.

Fix-Combe, Nathalie. "Sous les soleil de Solal: Regard brûlant sur la fémininité." *Cahiers Albert Cohen,* no. 8 (September 1998).

Flory, Emmanuel. "Des mythes antiques dans le roman cohéniens: Dionysos et Ariane." *Cahiers Albert Cohen,* no. 10 (2000): 103–22.

Goitein-Galperin D. R. *Visage de mon peuple: Essai sur Albert Cohen.* Paris: Nizet, 1982.

Kauffmann, Judith. *Grotesque et marginalité: Variation sur Albert Cohen et l'effet-Mangeclous.* Bern: Peter Lang, 1999.

———. "'Ma mère n'avait pas de moi mais un fils': Violence et celebration paradoxale dans Le Livre de ma mère." *Cahier Albert Cohen,* no. 13 (September 2003): 147–64.

Léwy-Bertaut, Evelyne. "L'Androgyne: Double, moitié ou zero?" *Cahiers Albert Cohen,* no. 5 (1995): 125–44.

———. *Albert Cohen mythobiographe: Une Démarche de création.* Grenoble: ELLUG, Université Stendhal, 2001.

Maisier-Eynon, Véronique. "L'inspiration picaresque dans l'œuvre d'Albert Cohen." *Cahiers Albert Cohen,* no. 11 (2001): 97–100

Michon-Bertout, Laure. "Cohen et l'antisémitisme." *Cahiers Albert Cohen,* no. 9 (September 1999).

Milkovitch-Rioux, Catherine. "Tristan et Iseut: Fortune et avatars du mythe dans Belle du Seigneur." In *Albert Cohen: Colloque du centenaire.* Villeneuve d'Ascq: Roman 20–50, 1997.

———. *L'Univers mythique d'Albert Cohen: Personnages, décors et mise en scène.* Presses universitaires du Septentrion, 1998.

Miernowska, Ewa. *Le Dialogue des discours dans les romans d'Albert Cohen.* New York: Peter Lang, 1998.

Morganroth-Schneider, Judith. "Struggle with Ambivalence: Representation of Misogyny and Jewish Self-Hatred in the Writing of Albert Cohen." *Shofar* 18, no. 3 (Spring 2000): 27–48.

Politis, Daisy. "La Bisexualité chez les personnages d'Albert Cohen." *Cahiers Albert Cohen,* no. 5 (1995): 145–54.

"Présence d'Albert Cohen dans le secondaire." *Cahiers Albert Cohen,* no. 3 (September 1993): 131–34.

Schaffner, Alain. *Albert Cohen.* Bibilographie des écrivains français, 1. Paris: Memini, 1995. Lists all press and scholarly articles on Albert Cohen up to 1994 by subject, including a useful software data base.

———. "Paroles juives: Cohen avant Cohen." In id., ed., *Albert Cohen: Colloque du centenaire, Université de Picardie Jules Verne, Amiens, 6–7 septembre 1995.* Villeneuve d'Ascq: Roman 20–50, 1997.

———. *Le Goût de l'absolu: L'Enjeu sacré de la littérature dans l'œuvre d'Albert Cohen.* Paris: Honoré Champion, 1999.

———. "Le Château gothique de Solal, sur l'imaginaire 'noir' d'Albert Cohen." *Cahiers Albert Cohen,* no. 11 (September 2001).

———, ed. *Albert Cohen: Colloque du centenaire, Université de Picardie Jules Verne, Amiens, 6–7 septembre 1995.* Villeneuve d'Ascq: Roman 20–50, 1997.

Stolz, Claire. *La Polyphonie dans "Belle du Seigneur" d'Albert Cohen: Pour une approche sémiostylisque.* Paris: Honoré Champion, 1998.

Weingrad, Michael. "Book Review: Juifs imaginaires." *Prooftexts* 21, no. 2 (2001): 255–76. http://iupjournals.org/prooftexts/pft21-2.html.

Zard, Philippe. *La Fiction de l'Occident: Thomas Mann, Franz Kafka, Albert Cohen.* Paris: Presses universitaires de France, 1999.

———. "Les Têtes-à-queue de l'histoire: Fiction et diction sionistes." *Cahiers Albert Cohen,* no. 13 (September 2003): 9–49.

Other Books and Articles

Abécassis, Armand. *La Pensée juive,* vol. 1: *Du désert au désir.* Paris: Librairie générale française (Livre de Poche), 1987.

———. *La Pensée juive,* vol. 2: *De l'état politique à l'éclat prophétique.* Paris: Librairie générale française (Livre de Poche), 1987.

———. *La Pensée juive,* vol. 3: *Espace de l'oubli et mémoires du temps.* Paris: Librairie générale française (Livre de Poche), 1989.

———. *La Pensée juive,* vol. 4: *Messiantés: Éclipse politique et éclosions apocalyptiques.* Paris: Librairie générale française (Livre de Poche), 1996.

Abecassis, Jack I. "Camus' Pulp Fiction." *Modern Language Notes* 112, no. 4 (September 1997).

Aciman, André. *Out of Egypt: A Memoir.* New York: Riverhead Books, 1996.

———. "Le Juif intérieur." In *Pardès (Le Juif caché),* no. 29 (2000): 39–56.

Allen, Barry. *Truth in Philosophy.* Cambridge, Mass.: Harvard University Press, 1993.

Alter, Robert. *Genesis: Translation and Commentary.* New York: Norton, 1997.

———. *Canon and Creativity: Modern Writings and the Authority of Scripture.* New Haven: Yale University Press, 2000.

Alter, Robert, and Frank Kermode, eds. *The Literary Guide to the Bible.* Cambridge, Mass.: Harvard University Press, Belknap Press, 1987.

Attali, Michel. "Les Marranes et Pourim, d'un confortable identification au problème éthique." *Pardès (Le Juif caché),* no. 29 (2000): 23–34.

Bakhtin, Mikhail. *The Dialogic Imagination: Four Essays.* Austin: University of Texas Press, 1981.

———. *Problems in Dostoevsky's Poetics.* Minneapolis: University of Minnesota Press, 1984.

———. *Rabelais and His World.* Translated by Hélène Iswolsky. Bloomington: Indiana University Press, 1984.

Barzel, Alexander. *On the Structure of Judaism.* In Hebrew. Tel Aviv: Sifriat Po-Halim, 1994.

Bean, Henry. *The Believer: Confronting Jewish Self-Hatred.* New York: Thunder's Mouth Press, 2002.

Birnbaum, Philip. *The Book of Jewish Concepts.* New York: Hebrew Publishing Co., 1975 [1964].

Bloom, Harold. *The Anxiety of Influence: A Theory of Poetry.* New York: Oxford University Press, 1997 [1973].

The Book of J. Translated from the Hebrew by David Rosenberg. Edited by Harold Bloom. New York: Vintage Books, 1991 [1990].

Boone, Joseph Allen. *Libidinal Currents: Sexuality and the Shaping of Modernism.* Chicago: University of Chicago Press, 1998.

Braud, Michel. *La Tentation du suicide dans les écrits autobiographiques, 1930–1970.* Paris: Presses universitaires de France, 1992.

Brooks, Peter. *Reading for the Plot: Design and Intention in Narrative.* Cambridge, Mass.: Harvard University Press, 1992 [1984].

Calasso, Roberto. *The Marriage of Cadmus and Harmony.* Translated by Tim Parks. New York: Vintage International, 1994 [1988].

Céline, Louis-Ferdinand. *Bagatelles pour un massacre.* Paris: Denoël, 1938.

Citati, Pietro. *Kafka.* Translated from the Italian by Raymond Rosenthal. New York: Knopf, 1989 [1987].

Cohen, Ted. *Jokes: Philosophical Thoughts on Joking Matters.* Chicago: University of Chicago Press, 1999.

Cohn, Dorrit. *Transparent Minds.* Princeton: Princeton University Press, 1978.

———. *The Distinction of Fiction.* Baltimore: Johns Hopkins University Press, 1999.

Delacampagne, Christian. *Une Histoire du racisme.* Paris: Librairie générale française, 2000.

———. *Le Philosophe et le tyran: Histoire d'une Illusion.* Paris: Presses universitaires de France, 2000.

Deleuze, Giles. *Difference and Repetition.* Translated by Paul Patton. New York: Columbia University Press, 1995. Originally published as *Différence et répétition* (Paris: Presses universitaires de France, 1968).

Díaz-Mas, Paloma. *Sephardim: The Jews from Spain.* Translated by George K. Zucker. Chicago: University of Chicago Press, 1992.

Dictionnaire de la psychanalyse. 2d ed. Paris: Albin Michel, 2001.

Doniach, N. S. *Purim, or, The Feast of Esther: An Historical Study.* Philadelphia: Jewish Publication Society of America, 1933.

Felstiner, John. *Paul Celan: Poet, Survivor, Jew.* New Haven: Yale University Press, 2001 [1995].

Finkielkraut, Alain. *Le Juif imaginaire.* Paris: Seuil, 1980.

———. *La Réprobation d'Israël.* Paris: Denoël, 1983.

Freud, Sigmund. *Collected Papers,* vol. 4: *Papers on Metapsychology, Papers on Applied Psychoanalysis.* London: Hogarth Press and the Institute of Psycho-Analysis, 1953.

———. "The Uncanny." In *The Standard Edition of the Complete Psychological Works of Sigmund Freud,* edited by James Strachey et al., 17: 219–52. London: Hogarth Press and the Institute of Psycho-Analysis, 1953–74.

———. *Jokes and Their Relation to the Unconscious.* New York: Norton, 1960 [1905].

———. *Beyond the Pleasure Principle.* New York: Norton, 1961 [1920].

Gary, Romain. *Education européenne.* Paris: Gallimard, 1972 [1945].

———. *Les Clowns lyriques.* Gallimard, 1979.

Gilman, Sander L. *Jewish Self-Hatred, Anti-Semitism and the Hidden Language of the Jews.* Baltimore: Johns Hopkins University Press, 1986.

Girard, René. *Deceit, Desire, and the Novel, Self and Other in Literary Structure.* Translated by Yvonne Freccaro. Baltimore: Johns Hopkins University Press, 1976.

Gopnik, Adam. "A Purim Story." *New Yorker,* February 18–25, 2002.

Halberstadt-Freud, Hendrika C. *Freud, Proust, Perversion and Love.* Amsterdam: Swets & Zeitlinger, 1991.

Hertzberg, Arthur. *The French Enlightenment and the Jews: The Origins of Modern Anti-Semitism.* New York: Columbia University Press, 1990 [1968].

Homer. *The Odyssey.* Translated by Robert Fagles. New York: Penguin Books, 1996.

Horn, Bernard. *Facing the Fires: Conversations with A. B. Yehoshua.* Syracuse, N.Y.: Syracuse University Press, 1997.

Humphrey, Robert. *Stream of Consciousness in the Modern Novel.* Berkeley: University of California Press, 1965 [1954].

Jama, Sophie. *L'Histoire juive de Montaigne.* Paris: Flammarion, 2001.

Jankélévitch, Vladimir. *La Mort.* Paris: Flammarion, 1997.

Joyce, James. *Ulysses.* New York: Vintage Books, 1986 [1921].

Itti, Eliane. *La Littérature française en 50 romans.* Paris: Ellipses, 1995.

Kafka, Franz. *The Metamorphosis, In the Penal Colony, and Other Stories.* Translated by Joachim Neugroschel. New York: Touchstone Books, 2000.

Kaplan, Alice. *French Lessons: A Memoir.* Chicago: University of Chicago Press, 1994.

———. *The Collaborator: The Trial and Execution of Robert Brasillach.* Chicago: University of Chicago Press, 2000.

Klein, Melanie, and Joan Riviere. *Love, Hate and Reparation.* New York: Norton, 1964.

———. *The Selected Melanie Klein.* Edited by Juliette Mitchell. New York: Free Press, 1987.

Kristeva, Julia. *Le Génie féminin,* vol. 2: *Melanie Klein.* Paris: Fayard, 2003.

Leibowitz, Yeshayahu. *Seven Years of Discourses on the Weekly Torah Reading.* In Hebrew. Jerusalem: Kether, 2000.

Lessing, Theodor. *Der jüdische Selbsthass.* Berlin: Jüdischer Verlag, 1930. Edited and translated by Maurice-Ruben Hayoun under the title *La Haine de soi: Le Refus d'être Juif* (Paris: Berg International, 2001).

Lilla, Mark. *The Reckless Mind: Intellectuals in Politics.* New York: New York Review Books, 2001.

The Living Talmud: The Wisdom of the Fathers and Its Classical Commentaries. Edited and translated by Judah Goldin. New York: New American Library, 1957.

Loewenstein, Rudolph. *Psychanalyse de l'antisemitisme.* Paris: Presses universitaires de France, 2001 [1952].

Mann, Paul. *Masocriticism.* Albany: State University of New York Press, 1999.

Mann, Thomas. *Joseph in Egypt.* New York: Knopf, 1938.

———. *Joseph the Provider.* New York, Knopf, 1944.

Marks, Elaine. *Marrano as Metaphor: The Jewish Presence in French Writing.* New York: Columbia University Press, 1996.

McGaha, Michael. *Coat of Many Cultures: The Story of Joseph in Spanish Literature, 1200–1492.* Philadelphia: Jewish Publication Society, 1997.

———. *The Story of Joseph in Spanish Golden Age Drama.* London: Bucknell University Press, 1998.

MeAm Lo'ez, Genessis I [People of Strange Language (The Torah Anthology)]. In Hebrew. New York: Maznaim Publishing Corp., 1977.

Mehlman, Jeffrey. *Legacies of Anti-Semitism in France.* Minneapolis: University of Minnesota Press, 1983.

Miles, Jack. *God: A Biography.* New York: Knopf, 1995.

The Oxford Companion to Music. Edited by Alison Latham. Oxford: Oxford University Press, 2002.

Peyrefitte, Christel. *Des rides à l'âme.* Paris: Gallimard, 1997.

Phillips, Adam. *Darwin's Worms: On Life Stories and Death Stories.* New York: Basic Books, 2000 [1999].

———. *Promises, Promises.* New York, Basic Books, 2001 [2000].

Philo of Alexandria. *De Iosepho.* French and Greek. Translated by Jean Laporte. Paris: Cerf, 1964.

Pirke Avot [The Ethics of the Fathers]. In *Daily Prayers,* trans. A. Th. Philips. New York: Hebrew Publishing Co.

Prager, Jeffrey. *Presenting the Past: Psychoanalysis and the Sociology of Misremembering.* Cambridge, Mass.: Harvard University Press, 1998.

Rabinovitch, Gérard. *Le Sourire d'Isaac: L'Humour juif comme art de l'esprit.* Paris: Arte, 2002.

Rosset, Clément. *L'Anti-Nature.* Paris: Presses universitaires de France, 1995 [1973].

Roth, Cecil. *A History of the Marranos.* New York: Harper & Row, 1958 [1932].

Roth, Philip. *American Pastoral.* New York: Vintage International, 1997.

———. *Reading Myself and Others.* New York: Vintage International, 2001.

Rougement, Denis de. *L'Amour et l'Occident.* Paris: Plon (10/18), 1972 [1939].

Sánchez-Pardo, Esther. *Cultures of the Death Drive: Melanie Klein and Modernist Melancholia.* Durham, N.C.: Duke University Press, 2003.

Schor, Ralph. *L'Antisémitisme en France pendant les années trente.* Brussels: Complexe, 1992.

Sibony, Daniel. *Entre-Deux: L'Origine en partage.* Paris: Seuil, 1991.

———. *Le Jeu et la passé.* Paris: Seuil, 1997.

———. *Le "Racisme": Une Haine identitaire.* Paris: Bourgeois, 1997.

———. *Les Trois Monothéismes: Juifs, Chrétiens, Musulmans entre leurs sources et leurs destins.* Paris: Seuil, 1997 [1992].

———. *Don de soi ou partage de soi: Le Drame Lévinas.* Paris: Odile Jacob, 2000.

———. *Perversions: Dialogues sur des folies "actuelles."* Paris: Seuil, 2000 [Grasset, 1987].

———. *Psychanalyse et Judaisme: Question de transmission.* Paris: Flammarion, 2001.

Simson, Otto von. *The Gothic Cathedral: Origins of Gothic Architecture and the Medieval Concept of Order.* London: Routledge & K. Paul, 1956.

Steiner, George. *Errata: An Examined Life.* New Haven: Yale University Press, 1997.

———. *No Passion Spent.* New Haven: Yale University Press, 1996.

Strauss, Leo. *Persecution and the Art of Writing.* Chicago: Chicago University Press, 1988 [1952].

Taguieff, Pierre-André. *La Nouvelle Judéophobie.* Paris: Mille et une nuits, 2001.

Trigano, Shmuel. *La Philosophie de la Loi: L'Origine de la politique dans la Tora.* Paris: CERF, 1991.

———. "Le Mystère d'Esther et de Josephe: La Mystique politique du marranisme." *Pardès (Le Juif caché),* no. 29 (2000): 11–22.

Tonnet-Lacrois, Eliane. *La Littérature française et francophone de 1945 à l'an 2000.* Paris: L'Harmattan, 2003.

Whedbee, William J. *The Bible and the Comic Vision.* Cambridge: Cambridge University Press, 1998.

Wimmers, Inge Crosman. *Poetics of Reading: Approaches to the Novel.* Princeton: Princeton University Press, 1988.

Winter, Jean-Pierre. *Les Errants de la chair: Études sur l'hystérie masculine.* Paris: Petite Bibliothèque Payot, 2001 [1998].

Yehoshua, A. B. *Mr. Mani.* Translated from the Hebrew by Hillel Halkin. New York : Doubleday, 1992 [1987].

Yovel, Yirmiyahu. *Spinoza and Other Heretics: The Marrano of Reason.* Princeton: Princeton University Press, 1989.

Index